W0114374

AP® COMPUTER SCIENCE PRINCIPLES

PREMIUM PREP

4th Edition

The Staff of The Princeton Review

PrincetonReview.com

Penguin
Random
House

The Princeton Review
110 East 42nd Street, 7th Floor
New York, NY 10017
princetonreview.com
penguinrandomhouse.com

Copyright © 2025 by TPR Education IP Holdings, LLC. All rights reserved.

Published in the United States by Penguin Random House LLC, New York.

Terms of Service: The Princeton Review Online Companion Tools ("Student Tools") for retail books are available for only the two most recent editions of that book. Student Tools may be activated only once per eligible book purchased for a total of 24 months of access. Activation of Student Tools more than once per book is in direct violation of these Terms of Service and may result in discontinuation of access to Student Tools Services.

Please note that no part of this book may be used or reproduced in any manner for the purpose of training artificial intelligence technologies or systems.

ISBN: 978-0-593-51824-3
ISSN: 2767-1321

AP is a trademark registered and owned by the College Board, which is not affiliated with, and does not endorse, this product.

The Princeton Review is not affiliated with Princeton University.

Editor: Chris Chimera
Production Editors: Emily Epstein White and Sarah Litt
Production Artist: Jennifer Chapman
Content Contributor: Melissa Estremera

Manufactured in the United States of America

10   9   8   7   6   5   4   3   2   1

4th Edition

EU Contact:
Penguin Random House Ireland
32 Nassau Street
Dublin D02 YH68
https://eu-contact.penguin.ie

The Princeton Review Publishing Team
Rob Franek, Editor-in-Chief
David Soto, Senior Director, Data Operations
Stephen Koch, Senior Manager, Data Operations
Deborah Weber, Director of Production
Jason Ullmeyer, Production Design Manager
Jennifer Chapman, Senior Production Artist
Selena Coppock, Director of Editorial
Aaron Riccio, Director, Editorial Admissions Content
Orion McBean, Senior Editor
Meave Shelton, Senior Editor
Chris Chimera, Editor
Patricia Murphy, Editor
Laura Rose, Editor
Isabelle Appleton, Editorial Assistant

Random House Publishing Team
Tom Russell, VP, Publisher
Alison Stoltzfus, Senior Director, Publishing
Emily Hoffman, Managing Editor
Mary Ellen Owens, Assistant Director of Production
Suzanne Lee, Senior Designer
Eugenia Lo, Publishing Assistant

For customer service, please contact **editorialsupport@review.com**, and be sure to include:

- full title of the book

- ISBN

- page number

ACKNOWLEDGMENTS

Special thanks to Melissa Estremera for her content development work on the 4th edition of this book. Additionally, The Princeton Review would like to thank Jennifer Chapman, Emily Epstein White, and Sarah Litt for their contributions to this title.

Contents

Get More (Free) Content viii

Part I: Using This Book to Improve Your AP Score................. 1

Preview: Your Knowledge, Your Expectations 2

Your Guide to Using This Book 2

How to Begin.. 4

Part II: Practice Test.. 7

Practice Test 1 9

Practice Test 1: Diagnostic Answer Key and Explanations 53

How to Score Practice Test 1 66

Part III: About the AP Computer Science Principles Exam.... 67

The Structure of the AP Computer Science Principles Exam 68

How the AP Computer Science Principles Exam Is Scored................ 69

The AP Computer Science Principles Exam Is Fully Digital 69

Past AP Computer Science Principles Score Distributions................ 70

How AP Exams Are Used.. 72

Other Resources 73

Part IV: Test-Taking Strategies for the AP Computer Science Principles Exam... 75

Preview.. 76

How to Use this Part... 76

1   How to Approach Multiple-Choice Questions........................ 77

The Basics... 78

Multiple Choice Strategies 79

2   How to Approach the Create Performance Task....................... 81

Create Task Scavenger Hunt Worksheet.. 82

What is the Create Performance Task?... 83

Create Task Checklist... 85

Possible Create Task Timeline 86

Common Questions about the Create Task....................................... 87

Create Task Scavenger Hunt Worksheet Answers............................. 88

Part V: Content Review for the AP Computer Science Principles Exam 89

3   **Creative Development** 91

    Collaboration 92

    Identifying and Correcting Errors 93

4   **Data** 97

    Binary Numbers 98

    Data Compression 102

    Extracting Information From Data 104

    Using Programs with Data 106

    Chapter 4 Key Terms 109

    Chapter 4 Review Drill 110

    Chapter 4 Summary 112

5   **Algorithms and Programming** 115

    Variables and Assignments 116

    Data Abstraction 117

    Mathematical Expressions 118

    Strings 120

    Boolean Expressions 121

    Conditionals 122

    Nested Conditionals 124

    Iteration 124

    Developing Algorithms 126

    Lists 127

    Binary Search 130

    Calling Procedures, Developing Procedures, and Libraries 130

    Random Values 132

    Simulations 133

    Algorithmic Efficiency 134

    Undecidable Problems 134

    Chapter 5 Key Terms 135

    Chapter 5 Review Drill 136

    Chapter 5 Summary 138

6   Computer Systems and Networks 141

    The Internet 142

    Fault Tolerance 144

    Parallel and Distributed Computing 145

    Chapter 6 Key Terms 148

    Chapter 6 Review Drill 149

    Chapter 6 Summary 150

7   Impact of Computing 153

    Beneficial and Harmful Effects 154

    Digital Divide 155

    Computing Bias 156

    Crowdsourcing 157

    Legal and Ethical Concerns 159

    Safe Computing 161

    Chapter 7 Key Terms 165

    Chapter 7 Review Drill 166

    Chapter 7 Summary 168

8   End of Chapter Drill Answers and Explanations 173

Part VI: Additional Practice Tests 179

    Practice Test 2 181

    Practice Test 2: Answers and Explanations 229

    How to Score Practice Test 2 239

    Practice Test 3 241

    Practice Test 3: Answers and Explanations 287

    How to Score Practice Test 3 305

Glossary 307

Exam Reference Sheet 313

Online Practice Tests

    Practice Test 4 .... Online

    Practice Test 4: Answers and Explanations .... Online

    Practice Test 5 .... Online

    Practice Test 5: Answers and Explanations .... Online

Get More (Free) Content
at **PrincetonReview.com/prep**

As easy as **1·2·3**

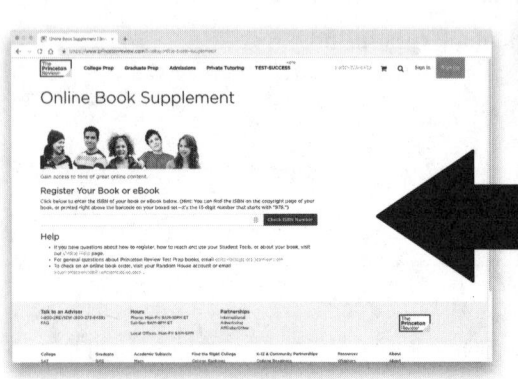

1 Go to PrincetonReview.com/prep or scan the **QR code** and enter the following ISBN to register your book:
9780593518243

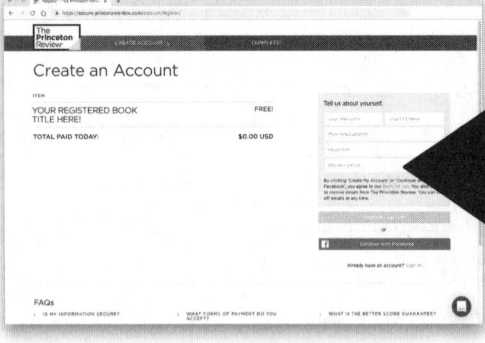

2 Answer a few simple questions to set up an exclusive Princeton Review account. *(If you already have one, you can just log in.)*

3 Enjoy access to your **FREE** content!

Access Your Online Test Practice

Your AP Prep book comes with new interactive practice exams to help you prepare for digital test-taking! Find these tests in your online Student Tools, provided in at least one of the following formats:

- Fully digital versions with a timer option to simulate the exam experience
- Downloadable interactive PDFs with digital features like clicking your answer in Section I

Check back often as we continue to update the included AP Student Tools.

PLUS, IN YOUR ACCOUNT YOU CAN:

- Get valuable advice about the college application process, tips for essay writing, and financial aid info

- Use our searchable rankings to learn more about your dream school

- Access additional practice tests, comprehensive study guides, AP Score Conversion charts, Key Terms lists, and the Glossary

- Check whether there have been any updates or corrections to this edition

Need to report a potential **content** issue?

Contact **EditorialSupport@review.com** and include:

- full title of the book
- ISBN
- page number

Need to report a **technical** issue?

Contact **TPRStudentTech@review.com** and provide:

- your full name
- email address used to register the book
- full book title and ISBN
- Operating system (Mac/PC) and browser (Chrome, Firefox, Safari, etc.)

Look For These Icons Throughout The Book

 PROVEN TECHNIQUES

 OTHER REFERENCES

 ONLINE ARTICLES

 APPLIED STRATEGIES

Learn From the Best

The Princeton Review®

With over 40 years of experience, The Princeton Review can help you achieve maximum results in minimal time.

Check out our complete line of books.

From test prep to financial aid, we've got you covered:

- ACT®, AP®, and SAT® prep—if it's on the test, it's in our books
- High school academics—put your learning on the fast track
- Admissions and financial aid guides—find and fund your perfect college match

...and much more!

PrincetonReviewBooks.com | **1-800-2-REVIEW**

©2025 TPR Education IP Holdings, LLC. All Rights Reserved. The Princeton Review is not affiliated with Princeton University. ACT® is a registered trademark of ACT, Inc. AP® and SAT® are trademarks registered by the College Board, which is not affiliated with, and does not endorse, these products.

Part I
Using This Book to Improve Your AP Score

- Preview: Your Knowledge, Your Expectations
- Your Guide to Using This Book
- How to Begin

PREVIEW: YOUR KNOWLEDGE, YOUR EXPECTATIONS

Your route to a high score on the AP Computer Science Principles Exam depends a lot on how you plan to use this book. Start thinking about your plan by responding to the following questions.

1. Rate your level of confidence in your knowledge of the content tested by the AP Computer Science Principles Exam:

   A. Very confident—I know it all
   B. I'm pretty confident, but there are topics for which I could use help
   C. Not confident—I need quite a bit of support
   D. I'm not sure.

2. If you have a goal score in mind, circle your goal score for the AP Computer Science Principles Exam:

   5   4   3   2   1   I'm not sure yet.

3. What do you expect to learn from this book? Circle all that apply to you.

   A. A general overview of the test and what to expect
   B. Strategies for how to approach the test
   C. The content tested by this exam
   D. I'm not sure yet.

YOUR GUIDE TO USING THIS BOOK

This book is organized to provide as much—or as little—support as you need, so you can use this book in whatever way will be most helpful to improving your score on the AP Computer Science Principles Exam.

- The remainder of **Part I** will provide guidance on how to use this book and help you determine your strengths and weaknesses.

- **Part II** of this book contains Practice Test 1, the Diagnostic Answer Key, answers and explanations for each question, and a scoring guide. We recommend that you take this test before going any further in order to realistically determine:
  o your starting point right now
  o which question types you're ready for and which you might need to practice
  o which content topics you are familiar with and which you will want to carefully review

Note that the answer key for Practice Test 1 has been specifically designed to help you self-diagnose any potential areas of weakness so that you can best focus your test preparation and be efficient with your time.

- **Part III** of this book will:
  - o provide information about the structure, scoring, and content of the AP Computer Science Principles Exam
  - o help you to make a study plan
  - o point you toward additional resources

- **Part IV** of this book will explore various strategies:
  - o how to answer multiple-choice questions (MCQs)
  - o how to approach the Create Performance Task
  - o how to manage your time to maximize the number of points available to you

- **Part V** of this book covers the content you need for the AP Computer Science Principles Exam.

- **Part VI** of this book contains two additional practice tests, along with their answers, explanations, and scoring guides. If you skipped Practice Test 1, we recommend that you do all three (waiting at least a day or two between them) so that you can compare your progress. Additionally, taking the practice tests will help to identify any external issues: if you consistently get a certain type of question wrong, you probably need to review it. If you got it wrong only once, you may have run out of time or been distracted by something. In either case, examining your test results will allow you to focus on the factors that caused the discrepancy in scores and to be as prepared as possible on test day.

- **Online Resources** contain two additional practice tests. Follow the study guide found there based on the amount of time you have to study for the exam.

You may choose to use some parts of this book over others, or you may work through the entire book. Your approach will depend on your needs and how much time you have. Now let's look at how to make this determination.

Once you register your book online, you can print the bubble sheets and scoring worksheets for your practice tests!

HOW TO BEGIN

Scoring Worksheets
We've included a scoring worksheet for each of the Practice Tests. Remember that these worksheets are meant to serve as a rough guideline only. AP exam scores are weighted according to a statistical process that varies slightly every year based on how students perform on the exam. But you can use the worksheets to approximate your score!

1. **Take Practice Test 1**

    Before you can decide how to use this book, you need to take a practice test. Doing so will give you insight into your strengths and weaknesses, and the test will also help you make an effective study plan. If you're feeling test-phobic, remind yourself that a practice test is a tool for diagnosing yourself—it's not how well you do that matters but how you use information gleaned from your performance to guide your preparation.

    So, before you read further, take Practice Test 1 starting on page 9 of this book. Be sure to finish it in one sitting, following the instructions that appear before the test.

2. **Check Your Answers**

    Using the Diagnostic Answer Key on page 54, follow our three-step process to determine how you did on each section of the test.

3. **Reflect on the Test**

    After you take your first test, respond to the following questions:

    *   How much time did you spend on the multiple-choice questions?

    *   How many multiple-choice questions did you miss?

    *   Did you find the multi-select or reading passage questions to be more difficult?

Most of the work on the Create Performance Task is not a part of the exam, but is a part of your class and score, and you should reflect on any topics you could improve that would help you there as well.

4. **Read Part III of This Book and Complete the Self-Evaluation**

    Part III will provide information on how the test is structured and scored. It will also set out areas of content that are tested.

    As you read Part III, re-evaluate your answers to the questions above. At the end of Part III, you will revisit and refine those questions. You will then be able to make a study plan, based on your needs and available time, that will allow you to use this book most effectively.

5. **Engage with Parts IV and V as Needed**

    Notice the word *engage*. You'll get more out of this book if you use it intentionally than if you read it passively, hoping for an improved score through osmosis.

Strategy chapters will help you think about your approach to the question types on this exam. Part IV will open with a reminder to think about how you approach questions now and then close with a reflection section asking you to think about how or whether you will change your approach in the future.

The content chapters in Part V are designed to provide a review of the content tested on the AP Computer Science Principles Exam, including the level of detail you need to know and how the content is tested. In addition, the content chapters are broken up to reflect the 5 Big Ideas structure of the AP Computer Science Principles course, as outlined by the College Board. You will have the opportunity to assess your proficiency in the content of each chapter through test-appropriate questions and a reflection section.

6. Take Another Test and Assess Your Performance

Once you feel you have developed the strategies you need and gained the knowledge you lacked, you should take Practice Test 2, which starts on page 181 of this book. You should do so in one sitting, following the instructions at the beginning of the test.

When you are finished, check your answers to the multiple-choice section with the correct responses on page 229.

Once you have taken the test, reflect on the areas on which you still need work, and revisit the chapters in this book that address those deficiencies. Part IV includes Practice Tests 2 and 3, and two more practice tests can be found in your online Student Tools. Finally, don't forget to consult your class materials (e.g., textbook, handouts) as well.

7. Keep Working

As discussed in Part III, there are other resources available to you, including a wealth of information on the official AP Students website. Here, you can continue to explore areas to improve upon and engage with right up until the day of the test. If you've followed our recommended approach, you'll have a total of five practice tests left at this point (three in the book, two online), and you should use a mix of Web resources and book review to solidify your understanding of any questions or subjects that you keep getting wrong.

Need Some Guidance?
If you're looking for a way to get the most out of your studying, check out our free study guide for this exam, which you can access via your online Student Tools. See the "Get More (Free) Content" page for details on accessing this great resource and more.

Part II
Practice Test

- Practice Test 1
- Practice Test 1: Diagnostic Answer Key and Explanations
- How to Score Practice Test 1

Practice Test 1

AP® Computer Science Principles Exam

SECTION I: Multiple-Choice Questions

DO NOT BEGIN THE EXAM UNTIL YOU ARE TOLD TO DO SO.

At a Glance
Total Time
2 hours
Number of Questions
70
Percent of Total Score
70%

DISCLAIMER: The official AP Computer Science Principles will be administered digitally. Instructions for the digital exam may differ from this practice test.

Instructions

Section I has 70 multiple-choice questions and lasts 2 hours.

Each question is followed by four suggested answers.

For questions 1–62, select the single best answer choice for each question.

For questions 63–70, **two** of the suggested answers are correct. **For each of these questions, you must select both correct choices to earn credit.** No partial credit will be earned if only one correct choice is selected. Select the two that are best in each case.

Reference information for programming questions is available in this application and can be accessed throughout Section I.

GO ON TO THE NEXT PAGE.

Quick Reference

Instruction	Explanation
Assignment, Display, and Input	
Text: a ← expression Block: `a ⟵ expression`	Evaluates `expression` and then assigns a copy of the result to the variable a.
Text: DISPLAY(expression) Block: `DISPLAY expression`	Displays the value of `expression`, followed by a space.
Text: INPUT() Block: INPUT	Accepts a value from the user and returns the input value.
Arithmetic Operators and Numeric Procedures	
Text and Block: a + b a - b a * b a / b	The arithmetic operators +, -, *, and / are used to perform arithmetic on a and b. For example, 17 / 5 evaluates to 3.4. The order of operations used in mathematics applies when evaluating expressions.
Text and Block: a MOD b	Evaluates to the remainder when a is divided by b. Assume that a is an integer greater than or equal to 0 and b is an integer greater than 0. For example, 17 MOD 5 evaluates to 2. The MOD operator has the same precedence as the * and / operators.
Text: RANDOM(a, b) Block: RANDOM `a, b`	Generates and returns a random integer from a to b, including a and b. Each result is equally likely to occur. For example, RANDOM(1, 3) could return 1, 2, or 3.

Instruction	Explanation
Relational and Boolean Operators	
Text and Block: a = b a ≠ b a > b a < b a ≥ b a ≤ b	The relational operators =, ≠, >, <, ≤, and ≥ are used to test the relationship between two variables, expressions, or values. A comparison using relational operators evaluates to a Boolean value. For example, a = b evaluates to true if a and b are equal; otherwise it evaluates to false.
Text: NOT condition Block: NOT condition	Evaluates to true if condition is false; otherwise evaluates to false.
Text: condition1 AND condition2 Block: condition1 AND condition2	Evaluates to true if both condition1 and condition2 are true; otherwise evaluates to false.
Text: condition1 OR condition2 Block: condition1 OR condition2	Evaluates to true if condition1 is true or if condition2 is true or if both condition1 and condition2 are true; otherwise evaluates to false.
Selection	

Text:
 	
IF(condition)
 	
{
 	
<block of statements>
 	
}
 	
Block:
 	
IF condition
 	
block of statements
	The code in block of statements is executed if the Boolean expression condition evaluates to true; no action is taken if condition evaluates to false.

Instruction	Explanation
Selection—Continued	

Text:
 	
`IF(condition)`
 	
`{`
 	
`<first block of statements>`
 	
`}`
 	
`ELSE`
 	
`{`
 	
`<second block of statements>`
 	
`}`
 	
Block:
 	
IF (condition)
    first block of statements
ELSE
    second block of statements
	The code in `first block of statements` is executed if the Boolean expression `condition` evaluates to `true`; otherwise the code in `second block of statements` is executed.

Iteration	

Text:
 	
`REPEAT n TIMES`
 	
`{`
 	
`<block of statements>`
 	
`}`
 	
Block:
 	
REPEAT n TIMES
    block of statements
	The code in `block of statements` is executed n times.

Text:
 	
`REPEAT UNTIL(condition)`
 	
`{`
 	
`<block of statements>`
 	
`}`
 	
Block:
 	
REPEAT UNTIL (condition)
    block of statements
	The code in `block of statements` is repeated until the Boolean expression `condition` evaluates to `true`.

Instruction	Explanation
List Operations	
For all list operations, if a list index is less than 1 or greater than the length of the list, an error message is produced and the program terminates.	
Text: aList ← [value1, value2, value3, ...] Block: `aList ← value1, value2, value3`	Creates a new list that contains the values `value1`, `value2`, `value3`, and `...` at indices `1`, `2`, `3`, and `...` respectively and assigns it to `aList`.
Text: aList ← [] Block: `aList ← []`	Creates an empty list and assigns it to `aList`.
Text: aList ← bList Block: `aList ← bList`	Assigns a copy of the list `bList` to the list `aList`. For example, if `bList` contains [20, 40, 60], then `aList` will also contain [20, 40, 60] after the assignment.
Text: aList[i] Block: `aList i`	Accesses the element of `aList` at index `i`. The first element of `aList` is at index 1 and is accessed using the notation `aList[1]`.
Text: x ← aList[i] Block: `x ← aList i`	Assigns the value of `aList[i]` to the variable `x`.
Text: aList[i] ← x Block: `aList i ← x`	Assigns the value of `x` to `aList[i]`.
Text: aList[i] ← aList[j] Block: `aList i ← aList j`	Assigns the value of `aList[j]` to `aList[i]`.
Text: INSERT(aList, i, value) Block: `INSERT aList, i, value`	Any values in `aList` at indices greater than or equal to `i` are shifted one position to the right. The length of the list is increased by 1, and `value` is placed at index `i` in `aList`.

Instruction	Explanation
List Operations—Continued	

Text:
 	
`APPEND(aList, value)`
 	
Block:
 	
`APPEND` `aList, value`
	The length of `aList` is increased by 1, and `value` is placed at the end of `aList`.

Text:
 	
`REMOVE(aList, i)`
 	
Block:
 	
`REMOVE` `aList, i`
	Removes the item at index `i` in `aList` and shifts to the left any values at indices greater than `i`. The length of `aList` is decreased by 1.

Text:
 	
`LENGTH(aList)`
 	
Block:
 	
`LENGTH` `aList`
	Evaluates to the number of elements in `aList`.

Text:
 	
`FOR EACH item IN aList`
 	
`{`
 	
`<block of statements>`
 	
`}`
 	
Block:
 	
`FOR EACH item IN aList`
`block of statements`
	The variable `item` is assigned the value of each element of `aList` sequentially, in order, from the first element to the last element. The code in `block of statements` is executed once for each assignment of `item`.

Procedures and Procedure Calls	

Text:
 	
`PROCEDURE procName(parameter1,`
`                    parameter2, ...)`
 	
`{`
 	
`<block of statements>`
 	
`}`
 	
Block:
 	
`PROCEDURE procName` `parameter1,`
`parameter2, ...`
`block of statements`
	Defines `procName` as a procedure that takes zero or more arguments. The procedure contains `block of statements`.
	
	The procedure `procName` can be called using the following notation, where `arg1` is assigned to `parameter1`, `arg2` is assigned to `parameter2`, etc.:
	`procName(arg1, arg2, ...)`

Instruction	Explanation
Procedures and Procedure Calls—Continued	

Text:
 	
`PROCEDURE procName(parameter1,`
`                parameter2, ...)`
`{`
`<block of statements>`
`RETURN(expression)`
`}`
 	
Block:
 	
	Defines `procName` as a procedure that takes zero or more arguments. The procedure contains `block of statements` and returns the value of `expression`. The `RETURN` statement may appear at any point inside the procedure and causes an immediate return from the procedure back to the calling statement.
	
	The value returned by the procedure `procName` can be assigned to the variable `result` using the following notation:
	`result ← procName(arg1, arg2, ...)`

Text:
 	
`RETURN(expression)`
 	
Block:
 	
`RETURN expression`
	Returns the flow of control to the point where the procedure was called and returns the value of `expression`.

Robot	
If the robot attempts to move to a square that is not open or is beyond the edge of the grid, the robot will stay in its current location and the program will terminate.	

Text:
 	
`MOVE_FORWARD()`
 	
Block:
 	
`MOVE_FORWARD`
	The robot moves one square forward in the direction it is facing.

Text:
 	
`ROTATE_LEFT()`
 	
Block:
 	
`ROTATE_LEFT`
	The robot rotates in place 90 degrees counterclockwise (i.e., makes an in-place left turn).

Text:
 	
`ROTATE_RIGHT()`
 	
Block:
 	
`ROTATE_RIGHT`
	The robot rotates in place 90 degrees clockwise (i.e., makes an in-place right turn).

Text:
 	
`CAN_MOVE(direction)`
 	
Block:
 	
`CAN_MOVE direction`
	Evaluates to `true` if there is an open square one square in the direction relative to where the robot is facing; otherwise evaluates to `false`. The value of `direction` can be `left`, `right`, `forward`, or `backward`.

This page intentionally left blank.

GO ON TO THE NEXT PAGE.

AP COMPUTER SCIENCE PRINCIPLES

SECTION I

Time—2 hours

Number of Questions—70

Percent of total exam grade—70%

Directions: Choose one best answer for each question. Some questions at the end of the test will have more than one correct answer; for these, you will be instructed to choose two answer choices.

---

1 ☐ Mark for Review

Given the following code segment that should find the largest number in a list of numbers, it does not work as intended. What line of code needs to be changed to make it work correctly? You can assume that the numbers list is filled with whole numbers.

```
largest _ number ← numbers[0]        LINE 1
FOR EACH thing IN myList             LINE 2
{                                    LINE 3
    IF (n < largest _ number)        LINE 4
{                                    LINE 5
        largest _ number ← n         LINE 6
}                                    LINE 7
}                                    LINE 8
}                                    LINE 9
```

(A) Line 1 should be: `largest_number = 0`

(B) Line 2 should be: `FOR EACH myList in n`

(C) Line 4 should be: `if n > (largest_number)`

(D) The code is correct and does not need any changes.

---

2 ☐ Mark for Review

Which of the following scenarios best provides an example of citizen science?

(A) A team of professional researchers analyzing data from a climate change study collected from sensors at several hot spots around the world.

(B) A group of volunteers using a mobile app to identify and report invasive species in their neighborhood.

(C) A government agency collecting data on air pollution levels from universities in urban areas.

(D) A university professor leading a research team on artificial intelligence.

GO ON TO THE NEXT PAGE.

3 ☐ Mark for Review

Sam just took a picture of their homework with their phone. However, Sam's teacher is unable to open the file. Sam decides the best idea is to just delete the metadata and then resubmits the image. Why can't Sam's teacher open the file even though Sam deleted the metadata?

Ⓐ The metadata was too deeply embedded in the file to be completely removed.

Ⓑ Removing metadata does not change the underlying file format or structure.

Ⓒ The teacher's computer was incompatible with the file format.

Ⓓ The file was corrupted during the metadata removal process.

4 ☐ Mark for Review

A new company, CrimeTomorrow, is designing new AI software which allows city governments to predict areas that are more likely to have crime of a particular type. The system uses past data, which disproportionately shows wealthier areas as higher areas for burglary and poor areas as higher areas for violent crimes. As a result, the system is failing to predict crime accurately for either area. This is an example of:

Ⓐ Data bias

Ⓑ Poor design of the algorithm

Ⓒ Human error

Ⓓ System failure

GO ON TO THE NEXT PAGE.

5 ☐ Mark for Review

A dog kennel needs to determine whether they have capacity to take in more dogs. The kennel has a fixed number of available spots, and they want to check if there's space available for a new dog based on the current number of dogs already staying there.

Here are two possible algorithms to check for availability:

Algorithm A:
The system checks if the number of dogs already in the kennel is less than the total capacity. If this condition is true, the system returns that there is capacity for more dogs. If not, it returns that the kennel is full.

Algorithm B:
The system checks if the number of dogs already in the kennel is equal to the total capacity. If this condition is true, the system returns that the kennel is full. Otherwise, it returns that there is space available for a new dog.

Which of the following is the correct answer based on the algorithms described?

(A) Only Algorithm B is correct

(B) Only Algorithm A is correct

(C) Both Algorithm A and Algorithm B are correct

(D) Neither Algorithm A nor Algorithm B is correct

6 ☐ Mark for Review

A student wrote the following procedure but did not provide any documentation. Looking at the code, what is the function of the procedure?

```
PROCEDURE testCode(myList)
{
    sum ← 0
    FOR EACH thing IN myList
    {
        IF(thing MOD 2 = 1)
        {
            sum ← sum + thing
        }
    }
    return sum
}
```

(A) The procedure calculates the average of all elements in the list.

(B) The procedure finds the largest odd number in the list.

(C) The procedure calculates the sum of all odd numbers in the list.

(D) The procedure counts the number of even numbers in the list.

GO ON TO THE NEXT PAGE.

7 ☐ Mark for Review

A digital artist creates a beautiful painting and wants to share it online, allowing others to use it for non-commercial purposes but not to modify it. What type of license should the artist use?

(A) The artist doesn't need to do anything; they were granted copyright when they created it.

(B) Artist should put the painting in public domain so that others can use it as the artist wants.

(C) Creative commons, since it allows the artist to share but allows restrictions.

(D) The artist doesn't need to do anything but publish it online; then, people will be free to use it as the artist wants.

8 ☐ Mark for Review

When you visit a secure website, your browser verifies the website's identity using a digital certificate. What is the primary role of a Certificate Authority (CA) in this process?

(A) To encrypt the data transmitted between the user's browser and the website.

(B) To decrypt the data transmitted between the user's browser and the website.

(C) To issue digital certificates that verify the identity of websites.

(D) To store user passwords and other sensitive information.

9 ☐ Mark for Review

A tech company launches a new product and invites users to submit ideas for new features. This is an example of:

(A) Crowdsourcing

(B) Artificial intelligence

(C) Machine learning

(D) Virtual reality

GO ON TO THE NEXT PAGE.

10 ☐ Mark for Review

A company is designing a system that needs to ensure high availability and reliability, even if part of the system fails. The company decides to implement additional hardware and software components to provide backup resources, ensuring the system can continue operating without disruption. Which of the following terms best describes this approach?

(A) Redundancy, which involves duplicating components to ensure continued operation in case of failure.

(B) Fault tolerance, which enables the system to detect and correct errors automatically without user intervention.

(C) Network, which refers to a group of interconnected systems that work together.

(D) Algorithm, which is a set of instructions to solve a problem or complete a task

11 ☐ Mark for Review

A rural community with limited internet access is struggling to provide quality education to its students. Which of the following strategies could help bridge the digital divide in this community?

(A) Implementing a system that requires all students to own personal laptops.

(B) Providing high-speed internet access to schools and community centers.

(C) Encouraging students to use mobile data plans for online learning.

(D) Limiting online learning to students with reliable internet access.

GO ON TO THE NEXT PAGE.

12 🔖 Mark for Review

Consider the code segment below:

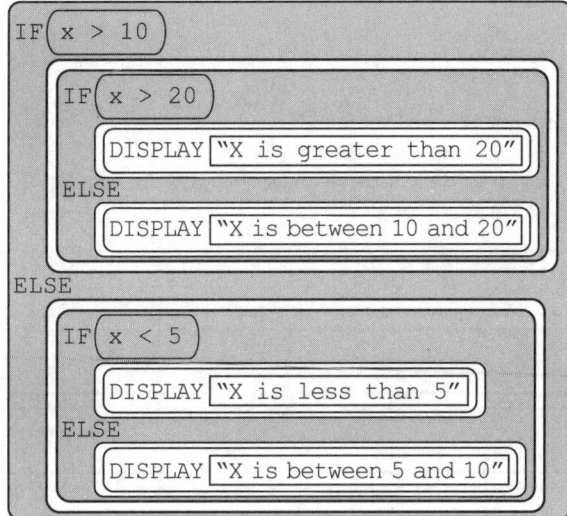

```
IF x > 10
    IF x > 20
        DISPLAY "X is greater than 20"
    ELSE
        DISPLAY "X is between 10 and 20"
ELSE
    IF x < 5
        DISPLAY "X is less than 5"
    ELSE
        DISPLAY "X is between 5 and 10"
```

If the value of x is 5, what will be the output of the code?

Ⓐ `X is greater than 20`

Ⓑ `X is between 10 and 20`

Ⓒ `X is less than 5`

Ⓓ `X is between 5 and 10`

13 🔖 Mark for Review

Which of the following is a potential ethical concern related to the use of AI algorithms that are trained on biased data?

Ⓐ Decreased accuracy in predictions and decision-making.

Ⓑ Increased risk of cyberattacks and data breaches.

Ⓒ Job displacement due to automation.

Ⓓ Environmental impact of AI development and deployment.

GO ON TO THE NEXT PAGE.

14 🔖 Mark for Review

A pet feeding system is designed to automatically feed a dog based on the time of day and whether the dog has already been fed that day. The feeding times are:

- Between 7 A.M. and 8 A.M. (morning feeding time)
- Between 5 P.M. and 6 P.M. (evening feeding time)

The system will feed the dog if it is during either feeding time and the dog has not been fed yet that day.

Which of the following Boolean expressions correctly represents when it's time to feed the dog if `time` represents the number of hours since midnight and `fedStatus` is true if the dog has been fed?

(A) `(time ≥ 7 AND time ≤ 8 OR time ≥ 17 AND time ≤ 18) AND fedStatus = false`

(B) `time ≥ 7 AND time ≤ 8 OR time ≥ 17 AND time ≤ 18`

(C) `time ≥ 7 && time ≤ 8 AND fedStatus = true`

(D) `time ≥ 6 && time ≤ 8 AND fedStatus = false`

15 🔖 Mark for Review

A computer program needs to search for a specific value in a list of numbers. Two algorithms are considered for the task: binary search and linear search.

Which of the following statements correctly compares binary search and linear search?

(A) Binary search is more efficient than linear search for all lists.

(B) Linear search requires the list to be sorted, while binary search does not, but it is less efficient.

(C) Binary search is more efficient than linear search, but it requires the list to be sorted.

(D) Linear search is faster than binary search for all input sizes and list types.

16 🔖 Mark for Review

Which of the following is a key characteristic of lossless data compression?

(A) It reduces file size by discarding unnecessary data.

(B) It is commonly used for images and videos.

(C) It preserves the original data so that it can be perfectly reconstructed.

(D) It is more efficient than lossy compression for large files.

GO ON TO THE NEXT PAGE.

17 ⬚ Mark for Review

A team of engineers is designing a new type of bridge. To test the bridge's structural integrity under different conditions, they create a computer simulation that models the bridge's behavior in various scenarios, such as strong winds, earthquakes, and heavy traffic loads. How does this computer simulation demonstrate the use of computing to represent real-world phenomena?

(A) By providing a controlled environment for testing the bridge's design without the risks and costs associated with building and testing a physical prototype.

(B) By allowing engineers to visualize the bridge's construction process in real-time.

(C) By collecting data from real-world bridges to create a realistic simulation.

(D) By automating the process of building and testing physical bridge models.

18 ⬚ Mark for Review

Which of the following best describes the role of the World Wide Web in the context of the internet?

(A) It provides the infrastructure for communication between devices over the internet using IP addresses.

(B) It is a service that allows users to search for websites using search engines.

(C) They are the same thing—both the World Wide Web and the internet refer to the same global network.

(D) It is a system of interconnected documents and resources accessed through web browsers using HTTP or HTTPS protocols.

19 ⬚ Mark for Review

A study found a strong correlation between getting certified as an IT technician and crime rates. Which of the following conclusions can be drawn from this data?

(A) Getting certified as an IT technician causes people to commit crimes.

(B) Committing crimes causes people to get certified as an IT technician.

(C) There may be a third factor, such as location, that influences both certification rates and crime rates.

(D) There is no relationship between IT certification and crime rates.

GO ON TO THE NEXT PAGE.

20 ▢ Mark for Review

What is displayed as a result of the following code segment?

```
x ← 10
y ← 5
x ← x + y
y ← x - y
x ← x - y
y ← y * 2
DISPLAY(x)
DISPLAY(y)
```

(A) 5
20

(B) 10
20

(C) 5
10

(D) 10
5

21 ▢ Mark for Review

Which of the following statements best describes the process of converting analog data into digital data?

(A) Analog data is directly converted into digital data without any loss of information.

(B) Analog data is divided into discrete samples, and each sample is assigned a binary code.

(C) Analog data is filtered to remove high-frequency components before digitization.

(D) Analog data is transmitted over a digital network without any conversion.

GO ON TO THE NEXT PAGE.

22 ☐ Mark for Review

Which of the following expressions is equivalent to NOT(A OR B)?

Ⓐ NOT(A) OR NOT(B)

Ⓑ NOT(A) AND NOT(B)

Ⓒ A OR NOT(B)

Ⓓ A AND NOT(B)

23 ☐ Mark for Review

A researcher develops a new algorithm for image recognition and shares the code publicly under an open-source license. Which of the following is a potential ethical concern associated with this action?

Ⓐ The algorithm could be used to create deep fakes, leading to misinformation and harm.

Ⓑ The researcher could lose control over the algorithm's future development.

Ⓒ The algorithm could be used to infringe on copyright laws.

Ⓓ The algorithm could be used to develop autonomous weapons.

24 ☐ Mark for Review

A warehouse assigns unique 5-bit binary codes to its inventory items. The warehouse plans to expand its catalog and is considering switching to 6-bit binary codes.

Which of the following best describes the impact of switching from 5-bit to 6-bit binary codes?

Ⓐ The number of unique item codes doubles.

Ⓑ The number of unique item codes increases by 64.

Ⓒ The number of unique item codes becomes six times larger.

Ⓓ The number of unique item codes is quadrupled.

GO ON TO THE NEXT PAGE.

25 ☐ Mark for Review

Which of the following situations is best suited to be solved using a heuristic algorithm, which prioritizes speed and approximation over precise solutions?

Ⓐ Designing an app to help college students calculate their exact grade point average.

Ⓑ Analyzing a large set of data to recommend recipes users could cook for dinner based on available ingredients.

Ⓒ Creating a program for engineers requiring precise calculations in designing aircraft components.

Ⓓ Writing software to control the exact output of a car's odometer reading.

26 ☐ Mark for Review

Josh and Lynn both completed the following coding challenge which is supposed to take in grades from a user until the user inputs −1, adding each number to a list. Below are their submissions. Which of the following is true about the code segments?

Josh's Code

```
numbers ← []
DISPLAY("Enter a number (-1 to stop): ")
num = INPUT()

REPEAT UNTIL (num = -1)
{
    DISPLAY("Enter a number (-1 to stop): ")
    APPEND(numbers, num)
    num = INPUT()
}
```

Lynn's Code

```
numbers ← []
DISPLAY("Enter a number (-1 to stop): ")
num = INPUT()
REPEAT UNTIL (num = -1)
{
    DISPLAY("Enter a number (-1 to stop): ")
    num = INPUT()
    APPEND(numbers, num)
}
```

Ⓐ Both Josh's and Lynn's code will always produce the correct list of all entered numbers.

Ⓑ Josh's code will always produce the correct list, while Lynn's will miss the first input number and append −1.

Ⓒ Lynn's code will always produce the correct list, while Josh's will miss the last input number.

Ⓓ Both Josh's and Lynn's code segments will always produce incorrect results.

GO ON TO THE NEXT PAGE.

27 ⬚ Mark for Review

Ryan is experimenting with different color combinations. He has three colors, each represented by a 24-bit RGB value.

- Color 1: 01110111 1110101 10101010
- Color 2: 11001011 01011110 10110110
- Color 3: 10001100 1111001 10101101

Which of the following correctly orders the colors from most blue to least blue?

(A) Color 2, Color 3, Color 1

(B) Color 2, Color 1, Color 3

(C) Color 3, Color 1, Color 2

(D) Color 3, Color 2, Color 1

GO ON TO THE NEXT PAGE.

28 ☐ Mark for Review

Sally is writing a guessing game to play with the computer. She has the computer choose a random number, and she is hoping the game will have her try to guess the number until she gets it right, telling her too low or too high until she gets it correct. Why doesn't her code work as intended?

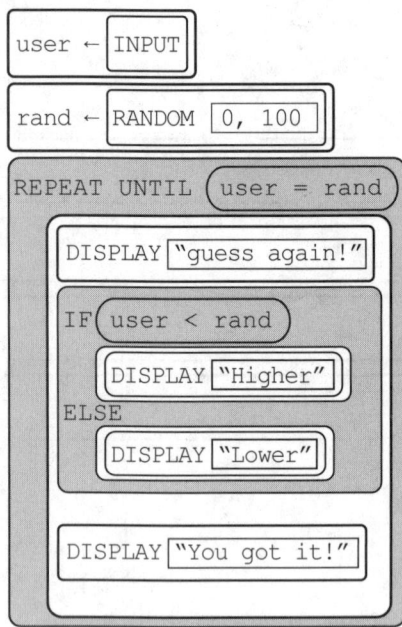

(A) She has to have the computer generate the number before the user enters a guess.

(B) The user currently only gets one guess, which causes the loop to be infinite.

(C) She is using the wrong type of iteration.

(D) Her selection statement should be outside the loop.

29 ☐ Mark for Review

A financial application is performing a series of calculations involving very small decimal values. Over time, the results of these calculations become increasingly inaccurate. What type of error is most likely causing this issue?

(A) Syntax error

(B) Logic error

(C) Round-off error

(D) Runtime error

GO ON TO THE NEXT PAGE.

30 ◻ Mark for Review

Ben has recently discovered that his identity has been stolen. The police have asked him to consider if any of his online activities may have put him at risk. Which of the following scenarios presents the greatest risk of identity theft:

(A) Sharing your full name and email address on a public forum.

(B) Posting a photo of your eye color and hair color on social media.

(C) Emailing your social security number and address to your mother.

(D) Sharing your full name and date of birth to an online retailer.

31 ◻ Mark for Review

A network administrator is tasked with improving the reliability of a network connecting two remote offices. Which of the following strategies would best enhance network redundancy and minimize downtime in case of a network failure?

(A) Implementing a single, high-speed fiber optic cable between the two offices.

(B) Using multiple, diverse network paths (e.g., fiber optic, copper, wireless) between the two offices.

(C) Configuring a single, dedicated server to handle all network traffic.

(D) Relying on a single internet service provider (ISP) for connectivity.

GO ON TO THE NEXT PAGE.

32 ☐ Mark for Review

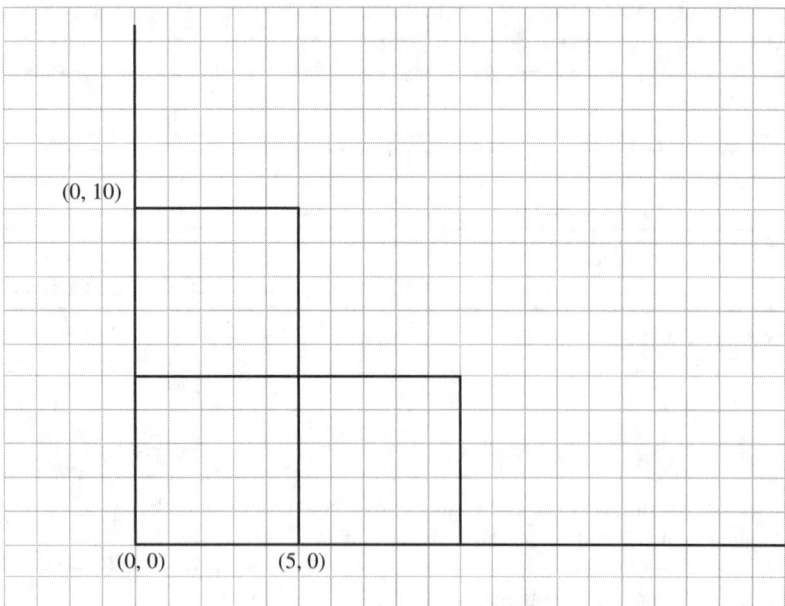

Given the following drawing and a procedure called `DRAW _ SQUARE(x,y,s)` where the `DRAW _ SQUARE` procedure draws a square on a grid based on the following input parameters:

1. **x (number):**
   The x-coordinate of the **bottom-left corner** of the square. This defines how far horizontally the square is positioned from the left edge of the grid.
2. **y (number):**
   The y-coordinate of the **bottom-left corner** of the square. This defines how far vertically the square is positioned from the bottom edge of the grid.
3. **s (number):**
   The size of the square, which corresponds to the length of each of its sides.

Which of the following will correctly make this drawing?

Ⓐ
```
DRAW_SQUARE(0,0,5)
DRAW_SQUARE(5,5,5)
DRAW_SQUARE(0,0,5)
```

Ⓑ
```
DRAW_SQUARE(0,5,1)
DRAW_SQUARE(5,0,1)
DRAW_SQUARE(0,0,1)
```

Ⓒ
```
DRAW_SQUARE(0,5,0)
DRAW_SQUARE(5,0,5)
DRAW_SQUARE(0,0,5)
```

Ⓓ
```
DRAW_SQUARE(0,5,5)
DRAW_SQUARE(5,0,5)
DRAW_SQUARE(0,0,5)
```

GO ON TO THE NEXT PAGE.

33 ▢ Mark for Review

A computer system has two processors that can work simultaneously. The table below shows the amount of time it takes a processor to complete four different tasks.

Task	Processing Time (Seconds)
A	20
B	30
C	45
D	50

Assuming these tasks can be divided and processed independently, what is the minimum total time needed to complete all four tasks utilizing parallel processing?

(A) 75 seconds

(B) 95 seconds

(C) 100 seconds

(D) 145 seconds

34 ▢ Mark for Review

Henry is designing a new game that involves rolling two dice and multiplying their results. The first die is a 4-sided die (with faces numbered 1 to 4), and the second is an 8-sided die (with faces numbered 1 to 8). He needs code to simulate this part of the game.

Which of the following code snippets could simulate the rolling of these dice?

(A)
```
dice1 ← RANDOM(1,8)
dice2 ← RANDOM(1,4)
diceRoll ← dice1 + dice2
```

(B)
```
dice1 ← RANDOM(1,9)
dice2 ← RANDOM(1,5)
diceRoll ← dice1 * dice2
```

(C)
```
dice1 ← RANDOM(0,8)
dice2 ← RANDOM(0,4)
diceRoll ← dice1 * dice2
```

(D)
```
dice1 ← RANDOM(1,8)
dice2 ← RANDOM(1,4)
diceRoll ← dice1 * dice2
```

GO ON TO THE NEXT PAGE.

35 ☐ Mark for Review

Consider the following method for string manipulation:

`IndexOf(str1, str2)`	Returns the index (position) of the first occurrence of `str2` within the `str1`. If `str2` is not found in `str1` it would return –1
	Example:
	`indexOf("computer", "put")` returns 4
`Substring (str, start)`	Returns a substring of consecutive characters from `str`, starting with the character at position start and going until the end of the string. The first character of `str` is located at position 1. For example, `Substring("computer", 4)` returns `"puter"`.

Which of the following code can be used to print out the rest of the string after the first "A" in the word "BANANA"?

Ⓐ `DISPLAY(Substring("BANANA", IndexOf("BANANA", "A")+1))`

Ⓑ `DISPLAY(Substring("BANANA", IndexOf("BANANA", "A")))`

Ⓒ `DISPLAY(Substring("BANANA", IndexOf("BANANA", "A")-1))`

Ⓓ `DISPLAY(Substring("BANANA", IndexOf("A", "BANANA")+1))`

36 ☐ Mark for Review

```
ans ← RANDOM (2,4) * RANDOM (3,6)
ans ← ans * RANDOM (1,3)
```

Which of the following describes the possible values of `ans` as a result of executing the code segment?

Ⓐ 6 to 72

Ⓑ 6 to 72 or 12 to 96

Ⓒ 12 to 72

Ⓓ 6 to 96

GO ON TO THE NEXT PAGE.

37 ☐ Mark for Review

Why are protocols like TCP and UDP essential for internet communication?

(A) They ensure all data is transmitted in a specific format.

(B) They regulate the speed of data transmission.

(C) They provide a standardized way for devices to communicate.

(D) They encrypt data to protect it from unauthorized access.

38 ☐ Mark for Review

A school district is analyzing student data to improve extracurricular program participation. The district has access to a data set that includes student names, grades, extracurricular activities, and parent contact information. They aim to identify students who participate in no extracurricular activities and notify their parents about available programs. Which programming process would best help the district achieve their goals?

(A) Transforming every record by adding additional information about students' classes.

(B) Filtering the data set to find students who are not involved in any activities.

(C) Combining data to determine the total number of students in the school.

(D) Visualizing the data set through charts to display extracurricular activity participation.

GO ON TO THE NEXT PAGE.

39 ⬚ Mark for Review

A coordinator of a community garden program wants to determine whether participants who attend more gardening workshops are more likely to grow a larger variety of plants. The coordinator has the following spreadsheets available:

- Spreadsheet A contains information on all participants in the community garden program, including their name, participant ID, and the total number of plants they have grown.

- Spreadsheet B contains information on participants who have attended at least one gardening workshop. For each entry, the participant ID and the number of workshops attended are listed.

- Spreadsheet C contains information on participants who have grown at least 5 different types of plants. It includes the participant name, participant ID, and the number of plant varieties they have grown.

- Spreadsheet D contains information on participants who have attended more than 3 workshops. For each entry, the participant name and participant ID are listed.

The coordinator wants to determine if there is a relationship between the number of workshops attended and the diversity of plants grown. Which of the following pairs of spreadsheets can be combined and analyzed to determine the desired information?

   I.   Spreadsheet A
  II.   Spreadsheet B
 III.   Spreadsheet C
 IV.   Spreadsheet D

Ⓐ I and II

Ⓑ I and III

Ⓒ II and IV

Ⓓ I, II, III, and IV

GO ON TO THE NEXT PAGE.

40 ☐ Mark for Review

A researcher at the local university developed a program to count the number of live cells on a slide. Below is a table showing runtime in seconds as a function of the number of cells analyzed.

Number of Cells	Time (seconds)
100	0.5
1000	2
10000	20
100,000	2,000
1,000,000	2,000,000

Given the trend in runtime values, which statement best describes the program?

Ⓐ The program demonstrates characteristics of a heuristic algorithm.

Ⓑ The program runs, but it does not run in reasonable time as the input grows.

Ⓒ The program runs efficiently, scaling within reasonable time as the input grows.

Ⓓ The program attempts to solve an undecidable problem, leading to erratic behavior.

41 ☐ Mark for Review

A company installs an employee monitoring program on company-issued laptops to track productivity. However, this program also records every keystroke made by the employees, including sensitive information such as passwords and personal messages. Employees were not informed that their keystrokes were being tracked. What ethical and privacy concern does this practice raise?

Ⓐ The program is a type of plagiarism, where employees' work is copied without proper credit.

Ⓑ The program is a keylogger, which records every keystroke typed by employees, potentially violating their privacy.

Ⓒ The program is a phishing attack, where employees are tricked into providing sensitive information.

Ⓓ The program is a copyright infringement, as it violates intellectual property rights by tracking and recording employees' personal data.

GO ON TO THE NEXT PAGE.

42 ☐ Mark for Review

A researcher at an environmental nonprofit is analyzing data to calculate the total amount of carbon dioxide (CO_2) emissions avoided by the organization's tree planting program. Below is part of the spreadsheet showing data for different regions:

Region	Trees Planted	Area (hectares)	CO_2 Absorbed per Tree (kg)	Planting Date	Project Duration (Years)
North Region	1,200	50	22	2020-05-01	5
South Region	2,500	100	20	2021-03-15	4
East Region	1,800	75	19	2022-06-30	3
West Region	3,000	120	21	2019-11-10	6
Central Region	1,000	40	24	2020-08-22	5

The researcher wants to calculate the total amount of CO_2 absorbed by all trees planted across all regions.

Which columns in the database can be ignored and still allow the researcher to perform this calculation?

Ⓐ Region, Area (hectares), Planting Date, Project Duration (Years)

Ⓑ Region, Trees Planted, Area (hectares), Project Duration (Years)

Ⓒ CO_2 Absorbed per Tree (kg), Area (hectares), Planting Date

Ⓓ Trees Planted, Area (hectares), Planting Date, Project Duration (Years)

43 ☐ Mark for Review

Which of the following scenarios would benefit most from lossy compression?

Ⓐ Storing a medical image for diagnostic purposes.

Ⓑ Archiving historical documents.

Ⓒ Compressing a text document.

Ⓓ Compressing a digital photograph for sharing online.

GO ON TO THE NEXT PAGE.

44 ☐ Mark for Review

A new AI-powered chatbot is released to the public. Initially designed to provide information and assistance, the chatbot quickly evolves as users interact with it.

Which of the following is a potential negative consequence of this rapid evolution?

(A) Improved customer service and support

(B) Increased efficiency and productivity

(C) The generation of harmful or biased content

(D) Enhanced creativity and innovation

45 ☐ Mark for Review

In a library, a student finds the following 2 procedures:

MIN(a) which takes a list and returns the smallest value
SORT(a) which takes a list returns the list sorted from least to greatest.

If the student wants to determine whether two lists (list1 and list2) have the same smallest value, which of the following uses of these procedures would work to complete this task.

(A)
```
IF (SORT(list2) = MIN(list1))
{
    DISPLAY(MIN(list1))
}
```

(B)
```
a ← SORT(list1)
IF (a[1] = MIN(list1))
{
    DISPLAY(a[1])
}
```

(C)
```
a ←SORT(list1)
IF (a[1] = MIN(list2))
{
    DISPLAY(a[1])
}
```

(D)
```
IF (SORT(list1) = MIN(list2))
{
    DISPLAY(MIN(list1))
}
```

GO ON TO THE NEXT PAGE.

46 ☐ Mark for Review

Which of the following is a key benefit of using an iterative development process?

(A) It guarantees that the final product will be perfect.

(B) It reduces the overall development time.

(C) It allows for early and frequent feedback and adjustments.

(D) It eliminates the need for testing and debugging.

47 ☐ Mark for Review

Algorithm A and Algorithm B are two different algorithms used to solve the same problem. The execution time for Algorithm A is 10 seconds, and the execution time for Algorithm B is 25 seconds. Based on these times, which of the following statements best describes the meaning of the speedup value?

(A) Algorithm A is 0.4 times faster than Algorithm B.

(B) Algorithm A is 1.5 times faster than Algorithm B.

(C) Algorithm A is 2.5 times faster than Algorithm B.

(D) Algorithm B is 3.5 times faster than Algorithm A.

GO ON TO THE NEXT PAGE.

48 ☐ Mark for Review

Which of the following network diagrams does NOT depict a redundant network?

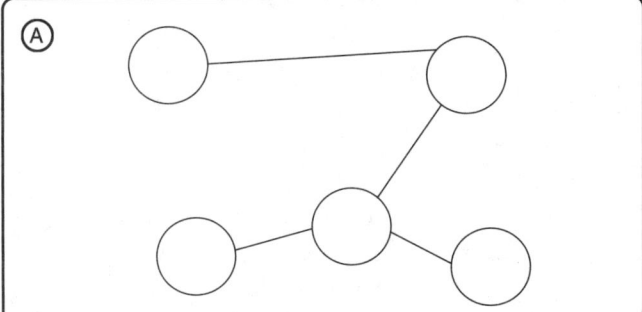

Ⓐ

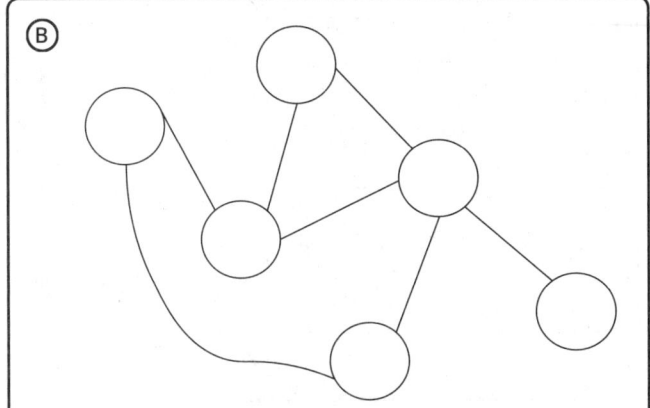

Ⓑ

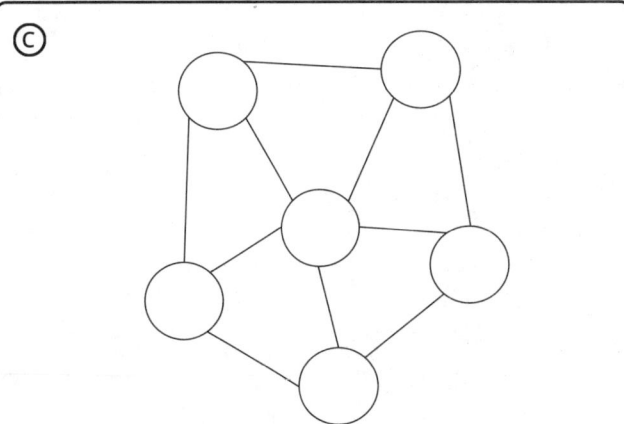

Ⓒ

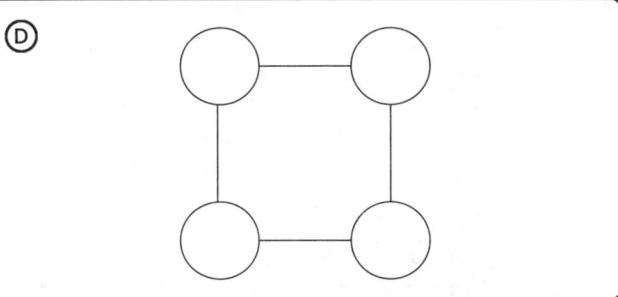

Ⓓ

GO ON TO THE NEXT PAGE.

49 ☐ Mark for Review

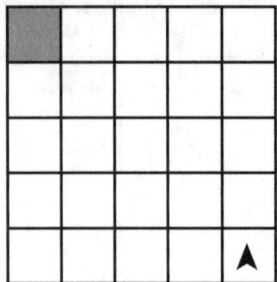

Alex's algorithm	Jordan's algorithm
| ```
REPEAT 5 TIMES
{
    MOVE_FORWARD()
    ROTATE_LEFT()
}
MOVE_FORWARD()
REPEAT 4 TIMES
{
    MOVE_FORWARD()
    ROTATE_RIGHT()
}
``` | ```
REPEAT 5 TIMES
{
  MOVE_FORWARD()
  ROTATE_LEFT()
  MOVE_FORWARD()
  ROTATE_RIGHT()
}
``` |

Which of the following is true?

(A) Both Alex's and Jordan's programs will correctly move the robot to the gray square.

(B) Only Alex's program will correctly move the robot to the gray square.

(C) Only Jordan's program will correctly move the robot to the gray square.

(D) Neither Alex's nor Jordan's program will correctly move the robot to the gray square.

50 ☐ Mark for Review

Which of the following best describes metadata?

(A) The physical hardware components of a computer system.

(B) The software programs that run on a computer.

(C) Data about data, such as author, creation date, and file size.

(D) The process of converting analog data into digital data.

GO ON TO THE NEXT PAGE.

51 ☐ Mark for Review

A company is looking to secure access to their employee onboarding system, which stores sensitive personal information. The system must require Multi Factor Authentication (MFA) to provide strong security. Which of the following authentication combinations would provide the strongest MFA for user accounts?

(A) A username and password combined with a visual CAPTCHA.

(B) An RFID keycard and a fingerprint scan.

(C) A username and password combined with a security question.

(D) Adding a text message verification code.

52 ☐ Mark for Review

A company's IT department notices that several employees' devices are showing connectivity issues on the company's Wi-Fi network. Upon investigation, it is discovered that a nearby employee has set up a personal Wi-Fi hotspot with the same network name (SSID) as the company's official network. Employees, unaware of the difference, are connecting to this unauthorized network instead of the company's secure Wi-Fi. What is this security risk called?

(A) Malware, which infects devices on the network and disrupts communication.

(B) Rogue access point, which allows unauthorized devices to connect to the network.

(C) Phishing attack, where attackers steal login credentials through deceptive emails.

(D) Virus, which spreads across the network and damages devices.

53 ☐ Mark for Review

What is the primary difference between data and information?

(A) Data is raw, unorganized facts, while information is processed data that is meaningful and useful.

(B) Data is more valuable than information.

(C) Information is always more accurate than data.

(D) Data is the processed form of information.

GO ON TO THE NEXT PAGE.

54 ☐ Mark for Review

A grocery store collected data on what shoppers bought for all of 2024. The manager is struggling to make sense of what information can be obtained from the data.

Which could be the biggest issue that the manager is struggling with?

(A) The data is probably too small for much information to be extracted from it.

(B) The manager can't use a single computer to process the data since large data always requires parallel processing.

(C) The data is likely very large and complex, requiring sophisticated data analysis techniques, such as machine learning or data mining, to extract meaningful insights.

(D) The data is probably biased, as it only reflects the purchasing behavior of the store's customers.

55 ☐ Mark for Review

A data analyst is working with a large data set of customer information. They want to identify customers who have made purchases over $100. Which data analysis technique should they use?

(A) Data transformation

(B) Data filtering

(C) Data aggregation

(D) Data visualization

GO ON TO THE NEXT PAGE.

56 ☐ Mark for Review

A social media platform maintains a single database containing records with the following information about each user on the platform:

- User identification number
- Username
- Account creation date
- Location
- Age
- Number of followers
- Number of posts

Using only the database, which of the following can be determined?

Ⓐ The average number of followers for users under the age of 30.

Ⓑ The most popular content type on the platform (e.g., images, videos, text posts).

Ⓒ The amount of time a user spends on the platform daily.

Ⓓ Whether a user is following another user.

57 ☐ Mark for Review

Social media platforms were originally designed to facilitate communication and connection between people. However, they have also been used for unintended purposes. Which of the following is an example of an unintended consequence of social media platforms?

Ⓐ Increased access to information and news

Ⓑ The ability to connect with people from around the world

Ⓒ The spread of misinformation and fake news

Ⓓ The creation of online communities and support groups

GO ON TO THE NEXT PAGE.

Questions 58 through 62 refer to the following.

SpendHere is trying to update their e-commerce platform from a desktop-only system to a web-based application. Currently, SpendHere is only a desktop application that requires both downloading and installing software. The updates create a web-based application, which allows users to shop from any device with an internet connection.

Both platforms will offer similar features, including product search, shopping cart functionality, and secure checkout. However, the new web-based application will introduce additional features like personalized product recommendations and real-time inventory updates. To allow users to get personalized recommendations, the platform will use cookies which contain user data including IP address, browsing history, and purchase history.

58 ☐ Mark for Review

Which of the following statements is MOST likely to be true about the trade-offs of the new web-based e-commerce platform?

- Ⓐ The platform will have higher costs compared to a desktop application.

- Ⓑ The platform will offer users the same experience across different devices.

- Ⓒ The platform will be less likely to be attacked by cyberthreats since it will be web-based application.

- Ⓓ The platform will not require as many updates in comparison to the desktop application.

59 ☐ Mark for Review

Which of the following data is not directly provided by the user but is necessary for the upgraded system to operate as described?

- Ⓐ Product preferences

- Ⓑ User's IP address

- Ⓒ Shipping address

- Ⓓ Payment information

60 ☐ Mark for Review

Which of the following is LEAST likely to be a potential privacy concern associated with the new e-commerce platform?

- Ⓐ Accidental data breaches

- Ⓑ Unauthorized access to user data

- Ⓒ Data misuse for targeted advertising

- Ⓓ User unable to retrieve lost password

GO ON TO THE NEXT PAGE.

61 ☐ Mark for Review

Which of the following groups is most likely to be targeted with personalized advertisements based on their browsing history?

(A) Users who have never visited the new platform

(B) Users who have made multiple purchases on new platform

(C) Users who have only visited the platform once

(D) Users who have blocked all cookies

62 ☐ Mark for Review

Which of the following is LEAST likely to be a benefit of the new web-based e-commerce platform?

(A) Increased ability for customers to access and use the system

(B) Better security features

(C) Personalized product recommendations

(D) Real-time inventory updates

GO ON TO THE NEXT PAGE.

63 ▢ Mark for Review

A neighborhood in Texas has been collecting data on the amount of trash collected each week for the past year. The following graph shows the amount of trash collected each week, measured in pounds.

Weekly Trash Collected in a Texas Neighborhood

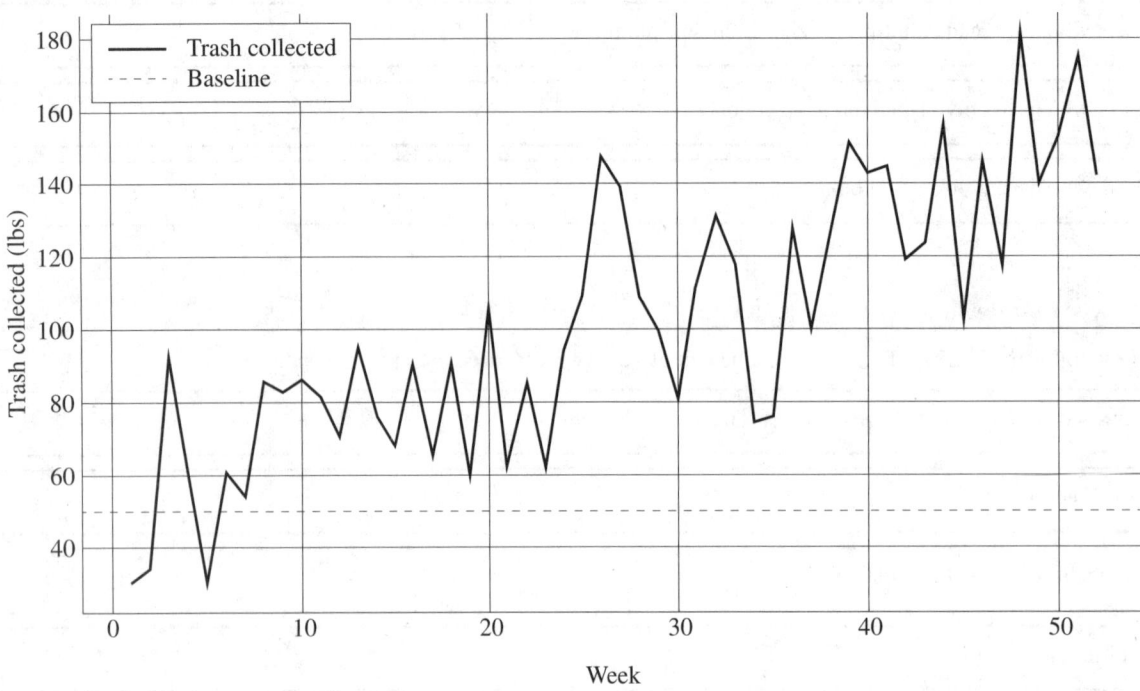

Based on the graph, which of the following conclusions can be drawn about the amount of trash collected in the neighborhood?

Select <u>two</u> answers.

▢ The amount of trash collected has increased steadily over the year.

▢ The amount of trash collected has decreased steadily over the year.

▢ The amount of trash collected has fluctuated significantly throughout the year.

▢ The amount of trash collected has remained relatively constant throughout the year.

GO ON TO THE NEXT PAGE.

64 🔖 Mark for Review

Given the following, which code will correctly move the robot to the gray square.

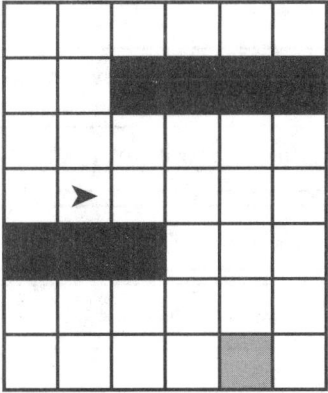

Select <u>two</u> answers.

☐
```
REPEAT 3 TIMES
{
    MOVE _ FORWARD()
}
REPEAT 3 TIMES
{
    ROTATE _ LEFT()
}
REPEAT 3 TIMES
{
    MOVE _ FORWARD()
}
```

☐
```
ROTATE _ LEFT()

MOVE _ FORWARD()

ROTATE _ RIGHT()

REPEAT 3 TIMES
{
    MOVE _ FORWARD()
}
ROTATE _ RIGHT()
REPEAT 4 TIMES
{
    MOVE _ FORWARD()
}
```

☐
```
REPEAT 2 TIMES
{
    ROTATE _ LEFT()
}
REPEAT 3 TIMES
{
    MOVE _ FORWARD()
}
REPEAT 2 TIMES
{
    ROTATE _ LEFT()
}
REPEAT 2 TIMES
{
    MOVE _ FORWARD()
}
```

☐
```
ROTATE _ LEFT()
REPEAT 3 TIMES {
    MOVE _ FORWARD()
}
REPEAT 2 TIMES {
    ROTATE _ RIGHT()
}
REPEAT 2 TIMES {
    MOVE _ FORWARD()
}
```

GO ON TO THE NEXT PAGE.

65 ☐ Mark for Review

Which of the following scenarios demonstrate the use of both iteration and selection in an algorithm?

Select two answers.

☐ A program that asks the user to enter their name and greets them with a personalized message.

☐ A program that processes a list of students' grades, checks if each grade is a passing grade, and prints a message for each.

☐ A program that calculates the sum of the first 100 even integers from a list.

☐ A program that uses a loop to repeatedly roll a die until a 6 is rolled.

66 ☐ Mark for Review

Why is data compression a valuable technique in computer science?

Select two answers.

☐ It increases the amount of information that can be stored in a given amount of space.

☐ It can improve the speed of data transmission over networks.

☐ It makes data more secure by encrypting it.

☐ It reduces the quality of data to save storage space.

67 ☐ Mark for Review

What are the primary functions of an IP address in networking?

Select two answers.

☐ To establish a secure connection between two devices.

☐ To identify a device or network on the internet.

☐ To store and manage website content.

☐ To route traffic between different networks.

GO ON TO THE NEXT PAGE.

68 ☐ Mark for Review

Which of the following are significant factors contributing to the digital divide?

Select <u>two</u> answers.

☐ Universal access to high-speed internet.

☐ Differences in technological literacy and skills.

☐ The affordability of technology devices.

☐ The dominance of English as the primary language of the internet.

69 ☐ Mark for Review

A student is working on a programming project and finds a code snippet online that perfectly solves a specific problem they are facing. The student decides to copy and paste the code directly into their project without citing the source or modifying the code.

Which of the following statements accurately describes the student's actions?

Select <u>two</u> answers.

☐ The student has acted ethically, as the code is freely available online because of Creative Commons.

☐ The student has committed plagiarism, as they have used someone else's work without proper attribution.

☐ The student has violated copyright law, as the code is protected by intellectual property rights.

☐ The student has acted legally, as the code is open-source and can be used without permission.

70 ☐ Mark for Review

A software development team is working on a large project. One developer writes a function to calculate the total price of items in a shopping cart but does not include any comments or documentation to explain how the function works. Another developer, unfamiliar with the code, needs to debug and make updates to this function. What are the primary risks of not including comments or documentation in this function?

Select <u>two</u> answers.

☐ The function may be more efficient, as no time is spent writing additional documentation.

☐ The lack of documentation may make it difficult for other developers to understand and modify the code in the future.

☐ Without documentation, developers may make incorrect assumptions about the function's behavior and introduce bugs.

☐ The code will automatically be optimized by the computer, making additional documentation unnecessary.

STOP

END OF EXAM

Practice Test 1: Diagnostic Answer Key and Explanations

PRACTICE TEST 1: DIAGNOSTIC ANSWER KEY

Let's take a look at how you did on Practice Test 1. Follow the three-step process in the diagnostic answer key below and go read the explanations for any questions you got wrong, or you struggled with but got correct. Once you finish working through the answer key and the explanations, go to the next chapter to make your study plan.

STEP 1 » Check your answers and mark any correct answers with a ✔ in the appropriate column.

Multiple Choice							
Q #	Ans.	✔	Chapter #, Section Title	Q #	Ans.	✔	Chapter #, Section Title
1	C		**5**, Iteration	28	B		**5**, Iteration
2	B		**7**, Citizen Science	29	C		**3**, Identifying and Correcting Errors
3	B		**4**, Extracting Information from Data	30	C		**7**, Safe Computing
4	A		**7**, Computing Bias	31	B		**6**, Fault Tolerance
5	C		**5**, Developing Algorithms	32	D		**5**, Developing Algorithms
6	C		**5**, Mathematical Expressions	33	A		**6**, Parallel and Distributed Computing
7	C		**7**, Legal and Ethical Concerns	34	D		**5**, Random Values
8	C		**7**, Safe Computing	35	A		**5**, Strings
9	A		**7**, Citizen Science	36	A		**5**, Random Values
10	A		**6**, Fault Tolerance	37	C		**6**, The Internet
11	B		**7**, Digital Divide	38	B		**4**, Extracting Information from Data
12	D		**5**, Nested Conditionals	39	A		**4**, Extracting Information from Data
13	A		**7**, Computing Bias	40	B		**5**, Algorithmic Efficiency
14	A		**5**, Boolean Expressions	41	B		**7**, Legal and Ethical Concerns
15	C		**5**, Binary Search	42	A		**4**, Extracting Information from Data
16	C		**4**, Data Compression	43	D		**4**, Data Compression
17	A		**5**, Simulations	44	C		**7**, Beneficial and Harmful Effects
18	D		**6**, The Internet	45	C		**5**, Lists
19	C		**4**, Extracting Information from Data	46	C		**5**, Iteration
20	A		**5**, Variables and Assignments	47	C		**5**, Algorithmic Efficiency
21	B		**4**, Binary Numbers	48	A		**6**, Fault Tolerance
22	B		**5**, Boolean Expressions	49	C		**5**, Developing Algorithms
23	A		**7**, Legal and Ethical Concerns	50	C		**4**, Extracting Information from Data
24	A		**4**, Binary Numbers	51	B		**7**, Safe Computing
25	B		**5**, Algorithmic Efficiency	52	B		**7**, Safe Computing
26	B		**5**, Iteration	53	A		**4**, Extracting Information from Data
27	A		**4**, Binary Numbers	54	C		**4**, Extracting Information from Data

Multiple Choice—Continued							
Q #	Ans.	✔	Chapter #, Section Title	Q #	Ans.	✔	Chapter #, Section Title
55	B		**4**, Extracting Information from Data	63	A, C		**4**, Extracting Information from Data
56	A		**4**, Extracting Information from Data	64	A, C		**5**, Iteration
57	C		**7**, Beneficial and Harmful Effects	65	B, C		**5**, Iteration
58	B		**7**, Beneficial and Harmful Effects	66	A, B		**4**, Data Compression
59	B		**4**, Extracting Information from Data	67	B, D		**6**, The Internet
60	D		**7**, Safe Computing	68	B, D		**7**, Digital Divide
61	B		**7**, Safe Computing	69	B, C		**7**, Legal and Ethical Concerns
62	B		**7**, Beneficial and Harmful Effects	70	B, C		**3**, Collaboration

 **Tally your correct answers from Step 1 by chapter. For each chapter, write the number of correct answers in the appropriate box. Then, divide your correct answers by the number of total questions (which we've provided) to get your percent correct.**

CHAPTER 3 TEST SCORE SELF-EVALUATION

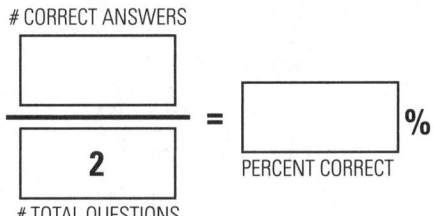

CORRECT ANSWERS / **2** # TOTAL QUESTIONS = ___ % PERCENT CORRECT

CHAPTER 4 TEST SCORE SELF-EVALUATION

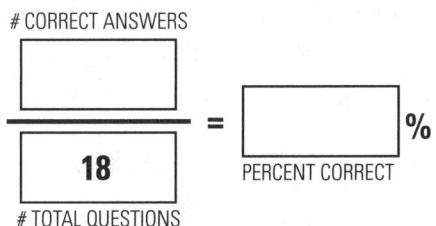

CORRECT ANSWERS / **18** # TOTAL QUESTIONS = ___ % PERCENT CORRECT

CHAPTER 5 TEST SCORE SELF-EVALUATION

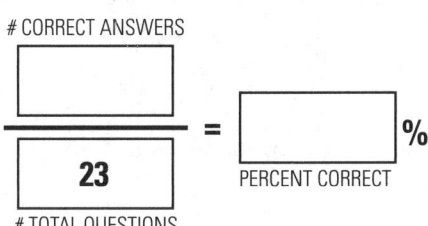

CORRECT ANSWERS / **23** # TOTAL QUESTIONS = ___ % PERCENT CORRECT

CHAPTER 6 TEST SCORE SELF-EVALUATION

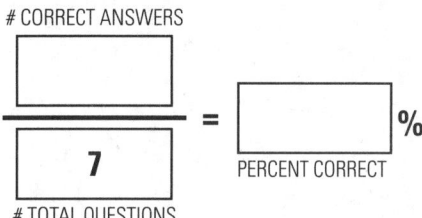

CORRECT ANSWERS / **7** # TOTAL QUESTIONS = ___ % PERCENT CORRECT

CHAPTER 7 TEST SCORE SELF-EVALUATION

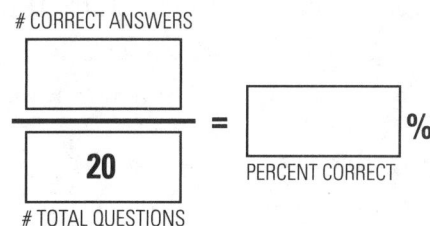

CORRECT ANSWERS / **20** # TOTAL QUESTIONS = ___ % PERCENT CORRECT

 **Use the results above to customize your study plan. You may want to start with, or give more attention to, the chapters with the lowest percents correct.**

PRACTICE TEST 1: ANSWERS AND EXPLANATIONS

1. **C** To find the largest number, we need to compare each number in the list to the current `largest_number` and update `largest_number` if a larger number is found. The given code incorrectly updates `largest_number` when it finds a smaller number. By changing the condition in line 4 to `if n > largest_number`, we ensure that only larger numbers are considered for updating the `largest_number`, otherwise `largest_number` would contain the smallest number in the list. The answer is (C).

2. **B** By definition, citizen science individuals are actively participating in scientific research by collecting and providing data using technology. Choices (A), (C), and (D) involve professionals or institutions conducting research, which is not the core concept of citizen science. A group of volunteers using a mobile app to identify and report invasive species in their neighborhood is the best example of citizen science. The answer is (B).

3. **B** Metadata can be removed, so eliminate (A). Removing the metadata would not change the compatibility of the file, so eliminate (C). Also, removing the metadata would not corrupt the file, so eliminate (D). Since removing the metadata does not affect compatibility, removing the metadata will not allow the teacher to open the file. The correct answer is (B).

4. **A** An AI system that is based on biased data will continue to develop models with similar data and assumptions, causing predictions to be inaccurate. The answer is (A).

5. **C** Algorithm A correctly checks if there are fewer dogs than the total capacity, which means there is space for more dogs if this condition is true. This is a valid way to check for capacity. Eliminate (A) and (D). Algorithm B is also correct. If the number of dogs equals the capacity, then the kennel is full. If not, there's space available. Eliminate (B). The answer is (C).

6. **C** The procedure calculates the sum of all odd numbers in the list by looking at each item in the list. When the item divided by 2 has a remainder of 1, it is added to the sum variable. After the loop finishes looking at each number in list the sum is returned. The answer is (C).

7. **C** While the artist automatically owns the copyright to their work, it doesn't necessarily allow others to use it without permission, so eliminate (A). Public domain would allow anyone to use the work in any way, including commercial use and modification, so eliminate (B). Publishing it online doesn't change copyright but opens it up for possible plagiarism, so eliminate (D). A Creative Commons License allows the artist to specify the terms of use, such as non-commercial use and no modification. The answer is (C).

8. **C** Certificate authorities issue digital certificates that validate the ownership of encryption keys used in secure communications and are based on a trust model. The answer is (C).

9. **A** The company is leveraging the collective intelligence of a large group of people to generate new ideas. All other options are not directly related to this idea. The answer is (A).

10. **A** The system described in the question utilizes redundancy by adding backup systems to ensure that if one part fails, another can take its place and keep the system running. Fault tolerance is related but focuses on the system's ability to handle failures seamlessly without user intervention, which may or may not involve redundancy. Redundancy is a key strategy for achieving fault tolerance, but they are not the same. The answer is (A).

11. **B** Choices (A) and (D) are incorrect because they could exacerbate the digital divide, as not all students may be able to afford a personal laptop or obtain reliable internet access. Choice (C) is also incorrect because relying on mobile data plans can be costly and unreliable, especially in rural areas. Choice (B) is the best solution to bridge the digital divide in this scenario, as it provides reliable internet access to the entire community, enabling equal access to education.

12. **D** Since 5 is not greater than 10, it goes to the `ELSE` statement. Once in the first `ELSE` statement, since 5 is not less than 5, it goes to the second `ELSE` statement and displays `X is between 5 and 10`. The answer is (D).

13. **A** While (B), (C) and (D) may be potential concerns with AI, they are not directly related to bias in training data. When AI algorithms are trained on biased data, they can learn and perpetuate those biases. This can lead to inaccurate predictions, unfair decisions, and discriminatory outcomes. For example, if a facial recognition algorithm is trained on a data set that primarily includes images of white people, it may struggle to accurately identify people of color. The answer is (A).

14. **A** Choice (B) does not check for `fedStatus = false`, meaning the dog could be fed even if it has already been fed. Choice (C) incorrectly uses `fedStatus = true`, which means the dog should only be fed if it has already been fed, which doesn't match the requirements. Choice (D) incorrectly includes times before 7 A.M. for the morning feeding. Choice (A) correctly checks that it's either between 7 A.M. and 8 A.M., or between 5 P.M. and 6 P.M., and that the dog has not been fed already. The answer is (A).

15. **C** A binary search starts in the middle of an ordered list as moves higher and lower on the list until it finds its target. Because a binary search requires an ordered list, eliminate (A) and (B). A linear search starts at the beginning of an ordered or unordered list and advances one item at a time until it finds its target. This can be an inefficient process. Eliminate (D). The answer is (C).

16. **C** By definition, lossless compression reduces file size by identifying and eliminating redundancy in data without discarding any information. This allows the original data to be perfectly reconstructed from the compressed file. Choices (A), (B), and (D) describe lossy compression. The answer is (C).

17. **A** While visualization can be a part of a simulation, it's not the primary purpose in this scenario, so eliminate (B). The scenario describes creating a simulation, not using real-world data to build one, so eliminate (C). The simulation aims to replace physical testing, not automate the physical construction process, so eliminate (D). By providing a controlled environment for testing the bridge's design without the risks and costs correctly highlights how simulations allow for experimentation in a safe and controlled environment, avoiding the potential risks and high costs of building and testing a physical bridge under various conditions. The answer is (A).

18. **D** The World Wide Web (WWW) is a system of linked documents and multimedia resources that are accessed through web browsers using HTTP or HTTPS. It is a service provided by the internet, not the same as the internet itself. Choice (C) incorrectly suggests that the World Wide Web and the internet are the same thing, which they are not. The answer is (D).

19. **C** Choices (A) and (B) are incorrect, as correlation does not imply causation. Choice (D) is incorrect because it contradicts what the data shows. Location could lead to both increased IT certification where the city has a lot of companies that need IT jobs and high population of people, which might increase the likelihood of crime. The answer is (C).

20. **A** Initially, x is given a value of 10 and y is given a value of 5. Then x is updated to be 10 plus 5 which is 15. Then, y is updated to be 15 − 5 = 10. Next, x is again updated to be 15 − 10 = 5. Finally, y updated to y * 2 which is 10 * 2 = 20. The values 5 and then 20 are displayed. The answer is (A).

21. **B** Converting analog signal to a digital signal inherently involves some loss of information, since the process of sampling and quantization, while precise, is not perfect. Eliminate (A). This process does not include filtering, so eliminate (C). This process must occur before transmission over a digital network, so eliminate (D). To convert an analog sound wave into a digital format, a process called sampling is used. In this process, the continuous analog wave is measured at regular intervals, and each measurement is assigned a binary code. This binary representation of the analog signal allows it to be stored and processed digitally. The answer is (B).

22. **B** Since A OR B is true when either A or B are true, NOT(A OR B) is true only when neither A nor B is true. In other words, it's true when both A and B are false. This is equivalent to NOT(A) AND NOT(B). The answer is (B).

23. **A** Choice (B) is a potential complication but not specifically an ethical concern. Choices (C) and (D) are less likely to be direct applications of image recognition technology. Choice (A) is correct as it is a potential ethical concern as the technology could be misused to create misleading or harmful content.

24. **A** A 5-bit binary code can store 2^5 = 32 different possible inventory item numbers, while a 6-bit binary code can store 2^6 = 64 different possible inventory item numbers. Since 64 is double 32, the answer is (A).

25. **B** A heuristic algorithm can quickly analyze available data and provide reasonable recommendations, although heuristic solutions are not precise or exhaustive. Choices (A), (C), and (D) require precise solutions. Choice (B) deals with a potentially large data set and does not require exact solutions, making it a good choice for a heuristic algorithm. The answer is (B).

26. **B** Lynn's code will not record the first number because if it is not −1 then it will immediately get input again before appending the first number to the list. Also, because the input is not the last step of the loop of Lynn's code, when −1 is entered it will append it to the list before exiting the loop. Josh's code does not make these errors and therefore produces the correct list. The answer is (B).

27. **A**   In RGB color, the blue component is represented by the last 8 bits.
    - Color 1: 10101010 (binary) = 160 (decimal)
    - Color 2: 10110110 (binary) = 182 (decimal)
    - Color 3: 10101101 (binary) = 173 (decimal)

    Therefore, Color 2 has the highest blue component, followed by Color 3, and then Color 1. The answer is (A).

28. **B**   Generating the number before the loop keeps that number consistent, which is the intention of the program, so eliminate (A). REPEAT UNTIL is an acceptable type of iteration for this program, so eliminate (C). Moving the selection statement outside the loop would cause the program not to display "Higher" or "Lower" for each guess, so eliminate (D). The user only enters a guess before the loop. Because the guess never changes, user will never match rand and the loop will continue infinitely. The answer is (B).

29. **C**   A logic error, although possible, occurs when the program's algorithm is incorrect or flawed, leading to incorrect results occurring in the same fashion each time, so eliminate (B). Eliminate (A) and (D), because syntax and runtime errors would both cause the program to halt execution. Round-off errors occur when a computer represents real numbers with a finite number of digits, leading to loss of precision. In financial calculations, even small rounding errors can accumulate over time, leading to significant inaccuracies in the final results. The answer is (C).

30. **C**   While sharing personal information online as in (A) and (D) can pose risks, these scenarios are relatively low risk. Sharing physical characteristics as in (B) is generally not considered sensitive information. Sharing your social security number and address, which are considered to be PII, over email creates the possibility of hacking and can significantly increase the risk of identity theft and stalking. The answer is (C).

31. **B**   Using a single cable would cause an outage with the impact of the path, so eliminate (A). Choices (C) and (D) would risk slow service or possible disruptions. Using multiple, different network paths between the two offices is the best strategy for enhancing network redundancy. That way, if one path is impacted, the network can continue to function. The answer is (B).

32. **D**   Choice (A) incorrectly draws a square at (5, 5) with a size of 5. Eliminate (A). Choice (B) incorrectly has the size of each square as 1. Eliminate (B). Choice (C) incorrectly draws its first square with a size of 0, which is incorrect. Choice (D) correctly three squares with a size of 5 and with bottom left corners at (0, 0), (5, 0), and (0, 5), respectively. The answer is (D).

33. **A**   To minimize the total time, we should assign the most time-consuming tasks to different processors.
    - Processor 1: Task C (45 seconds) and Task D (50 seconds)
    - Processor 2: Task A (20 seconds) and Task B (30 seconds)

    The longer of the two processor times will determine the total time, which in this case is 45 + 30 = 75 seconds. The answer is (A).

34. **D** The 8-sided die should produce random numbers between 1 and 8, and the 4-sided die should produce random numbers between 1 and 4. Based on the exam reference sheet, this requires RANDOM(1, 8) and RANDOM(1, 4), respectively. Eliminate (B) and (C). Then the 2 values should be multiplied together rather than added. Eliminate (A). The answer is (D).

35. **A** The code should initially find the first instance of "A" in "BANANA", which requires "BANANA" to be the first parameter and "A" to be the second parameter of IndexOf. Eliminate (D). The substring must begin with the index after the first "A", so 1 must be add to that index. Eliminate (B) and (C). The answer is (A).

36. **A** The first line of code ans is assigned a random value from multiplying a number between 2 and 4 by a random number between 3 and 6. This results in a value for ans to be between 6 and 24. In the second line of code, ans is multiplied by another random number between 1 and 3, giving the final range from 6 to 72. The answer is (A).

37. **C** While protocols do ensure a specific format for data transmission, this is just one aspect of their role which makes (A) incorrect. Protocols do not directly regulate the speed of data transmission. This is influenced by factors like network congestion and bandwidth, so (B) is incorrect. While encryption is important for data security, it's not a part of the protocol, so (D) is incorrect.

Protocols establish a common set of rules for communication between devices on the internet. This standardization ensures that different devices, operating systems, and applications can understand and interpret data correctly. Without protocols, devices would not be able to communicate effectively, leading to errors and data loss. TCP (Transmission Control Protocol) is a reliable, connection-oriented protocol that ensures data is delivered correctly and in order. UDP (User Datagram Protocol) is an unreliable, connectionless protocol that prioritizes speed over reliability, making it suitable for real-time applications. The answer is (C).

38. **B** While combining data might help determine overall numbers or summaries, it does not address the specific tasks outlined in the question, so (C) is incorrect. Visualization does not help identify students for parent notification and transforming data refers to changing data elements, such as adding new details to records. Therefore, neither (A) nor (D) are correct. Filtering the data set to find students who are not involved in any activities would allow the district to improve extracurricular involvement. The answer is (B).

39. **A** Spreadsheet A contains the number of plants grown by all participants. Spreadsheet B contains the number of workshops attended by all participants. These are the two pieces of information that are required. With this data, the coordinator can analyze whether participants who attend more workshops are growing more plants in total. The answer is (A).

40. **B** The table shows that runtime grows exponentially as the number of cells increases. For 1,000,000 cells, the runtime is 2,000,000 seconds (over 23 days), which is impractical for most applications. This clearly indicates that the program is not running in "reasonable time," often defined as scaling polynomially or better with input size. The answer is (B).

41. **B** The monitoring program was likely intended to track productivity; it functions like a keylogger by recording all keystrokes, including personal and sensitive information such as passwords. This creates significant privacy concerns, as employees were not informed that their every action was being monitored in such detail. Plagiarism and copyright issues are unrelated to this scenario, as the concern is about privacy and data collection without consent. The answer is (B).

42. **A** To find the total amount of CO_2 absorbed, multiply the average CO_2 absorbed per tree by the number of trees. These are the only two columns that are needed. Region, Area (hectares), Planting Date, Project Duration (Years) are not required to calculate the total amount of CO_2 absorbed by all trees planted across all regions. All other options show data that is required for the calculations. The answer is (A).

43. **D** Choices (A), (B), and (C) are processes that require precision and accuracy, and therefore would require lossless compression. Compressing a digital photograph for sharing online is the best answer. Lossy compression is ideal for images where a slight reduction in quality is acceptable in exchange for significant file size reduction. This is particularly beneficial for sharing photos online, as smaller file sizes lead to faster upload and download times. The answer is (D).

44. **C** As the chatbot evolves due to user interaction, if that interaction is harmful or biased, the chatbot will evolve accordingly. Choices (A), (B), and (D) all represent possible benefits of the chatbot. The answer is (C).

45. **C** A list cannot be compared to a single value. Since SORT(a) returns a list of MIN(a) returns a single value, (A) and (D) can be eliminated. Choice (B) makes no comparison between list1 and list2 so (B) can be eliminated. Choice (C) first sorts list1 and saves it to variable, a, putting the least value of list1 at the first index of a. Then it checks to determine if the first item is the same as what is returned from MIN(list2) procedure which returns the smallest value from list2. The answer is (C).

46. **C** Choice (A) is incorrect because no development process can guarantee a perfect product. Choice (B) is incorrect because iterative development doesn't make the overall development time shorter. Choice (D) is incorrect because testing and debugging are needed in any development process. Iterative development, by definition, involves breaking down the development process into smaller cycles, allowing for continuous testing, feedback, and refinement. This approach helps identify and fix issues early on, leading to a higher-quality product. The answer is (C).

47. **C** Speedup is calculated by dividing the execution time of Algorithm B by the execution time of Algorithm A. This means that Algorithm A is 2.5 times faster than Algorithm B. The answer is (C).

48. **A** Redundant routing is a system in which multiples paths between devices are possible. Choices (B), (C), and (D) all have multiple paths. Choice (A), however, has only one path from one device to another. The answer is (A).

49. **C** Jordan's algorithm moves the robot forward, turns the robot left, moves the robot another step, and turns the robot to the right. By repeating this pattern five times, the robot will reach the top-left corner. Alex's algorithm also involves a combination of forward movements and turns, both left and right, but it results in a specific pattern of movement on the grid, ending before it reaches the gray square. The answer is (C).

50. **C** Metadata is data that provides information about other data. It can include details such as the author, creation date, file size, and other relevant attributes. Metadata helps in organizing, searching, and understanding digital information. The answer is (C).

51. **B** The username relies on "something you know" and is coupled with visual CAPTCHA. The visual CAPTCHA is a challenge-response test to verify you're human, but it does not serve as an additional authentication factor. Eliminate (A). Username, password, and the answer to a security question only is information of the "something you know" category so it is not acceptable for MFA. Eliminate (C). While adding a verification code is better, it still relies solely on "something you know" and can be compromised and is not coupled with a second form of authentication. Eliminate (D). Choice (B) is correct because it requires both something you have, "an RFID card," and also something you are, which is your fingerprint. It is a strong implementation of multi-factor authentication. The answer is (B).

52. **B** In this scenario, the unauthorized personal hotspot is a rogue access point. It acts like the company's official Wi-Fi network (same SSID), causing employees to unknowingly connect to it. This can lead to security issues such as unauthorized access, data interception, and potentially malicious attacks. The answer is (B).

53. **A** Data is the raw material, and information is the product derived from processing and interpreting that data. Both (B) and (C) depend on the value of data and information depending on the source and how it's used. Choice (D) is a reversal of this idea. The answer is (A).

54. **C** Choice (A) is unlikely, as a year's worth of grocery store data would likely be quite large. Choice (B) is incorrect because while the data set may be large, computers can handle it and parallel processing is not always required. Choice (D) is incorrect because although the data may be biased, the bias is not likely to be a large issue because the data comes from the grocery store the manager is concerned with. Since large datasets require careful analysis and sophisticated tools to extract meaningful insights, the answer is (C).

55. **B** Data transformation only involves changing data to make it uniform for processing. It's not directly useful for identifying customers of a specific purchase amount, so eliminate (A). No data needs to be combined, so eliminate (C). Nothing to be displayed in a graph or chart, so eliminate (D). By applying a filter to the data set, the customers who did not make purchases over $100 can be determined. The answer is (B).

56. **A**   Eliminate (B) because the platform does not track content type. Eliminate (C) because it does not track time the platform is in use per user. Eliminate (D) because although the platform does track the number of followers, it does not track the usernames of those followers. The average number of followers for users under the age of 30 can be determined using age and number of followers, both of which are tracked by the platform. The answer is (A).

57. **C**   The spread of misinformation and fake news is an unintended consequence of social media platforms. While these platforms have many benefits, they can also be used to spread false information that can have negative impacts on individuals and society as a whole. The answer is (C).

58. **B**   While web-based applications may have some initial costs, they are often more cost friendly due to lower maintenance costs, so eliminate (A). Web-based applications, since they are on the internet, are more susceptible to cyberthreats, and due to that, often require more updates to protect the application, so eliminate (C) and (D). Web-based applications can be accessed from a variety of devices (computers, tablets, smartphones), ensuring a consistent user experience. The correct answer is (B).

59. **B**   Product preferences, shipping address, and payment information are all provided by the user, so eliminate (A), (C), and (D). The new system automatically collects and analyzes cookies, which will contain the user's IP address, browsing history, and purchase history without the user's direct input to create personalized product recommendations. The answer is (B).

60. **D**   While giving personalized recommendations can improve the user experience, the collection and analysis of user data does raise privacy concerns as presented in (A) and (B). There's a risk that this data could be misused for targeted advertising beyond what the user is anticipating as presented in (C). Choice (D) is just a possible feature of the system that is needed and not necessarily a privacy concern. The answer is (D).

61. **B**   Choices (A), (C), and (D) do not present sufficient data for targeted advertising. Choice (B) is correct, since as users make more purchases, there is more data available to predict future preferences.

62. **B**   Choice (A) is a likely benefit as a web-based application should be able to be used across more devices. Choices (C) and (D) are stated as improvements for the new application. Since the new, improved application is web-based, there are more risks to cyberattacks compared to the original desktop application, so better security features are unlikely to be a benefit. The answer is (B).

63. **A, C**   The upward trend in the graph indicates that the amount of trash collected has generally increased over the year, making (A) correct and eliminating (B). While there's an overall upward trend, the graph also shows fluctuations in the amount of trash collected from week to week. This suggests that there are factors influencing the amount of trash, such as seasonal changes or local events, making (C) correct and eliminating (D). The answers are (A) and (C).

64. **A, C** Choice (A) first moves forward (to the right) three times. Then it rotates left three times to face down. Lastly it moves 4 squares down to reach the target gray square. Choice (C) rotates 90 degrees left to face up, moves 1 square up, rotates 90 degrees right to face right, moves 3 squares right, rotates 90 degrees right to face down, and lastly moves 4 squares down to reach the gray target square. The answers are (A) and (C).

65. **B, C** Asking for a name and giving a personalized message does not use either iteration or selection. Eliminate (A). Using a loop to repeatedly roll a die does require iteration but does not require selection. Eliminate (D). Choice (B) uses iteration to check each grade and selection to determine whether the grade is a passing grade. Choice (C) uses iteration to check each number in the list and selection to determine which numbers are even. The answers are (B) and (C).

66. **A, B** Encryption is a separate technique from data compression and is used to protect data security, not to reduce its size, so eliminate (C). While some compression techniques can reduce data quality, this is not the primary goal. The aim is to reduce file size without significant loss of information. Eliminate (D). Data compression reduces the size of data, allowing more data to be stored in the same amount of space, making (A) correct. Files of smaller sizes can be transmitted faster over networks, so (B) is also correct. The answers are (A) and (B).

67. **B, D** Choice (A) is incorrect because securing data transmission is handled by protocols such as HTTPS. Choice (C) is incorrect because storing and managing website content is the responsibility of web servers and associated protocols like HTTP or HTTPS. Both (B) and (D) are correct answers as IP address is assigned to each device on the internet and IP addresses are integral to routing, directing packets of data from one network to another to reach their destination.

68. **B, D** The digital divide is primarily caused by:
    - Differences in technological literacy and skills: People with lower levels of digital literacy may struggle to use technology effectively, limiting their access to information and opportunities.
    - The dominance of English as the primary language of the internet: This can limit access for people who are not fluent in English, as many online resources and services are primarily available in English.
    - While universal access to high-speed internet and the affordability of technology devices are important factors in reducing the digital divide, they are not the primary causes.

    The answers are (B) and (D).

69. **B, C** Choice (A) appeals to a common misconception that if code is freely available online, it can be used without consequence. However, even if code is accessible, it still has ownership and copyright protections. Choice (D) is incorrect because it plays on the idea of open-source software, which often allows for reuse and modification under specific licenses. However, not all code is open-source, and even open-source code often requires attribution and adherence to specific licensing terms.

The student has used someone else's work (the code snippet) without acknowledging the original author. This is a form of academic dishonesty and is considered plagiarism, so (B) is correct. Even if the code is freely available online, it is still protected by copyright law. Copying and pasting the code without proper attribution or permission is a violation of copyright law, so (C) is also correct. The answers are (B) and (C).

70. **B, C** A lack of documentation is not related to efficiency or optimization, so eliminate (A) and (D). The lack of documentation may make it difficult for the second developer to understand the intentions and methods of the first developer, which could lead to further errors. The answers are (B) and (C).

HOW TO SCORE PRACTICE TEST 1

Section I: Multiple Choice

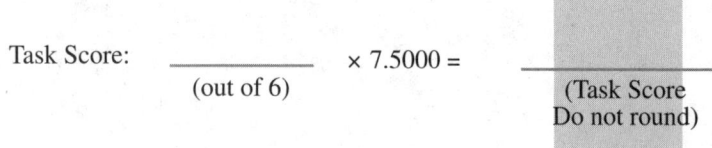

$$\underline{\hspace{3cm}} \times 1.5000 = \underline{\hspace{4cm}}$$

Number Correct
(out of 70)

Weighted
Section I Score
(Do not round)

Section II: Create Performance Task

(This is completed and submitted outside of test time. Do your best to score your Create Performance Task using the guidelines in Chapter 2.)

Task Score: $\underline{\hspace{2cm}} \times 7.5000 = \underline{\hspace{3cm}}$
(out of 6)

(Task Score
Do not round)

AP Score Conversion Chart Computer Science Principles	
Composite Score Range	AP Score
112–150	5
98–111	4
80–97	3
55–79	2
0–54	1

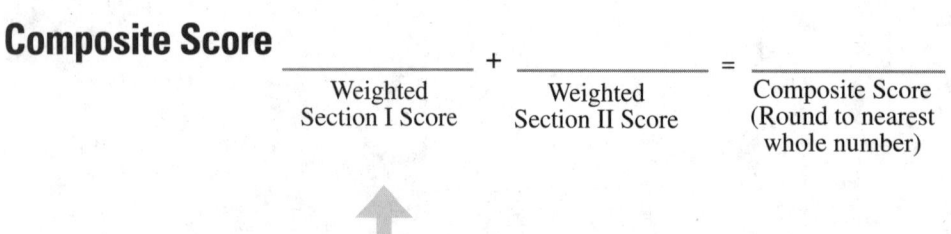

Composite Score

$$\underline{\hspace{3cm}} + \underline{\hspace{3cm}} = \underline{\hspace{3cm}}$$

Weighted
Section I Score

Weighted
Section II Score

Composite Score
(Round to nearest
whole number)

Part III
About the AP Computer Science Principles Exam

- The Structure of the AP Computer Science Principles Exam
- How the AP Computer Science Principles Exam Is Scored
- The AP Computer Science Principles Exam Is Fully Digital
- Past AP Computer Science Principles Score Distributions
- How AP Exams Are Used
- Other Resources

THE STRUCTURE OF THE AP COMPUTER SCIENCE PRINCIPLES EXAM

The AP Computer Science Principles Exam is a two-part test. The chart below illustrates the test's structure:

Section	Question Type	Number of Questions	Time Allowed	Percent of Final Grade
I	Multiple Choice	70	2 hours of test time	70%
II	Create Performance Task • Program code, video, and Personalized Project Reference • Written responses related to the Create Performance Task	4	9 hours of class time 1 hour of test time	30%

The AP Computer Science Principles course and exam require that potential solutions of problems be written in any programming language. You should be able to perform the following tasks:

- design, implement, and analyze solutions to problems
- use and implement commonly used algorithms
- use standard data structures
- develop and select appropriate algorithms and data structures to solve new problems
- write solutions fluently in your chosen language
- write, run, test, and debug solutions in your chosen programming language
- read and understand a description of the design and development process leading to such a program (examples of such solutions can be found in the AP Computer Science Labs)
- understand the ethical and social implications of computer use

The following table shows the classification categories and how they are represented in the multiple-choice section of the exam. Because questions can be classified as being in more than one category, the total of the percentages is greater than 100%.

Have You Noticed?
You may notice that our Part V content chapters align exactly with these units. You're welcome :)

Big Ideas	Exam Weighting
Big Idea 1: Creative Development	10–13%
Big Idea 2: Data	17–22%
Big Idea 3: Algorithms and Programming	30–35%
Big Idea 4: Computer Systems and Networks	11–15%
Big Idea 5: Impact of Computing	21–26%

In addition to the multiple-choice questions, there is also a Create Performance Task, for which you are required to create your own program. You must submit a PDF file of your program code, a video of your app running, and a written response to given prompts. You will be given a minimum of 9 hours of class time and it must be submitted by a given deadline. Be sure to check the College Board site for the deadline.

The multiple-choice questions are scored by machine, while the Create Performance Task is scored by thousands of college faculty and expert AP teachers at the annual AP Reading. Scores on the free-response questions are weighted and combined with the weighted results of the multiple-choice questions. These composite, weighted raw scores are then converted into the reported AP Exam scores of 5, 4, 3, 2, and 1. Each row in the rubric is given either a 0 or a 1 score; there is no partial credit.

HOW THE AP COMPUTER SCIENCE PRINCIPLES EXAM IS SCORED

A numeral score of 1 to 5 is going to be assigned to your test, based on the number of questions you've answered correctly.

- 5 = Extremely Well Qualified
- 4 = Well Qualified
- 3 = Qualified
- 2 = Possibly Qualified
- 1 = No Recommendation

Colleges decide for themselves the minimum score they will accept for college credit and/or advanced placement. The American Council on Education recommends the acceptance of grades 3 and above, and many colleges adhere to these standards. About 70 percent of students who take the AP Computer Science Principles Exam receive a score of 3 or higher. Check the website for each college you plan to apply to so that you can know its policy on granting credit or advanced placement.

THE AP COMPUTER SCIENCE PRINCIPLES EXAM IS FULLY DIGITAL

Both the multiple-choice and free-response sections of the AP Computer Science Principles exam are administered and completed digitally via the College Board's Bluebook testing app. To take the exam, you must have access to the testing app, available for Windows and Mac laptops/desktops, iPads, tablets, and Chromebooks. If your computer or tablet is owned or managed by your school, then a school official will likely have to install this app for you if it is not already on it. The test cannot be taken on a smartphone.

The Bluebook app allows you to annotate and highlight texts, eliminate answers, and flag questions for review later. You will also have access to scratch paper to plan responses to essay questions. Unlike other digital exams like the SAT, the digital AP exam will NOT be adaptive: this means that the difficulty of questions will not change depending on how well you do on earlier sections of the test.

PAST AP COMPUTER SCIENCE PRINCIPLES SCORE DISTRIBUTIONS

Score	2024 Percentage	Credit Recommendation	College Grade Equivalent
5	10.9%	Extremely Well Qualified	A
4	20.0%	Well Qualified	A–, B+, B
3	33.1%	Qualified	B–, C+, C
2	20.3%	Possibly Qualified	–
1	15.7%	No Recommendation	–

Scores taken from May 2024 test administration. Data taken from the College Board website.

Looking for More Help with Your APs?

We now offer specialized AP tutoring and course packages that guarantee a 4 or 5 on the AP. To see which courses are offered and available, and to learn more about the guarantee, visit PrincetonReview.com/college/ap-test-prep.

Create Performance Task

The other portion of the AP Computer Science Principles Exam is the Create Performance Task. This is a student-created app, and the task includes coding, video, creating references and, on test day, written responses. The Create Performance Task is scored from 0 to 6.

Unlike the multiple-choice questions on the AP Computer Science Principles Exam, the Create Performance Task doesn't change. You get to decide what task to complete as long as it fits within the requirements laid out by the College Board.

A minimum of 9 hours of in class time will be provided to complete an original program, supporting video, and Personalized Project Reference. The video must demonstrate input, output, and program functionality.

On Part II of the AP Computer Science Principles Exam (1 hour in length), you will write responses to 4 prompts related to your Create Performance Task. For Part II, you will have access to your student-authored Personalized Project Reference.

Program Design, Function, and Purpose	• Describe the purpose of a computing innovation. • Explain how a program or code segment functions. • Identify input(s) to a program. • Identify output(s) produced by a program. • Develop a program using a development process. • Design a program and its user interface. • Describe the purpose of a code segment or program by writing documentation.
Algorithm Development	• Explain how a program or code segment functions. • Evaluate expressions that use relational operators. • Evaluate expressions that use logic operators. • Determine the result of conditional statements. • Express an algorithm that uses iteration without using a programming language. • Determine the result or side effect of iteration statements. • Compare multiple algorithms to determine if they yield the same side effect or result. • Create algorithms. • Combine and modify existing algorithms.
Errors and Testing	• Identify the error. • Correct the error. • Identify inputs and corresponding expected outputs or behaviors that can be used to check the correctness of an algorithm or program.
Data and Procedural Abstraction	• Develop data abstraction using lists to store multiple elements. • Explain how the use of data abstraction manages complexity in program code. • Write iteration statements to traverse a list. • Determine the result of an algorithm that includes list traversals. • Explain how the use of procedural abstraction manages complexity in a program.

The second section of the AP Computer Science Principles Exam assesses Computational Thinking Practices 1, 2, 3, and 4 across six rubric rows.

Row 1	Video assesses students' ability to implement and apply an algorithm.
Row 2	Program Requirements assesses students' ability to implement and apply an algorithm.
Row 3	Program Design, Function, and Purpose assesses students' ability to investigate the situation, context, or task.
Row 4	Algorithm Development assesses students' ability to explain how a code segment of program functions.
Row 5	Errors and Testing assesses students' ability to identify and correct errors in algorithms and programs, including error discovery through testing.
Row 6	Data and Procedural Abstraction assesses students' ability to explain how abstraction manages complexity.

AP Exams Go Digital in 2025

College Board announced that in May 2025, a number of AP exams will go fully digital or hybrid digital! For the latest information regarding the specific AP subjects going digital and testing accommodations, visit the College Board website at apcentral.collegeboard.org/examadministration-orderingscores/digital-ap-exams.

How Will I Know?

Your dream college's website may explain how it uses the AP Exam scores, or you can contact the school's admissions department to verify AP Exam score acceptance information.

HOW AP EXAMS ARE USED

Different colleges use AP Exams in different ways, so it is important that you visit a particular college's website in order to determine how it accepts AP Exam scores. The three items below represent the main ways in which AP Exam scores can be used.

- **College Credit.** Some colleges will give you college credit if you receive a high score on an AP Exam. These credits count toward your graduation requirements, meaning that you can take fewer courses while in college. Given the cost of college, this could be quite a benefit, indeed.

- **Satisfy Requirements.** Some colleges will allow you to "place out" of certain requirements if you do well on an AP Exam, even if they do not give you actual college credits. For example, you might not need to take an introductory-level course, or perhaps you might not need to take a class in a certain discipline at all.

- **Admissions Plus.** Even if your AP Exam will not result in college credit or even allow you to place out of certain courses, most colleges will respect your decision to push yourself by taking an AP course. In addition, if you take an AP Exam outside of an AP course, they will likely respect that drive too. A high score on an AP Exam shows an understanding of more difficult content than is typically taught in high school courses, and colleges may take that into account during the admissions process.

Some people think that AP courses are reserved for high school seniors, but that is not the case. Don't be afraid to see about being placed into an AP course during your junior or even sophomore year. A good AP Exam score looks fantastic on a college application and can set you apart from other candidates.

OTHER RESOURCES

There are many resources available to help you improve your score on the AP Computer Science Principles Exam, not the least of which are your teachers. If you are taking an AP course, you may be able to request extra attention from your teacher, such as feedback on your essays. If you are not in an AP course, you can reach out to a teacher who teaches AP Computer Science Principles and ask if they will help you with the content.

Another wonderful resource is AP Students, the official website of the AP Exams (part of the College Board's website). The scope of information available on AP Central is quite broad and includes the following:

- a course description that includes further details on what content is covered by the exam
- sample questions from the AP Computer Science Principles Exam
- Create Performance Task sample responses and multiple-choice questions from previous years

The AP Students home page address is apstudents.collegeboard.org/what-is-ap.

For up-to-date information about the AP Computer Science Principles Exam, please visit apstudents.collegeboard.org/courses/ap-computer-science-principles.

Finally, The Princeton Review offers tutoring and small group instruction. Our expert instructors can help you refine your strategic approach and enhance your content knowledge. For more information, call 1-800-2REVIEW.

More Great Books
The Princeton Review writes tons of books to guide you through test preparation and college admissions. If you're thinking about college, check out our jampacked *The Best 391 Colleges* and visit our website PrincetonReview.com for gobs of college rankings and ratings.

Part IV
Test-Taking Strategies for the AP Computer Science Principles Exam

1   How to Approach Multiple-Choice Questions
2   How to Approach the Create Performance Task

PREVIEW

Review your Practice Test 1 results and then respond to the following questions:

- How many multiple-choice questions did you miss even though you knew the answer?

- On how many multiple-choice questions did you guess randomly?

- How many multiple-choice questions did you miss after eliminating some answers and guessing based on the remaining answers?

HOW TO USE THIS PART

Before reading the following strategy chapters, think about what you are doing now. As you read and engage in the directed practice, be sure to think critically about the ways you can change your approach.

Chapter 1
How to Approach Multiple-Choice Questions

THE BASICS

The directions for the multiple-choice section of the AP Computer Science Principles Exam are pretty simple. They read as follows:

Directions: Section I has 70 multiple-choice questions and lasts 2 hours. Each question is followed by four suggested answers.

For questions 1–62, selected the single best answer choice for each question.

For questions 63–70, two of the suggested answers are correct. For each of these questions, you must select both correct choices to earn credit. No partial credit will be earned if only one correct choice is selected. Select the best two in each case.

Reference information for programming questions is available in this application and can be accessed throughout Section I. You may use scratch paper for notes and planning, but credit will only be given for responses entered in this application.

In short, you're being asked to do what you've done on many other multiple-choice exams: pick the best answer (or answers) and then enter it into the application. You will not be given credit for answers you record in your scratch paper but do not enter into the application. The section consists of 70 questions, and you will be given 2 hours to complete it.

The College Board also provides a breakdown of the general subject matter covered on the exam. You will not see the information in the Bluebook application; it comes from the preparatory material that the College Board publishes. Here again is the chart we showed you in Part III:

Big Ideas	Exam Weighting
Big Idea 1: Creative Development	10–13%
Big Idea 2: Data	17–22%
Big Idea 3: Algorithms and Programming	30–35%
Big Idea 4: Computer Systems and Networks	11–15%
Big Idea 5: Impact of Computing	21–26%

A few important notes about the AP Computer Science Principles Exam directly from the College Board:

- Students will be given the Exam Reference Sheet, which contains both block-based and text-based programming constructs and establishes a common way to communicate programming concepts for the purpose of the exam.
- Questions in Big Ideas 1, 2, and 3 can be represented as algorithms with no problem code or as program code using the Exam Reference Sheet.
- The program code questions will contain some graphical representations, some of which use robots in a grid.

MULTIPLE-CHOICE STRATEGIES

Process of Elimination (POE)

As you work through the multiple-choice section, always keep in mind that you are not graded on your thinking process or scratchwork. All that ultimately matters is that you indicate the correct answer. Even if you aren't sure how to answer a question in a methodically "correct" way, see if you can eliminate any answers based on common sense and then take a guess.

Throughout the book, we will point out areas where you can use common sense to eliminate answers.

Although we all like to be able to solve problems the "correct" way, using Process of Elimination (POE) and guessing decisively can help earn you a few more points. It may be these points that make the difference between a 3 and a 4 or push you from a 4 to a 5.

The Two-Pass System

The AP Computer Science Principles Exam covers a broad range of topics. There's no way, even with our extensive review, that you will know everything about every topic in computer science. So, what should you do?

Adopt what we call the two-pass system. The two-pass system entails going through the test and answering the easy questions first. Save the more time-consuming questions for later. (Don't worry—you'll have time to do them later!) First, read the question and decide if it a "now" or "later" question. If you decide this is a "now" question, solve it in your scratch paper and click on the answer in the Bluebook app. If it is a "later" question, use the Mark for Review tool to add a little flag next to the question. Then keep on moving.

Once you've finished all the "now" questions, go back to the questions that you Marked for Review and start on those. Start with the easier questions first. These are the ones that require close attention or that require you to eliminate the answer choices (in essence, the correct answer does not jump out at you immediately).

Don't Be Afraid to Guess

If you don't know the answer, guess! There is no penalty for a wrong answer, so there is no reason to leave an answer blank. Obviously, the more incorrect answers you can eliminate, the better your odds of guessing the correct answer.

Don't Turn a Question into a Crusade!

Most people don't run out of time on standardized tests because they work too slowly. Instead, they run out of time because they spend half of the test wrestling with two or three particular questions.

You should never spend more than a minute or two on any question. If a question doesn't involve calculation, then you either know the answer, can take an educated guess at the answer, or don't know the answer. Figure out where you stand on a question, make a decision, and move on.

Any question that requires more than two minutes' worth of calculations probably isn't worth doing. Remember, skipping a question early in the section is a good thing if it means that you'll have time to get two right later on.

Watch for < vs. ≤ and > vs. ≥

The difference between < and ≤ or between > and ≥ can be huge, especially in loops. You can bet that this discrepancy will appear in multiple-choice questions!

Know How to Use the AP Computer Science Principles Exam Reference Sheet

This chapter offers strategies that will help make you a better test-taker and, hopefully, a better scorer on the AP Computer Science Principles Exam. However, there are some things you just have to know. Although you'll be provided the AP Computer Science Principles Exam Reference Sheet as part of the exam, review it beforehand and understand the pseudocode language before the exam.

Trial and Error

If a question asks about the result of a code segment based on the value of variables, pick simple values for the variables, and determine the results based on those values. Eliminate any choice that is inconsistent with that result. This is often easier than determining the results in more general terms.

Chapter 2
How to Approach the Create Performance Task

CREATE TASK SCAVENGER HUNT WORKSHEET

By the end of this chapter, you should be able to answer the following questions:

1. How many hours will you be given in class to complete the Create Performance Task?

2. Are you allowed to work with a partner for this task?

3. Are you allowed to get help from a teacher or anyone else for this task?

4. What are the three components that you'll have to submit for the Create Performance Task?

5. Which part of the 3 components must be done independently?

6. Can your entire program be collaborative?

7. Can you work on the entire task independently (Yes / No)? Explain your answer.

8. How large can your video file be?

9. What are the acceptable formats for the videos?

10. Are you allowed to have an audio narration in your video?

11. What information should your video contain?

12. How many written prompts about the Create Performance Task will appear on the end-of-course exam?

13. In what format should you turn in your program code?

14. What is the preferred way to give credit for code that you did not write in the Create Performance Task?

15. What other components of your submission should include appropriate acknowledgment?

WHAT IS THE CREATE PERFORMANCE TASK?

The Create Performance Task requires you to create your own computer program and then showcase this program with a video showing its functionality. In addition, on the end-of-course exam, you will have 1 hour to write responses to 4 prompts about your Create Performance Task. The Create Performance Task will constitute 30% of your final AP Computer Science Principles score.

What must you turn in to the College Board (in advance of the AP Computer Science Principles Exam)?

1. Final Program Code (PDF)
2. A video of your program running and demonstrating its functionality
3. Student-authored Personalized Project Reference

Required Elements in your Program Code:

1. Input from one of the following:
   - A file
   - The user
   - A device or sensor
   - A data stream
2. Output that is impacted by the following:
   - The input
   - The developed procedure/functionality
3. A list or collection data type that is important to the functionality of the program
4. Student Developed Procedure that includes the following:
   - A parameter that impacts functionality
   - Iteration
   - Selection
   - Sequencing

Video Requirements:

1. 60 seconds maximum
2. 30 MB max file size
3. Must be .webm, .mov, .mp4, .wmv or .avi
4. Cannot contain narration but captioning is optional
5. Must show input, output, and functionality of code
6. Does not need to show code at all, just program executing

While the code itself can be created collaboratively, the remaining parts of this task—functionality that you developed and written responses—must be done independently. Also note that if any code came from an external source (not you or your partners), it must be appropriately cited in the comments to your code.

The Personalized Project Reference, Part 1

The Personalized Project Reference must be submitted at the same time as your final program code and video. It will be made available to you for the 1 hour section of the end-of-course exam pertaining to the Create Performance Task.

For the Personalized Project Reference, you will need to do the following:

Procedure: Screen capture and paste 2 code segments from your program that contain a procedure that *you developed*, implementing an algorithm used in your program, as well as a call to that procedure. (Note: The capture font size must be at least 10 point.)

The **first** program code segment must be a procedure that *you developed* that:

- Defines the procedure's name and return type (if necessary)
- Contains and uses one or more parameters that have an effect on the functionality of the procedure
- Implements an algorithm that includes sequencing, selection, and iteration

The **second** program code segment must show where the procedure that *you developed* is being called in your program.

The Personalized Project Reference, Part 2

List: Screen capture and paste 2 code segments from your program that contain a list being used to handle complexity in your program. (Note: The capture font size must be at least 10 point.)

The *first* program code segment must show how data have been stored in the list.

The *second* program code segment must show the data in the same list being used.

For example

- Create new data from the existing data
- Access multiple elements in the list as part of fulfilling the program's purpose

Guidance on How to Respond to the Prompts to Get a High Score Using the Rubrics

- All criteria in each row should be met to get a full score. There is no partial scoring.
- Be sure to provide program code whenever asked. Otherwise, you may lose points for certain rows.
- All criteria required for the rubric should be clearly stated as a response to that prompt. (For example, score for Row 2 will be evaluated by the response provided by Prompt 3b.)

CREATE TASK CHECKLIST

Row 1	Video	• Shows input • Shows output • Shows functionality
Row 2	Programming Code Segments	• Code Segment showing data being stored in a list • Code Segment showing same list being used to fulfill the functionality of the program • Ensure both code segments show the SAME list • Ensure list is NOT trivial and is needed for the program to function effectively • If multiple lists are shown in code segments, only the first list will be considered for written response and all grading

Row 3	Programming Code Segments	• Code Segment showing data shows a student-developed procedure that meets all requirements:
		    Procedure must have a parameter
		    Parameter should influence the functionality of the code, so depending on the parameter, different parts of the code should be executed
		• Code Segment showing same procedure being called or used
		• Ensure that procedure is not the whole code of the program
		• Ensure the procedure is NOT trivial and is needed for the program to function effectively
		• If multiple procedures are shown in code segment, only the first list will be considered for written response and all grading

Row 4	Programming Code Segments	• Uses same Programming Code Segment referred to in Row 3 but has additional considerations
		• Code Segment additional procedure requirements:
		    Must have selection (conditional statements, IF-ELSE statements, etc.)
		    Must have iteration (any type of loop or recursion)
		    Must have sequencing

For sample responses and scoring commentaries please visit: apcentral.collegeboard. org/courses/ap-computer-science-principles/exam/ past-exam-questions

Row 5	Personalized Project Reference	Paste screen captures of
		
		• Procedure
		    o Code for the procedure that you developed showing:
		      ■ Name and return type
		      ■ Parameters
		      ■ Algorithm that includes sequencing, selection, and iteration
		    o Where in your program this procedure is called
		• List
		    o Data being stored in your list
		    o How data in your list is being used

POSSIBLE CREATE TASK TIMELINE

Day 1	• Outline ideas for Create Task • Ensure it will require a list that is critical to functionality • Will it contain procedure with a parameter?
Day 2	• Create a more detailed pseudocode • Determine what variables are needed • Decide how you will use iteration and selection in your procedure • Check to see whether the parameter affects which portion of the code will be executed
Day 3–4	• Program the list • Program the procedure and determine how it will be used in the main program code
Day 5–7	• Finalize all programming code, ensure your procedure is called and is required for program functionality • Debug code vs. adding features
Day 8	• Record video; possible software includes Screencastify, Quicktime, etc. • Ensure all video requirements are met
Day 9	• Prepare the Personalized Project Reference
Day 10	• Proofread submission and confirm your submission meets all components of checklist • Submit submission to College Board via Digital Portfolio

COMMON QUESTIONS ABOUT THE CREATE TASK

Do I put my name on my Create Task project?

Your name should NOT appear on your submission in any place.

Is there a specific language that you need to use for the Create Task?

No, the Create Task is language agnostic. Any computer science language can be utilized that will allow you to create procedures and complete all other requirements of the task.

What parts of the Create Task can you work with your peers?

You can work independently or collaboratively on the program code, but all other parts (video and written response) must be completed independently.

Can your teacher help you with your Create Task project?

Your teacher cannot give you feedback or help troubleshoot your code.

How long will you have to complete your Create Task?

In class, you will have a minimum of 9 hours to complete the Create Task, including the program code, written response, and video creation.

Can you work on it at home, outside of the classroom?

You can also utilize any time outside of class to complete the task.

Can you submit an assignment you already created in class?

You cannot submit work that has been submitted for assignments or received feedback from your teacher or another student other than your collaborative partner.

Can you use libraries and other resources for your Create Task project?

Yes; any library or other resources you use should be documented. If your language allows commenting, using a comment to give credit or citation is preferred by the College Board.

CREATE TASK SCAVENGER HUNT WORKSHEET ANSWERS

1. A minimum of 9 hours

2. Yes

3. No—other than your collaborative partner (student from your class)

4. a. Video

   b. Written response

   c. PDF of the source code

5. The video and the written responses

6. Yes. This includes design and testing phases as well.

7. Yes. It is quite okay for the program to have been worked by one person with no collaboration at all.

8. 30 MB in size and not exceeding 1 minute in length

9. .webm, .mp4, .wmv, .avi, or .mov

10. No. However, text captions are encouraged.

11. Input to the program, one aspect of the functionality of the program, and output of the program

12. 4 prompts

13. PDF

14. Write comments in the program code citing references, giving credit to the external sources. If the programming environment does not support comments, then it can be documented in the editor when the program code is captured for submission in the written responses. This includes APIs and open source code.

15. Any media or data sources that have not been created by you or your partner should be acknowledged (citation, attribution, and/or references) to avoid plagiarism.

Another Course? Of Course!

If you can't get enough AP Computer Science Principles and want to review this material with an expert, we also offer an online Cram Course that you can sign up for here: PrincetonReview.com/college/ap-test-prep.

Part V
Content Review for the AP Computer Science Principles Exam

3 Creative Development
4 Data
5 Algorithms and Programming
6 Computer Systems and Networks
7 Impact of Computing
8 End of Chapter Drill Answers and Explanations

Chapter 3
Creative
Development

This Big Idea is primarily to find a way to tap into a student's creative talents and bring them to the forefront. Creativity, by definition, is a way of transforming one's ideas into reality. A product created as a result of personal creativity is a form of personal expression.

Programs can help solve problems, enable innovations, or express personal interests.

COLLABORATION

Programming is a collaborative and creative process that brings ideas to life through the development of software. Software development processes used in the industry often require students to work together in teams. Collaboration can take place at various points and in various ways.

An important concept that is discussed throughout the entire course is the idea of computing innovations. A computing innovation uses a computer program to take in data, transform data, and output data. Smart Assistants such as Siri or Alexa are good examples. These devices have software running inside them. In contrast, a T-shirt labeled "tech shirt" made up of material that absorbs sweat well or keeps a runner warm in winter cannot be considered a computing innovation despite a catchy name. A social media website, though non-physical, is a computing innovation because many computer programs run collectively to make the website work.

To develop functional, robust software, teams must work together collaboratively to produce effective, functional programs. Getting multiple perspectives allows for improvements in the software. Collaboration can occur in the planning, designing, or testing (debugging) part of the development process. Collaboration tools allow students and teachers to exchange resources in several different ways, depending on what suits a particular task.

Many tools help the collaborative process be effective. One such example is Google Docs, which allows multiple users to edit the document simultaneously. Discussion boards such as Piazza (piazza.com/) let team members collaborate in an online space to exchange ideas and discuss solutions to different problems.

Collaborative learning can occur peer-to-peer or in larger groups. Peer instruction involves students working in pairs or small groups to discuss concepts to find solutions to problems.

The idea that two or three heads are better than one facilitates students collaborating by addressing misunderstandings and clarifying misconceptions.

The benefits of collaborative learning include the development of thinking skills, increased student responsibility, exposure to other perspectives, and an increase in understanding of diverse perspectives. This can help eliminate bias. People with different backgrounds and experiences may be able to identify different flaws in algorithms. It helps prepare students for real-life situations. A popular collaborative style of programming is called pair programming. Pair or collaborative programming is where two programmers develop software side by side at one computer, on the same algorithm, design, or programming task. Pair programming leads to greater satisfaction when the project is complete, is better designed, and both participants learn from each other. Research has shown even when pairing a novice programmer with an expert programmer, the novice programmer can contribute effectively to the project. Even collaboration with users can help the programmers understand that perspective in a project.

IDENTIFYING AND CORRECTING ERRORS

There are 4 main types of errors in programming:

- **Syntax Error:** A mistake in which the rules of the programming language are not followed. For example:

```
a ← expression
DISPLAY (A)
```

A syntax error in this example occurs because the second statement attempts to display the variable A, which is not the defined variable. Variable names are case sensitive. While the variable with a lowercase a is defined by the first statement, the variable with a capital A in the second is not defined. Therefore, the rules of the programming language were violated.

- **Run-time Error:** A mistake that occurs during the execution of a program that ceases the execution. For example:

```
DISPLAY (5/0)
```

In this example, there is no syntax error because the language of the code is used correctly. However, this causes a run-time error because you cannot divide by zero. The execution of the program will halt at this line.

- **Logic Error:** A mistake in the algorithm or program that causes it to behave incorrectly or unexpectedly. For example:

```
a ← 95
IF (a > 90)
{
  DISPLAY("You got an A.")
}
IF (a > 80)
{
  DISPLAY("You got a B.")
}
IF (a > 70)
{
  DISPLAY("You got a C.")
}
```

The code is intended to correctly print out what grade the student got. Since this particular student's score was a 95, which is greater than 90, the program *should* display You got an A. However, the program actually prints out the following:

```
You got an A.
You got a B.
You got a C.
```

This logic error occurs because the student's score is also greater than 80 and 70, with no restriction that prevents multiple grades from being printed.

- **Overflow Error:** A mistake that occurs when a computer attempts to handle a number that is outside of the defined range of values. For example:

```
x ← 2000 * 365
DISPLAY (x)
```

The result is the multiplication of a large number. In many languages, this product would be large enough to be outside the range of certain data types. Therefore, if x is defined as a variable of one of those data types, this multiplication will cause an overflow error.

Debugging is the process of finding and fixing errors. You should use test cases, extra output statements, examination for syntax errors, and other debugging tools to find and fix any errors.

Brainstorming

Whenever you create a program, you should start to brainstorm on a topic for designing the program in a way that efficiently accomplishes the goal of the program. Below is a sheet that you can use to aid the brainstorming process.

Preliminary Topic Selection Guide

Program Topic: _____

Program Requirement	No	Probably Not	Probably Yes	Yes
The program will take about 5 hours to complete.				
The program would make use of lists or collections.				
The program should have features that support the design of an algorithm that can be made into a procedure that can be called from the main program. The procedure must have at least one parameter that must be used in a meaningful way, preferably for selection inside the loop.				
The parameter should affect which portion of the code is run. In other words, different parameters should cause a conditional statement or loop to run different code.				
The program needs to use decision statements. It should be part of the identified procedure.				
The program needs to use loops. The loop should be used inside the procedure to iterate the list or collection.				
The program needs to have user input and output. The user input should affect what is output by the program.				

Chapter 4
Data

BINARY NUMBERS

Any digital data has a numerical representation using binary numbers. A **bit** is the smallest unit of information stored or manipulated on a computer; it consists of either zero or one. Depending on meaning, it could instead be described as false/true, off/on, no/yes, or anything else that has two possible values. We can also call a bit a **binary digit,** especially when working with the 0 or 1 values. Everything in a computer is 0s and 1s. The bit stores just a 0 or 1: it is the smallest building block of storage. However, it can be said that a bit is also the largest unit of information a computer can manipulate.

A group of bits is combined so that the computer can use several bits simultaneously for calculating numbers. When a group has eight bits, it is called a **byte**. A bit can represent anything we want, perhaps yes and no, but it has only two possible values. So, to represent more things, we have always grouped bits into larger chunks.

A group of 8 bits has 256 (2^8) possible unique combinations, where each combination can have its predetermined meaning. The number of bits determines some maximum number of unique combinations of bits.

Base Conversion

Binary to Decimal Conversion

Of course, binary numbers are rarely used in real life. Therefore, programmers must be able to go back and forth between the binary numbers we use in computing and the decimal numbers that we use in everyday life. The key is to remember that the different binary digits represent different powers of 2. For example, let's use the binary number 1101.

Use this table:

2^7	2^6	2^5	2^4	2^3	2^2	2^1	2^0	
128	64	32	16	8	4	2	1	
0	0	0	0	1	1	0	1	
0	0	0	0	8×1	4×1	2×0	1×1	
0	0	0	0	8	+ 4	+ 0	+ 1	= 13

Therefore, $(1101)_2 = (13)_{10}$.

Decimal to Binary Conversion

Similarly, in order to make the numbers we use in our everyday lives processable by computers, we need to be able to convert decimal numbers into binary numbers. To do this, we reverse the process. We need to find the powers of 2 that add up to the given decimal number. Start by finding the largest power of 2 that is less than the number. Subtract that number from the original, and repeat until you're down to 0. Try the example of the decimal number 200.

Use this table:

2^8	2^7	2^6	2^5	2^4	2^3	2^2	2^1	2^0
256	128	64	32	16	8	4	2	1
0	1	1	0	0	1	0	0	0

$$
\begin{array}{r}
200 \\
-128 \\
\hline
72 \\
-\ 64 \\
\hline
8 \\
-\ 8 \\
\hline
0
\end{array}
$$

Therefore, the decimal number 200 is equivalent to the binary number 1100 1000.

Using Bits

There are many things the same pattern of bits could represent, like part of one pixel in an image.

> A computer representing data within the computer is different from data interpretation by the computer and representation to the user. Programs translate data into a representation more easily understood by people.

Digital Images as Bits

Images displayed on the screen are converted into binary formats and then processed by a computer displayed on our screen. Digital images are a collection of pixels, where each pixel consists of binary numbers. If we say that 1 is black (or on) and 0 is white (or off), then a simple black and white picture can be created using binary. Draw a grid and color the squares (1—black and 0—white) to create the picture. However, before creating the grid, the size of the grid needs to be known. This data is called metadata, and computers need metadata to know the size of an image. The metadata for the image to be created is 6 × 6; this means the picture will be 6 pixels across and 6 pixels down.

1	1	1	1	1	1
1		1	1		1
1	1	1	1	1	1
1		1	1		1
1					1
1	1	1	1	1	1

Binary and Color Representation

Images are not often just black and white. To represent colors, computers also use binary numbers. Color is based on light. Any color can be created using red, green, and blue light. The maximum value for any color in decimal is 255, which is represented by 11111111 in binary. The minimum number is 0.

Here are some examples of color representation showing both the decimal values and the binary values:

White = [255, 255, 255]   [11111111, 11111111, 11111111]

Black = [0, 0, 0]   [0, 0, 0]

Blue = [0, 0, 255]   [0, 0, 11111111]

Red = [255, 0, 0]   [11111111, 0, 0]

Each color is 3 bytes of data. Engineers, computer scientists, and analysts often need to understand larger amounts of data. The measurement of data is based on the byte.

Music as Bits

An analog signal exists throughout a continuous interval of time and takes on a continuous range of values. A digital signal is a sequence of discrete symbols. If these symbols are zeros and ones, we call them bits. As such, a digital signal is neither continuous in time nor continuous in its range of values. Furthermore, it cannot correctly represent arbitrary analog signals. Sampling is recording an analog signal at regular discrete moments and converting them to a digital signal. Digital signals are resilient against noise. A digital signal representing an analog signal at discrete moments is an abstraction since it hides the continuous analog data. Digital signals can be stored on digital media (like a compact disc) and manipulated on digital systems (like the integrated circuit in a CD player). **Data abstraction** is filtering out specific details to focus on the information needed to process the data. The lowest level of data abstraction is bits. Higher abstraction is with numbers, letters, symbols, video, sound, and audio.

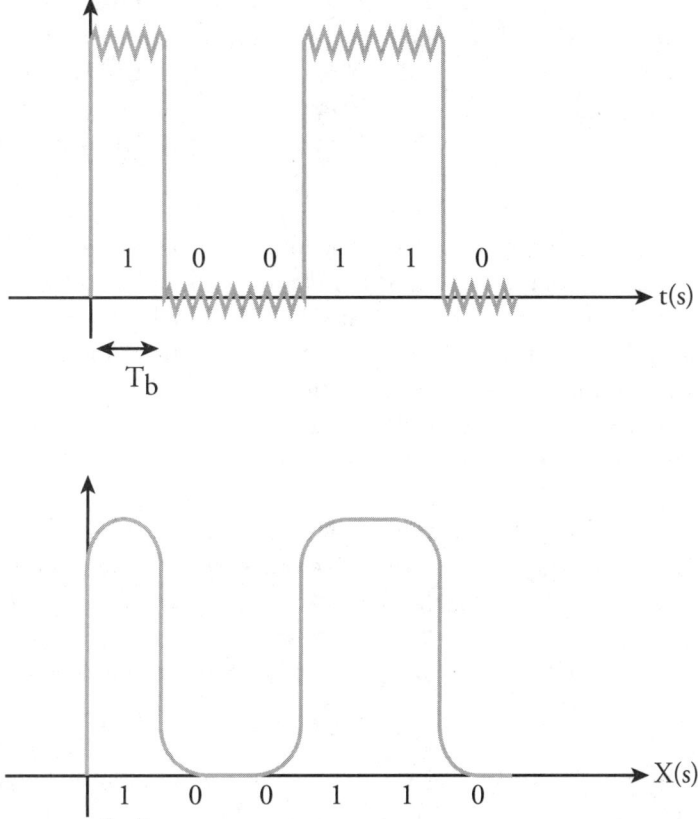

The above illustration is an example of an analog transmission of a digital signal. Consider a digital signal 100110 converted to an analog signal for radio transmission. The received signal suffers from noise, but it is still easy to read off the original sequence 100110 correctly given sufficient bit duration X_a.

DATA COMPRESSION

Data compression is used everywhere. File types like mp3, mp4, rar, zip, jpg, and png (along with many others) all use compressed data. Without data compression, a 3-minute song would be over 100MB, and a 10-minute video would easily be over 1GB. Data compression is a set of steps for packing data into a smaller space while allowing for the original data to be seen again. Whether it's the music that we listen to through our music players or the movies we stream or watch on disc, digital data files are often compressed so that they can fit on your storage devices. Whether you're buying movies or music for downloading online, data compression is a particularly important concern since it determines the quality and file size of the downloads. Compression is also an important consideration when it comes to backing up and archiving your important files, particularly for uploading over the Internet. Compression is a two-way process: a compression algorithm can be used to make a data package smaller, but it can also run the other way, to decompress the package into its original form. Data compression is useful in computing to save disk space or to reduce the bandwidth used when sending data (e.g., over the Internet). Data compression deals with taking a string of bytes and compressing it down to a smaller set of bytes, whereby it takes less bandwidth to either transmit the string or to store it to disk.

Data compression condenses large files into much smaller ones. It does this by getting rid of data that isn't needed while retaining the information in the file. Thus, you could say, data compression involves the development of a compact representation of information. Most representations of information contain large amounts of redundancy. Compression algorithms exploit this redundancy in the data to get a compact representation of the data. This, when achieved, aids in accurate reconstruction of the data.

The task of compression consists of two components: an encoding algorithm that takes a message or image and generates a "compressed" representation (hopefully with fewer bits), and a decoding algorithm that reconstructs the original message or some approximation of it from the compressed representation. These two components are typically intricately tied together since they both must understand the shared compressed representation.

Lossless algorithms are those that can reconstruct the original message exactly from the compressed message, and lossy algorithms can only reconstruct an approximation of the original message. Lossless algorithms are typically used for text, and lossy algorithms for images and sound where a little bit of loss in resolution is often undetectable or at least acceptable. Lossless compression packs data in such a way that the compressed package can be decompressed, and the data can be pulled out exactly the same as it went in. This is very important for computer programs and archives where even a very small change in a computer program will make it unusable.

This type of compression works by reducing how much wasted space is in a piece of data. For example, consider this string which contains "XXXXXZZZZYYY." It can be compressed into "5X4Z3Y," which has the same meaning but takes up less space. This type of compression is called "run-length encoding," because you define how long the "run" of a character is. In the above example, there are two runs: a run of 5 Xs, 4 Zs, and 3 Ys. This algorithm is an excellent example of a lossless compression working with a string of data.

Text compression is another important area for lossless compression. It is very important that the reconstruction is identical to the original text, as very small differences can result in statements with very different meanings. For example, in these two sentences, *"All is now well."* and *"All is not well."* the algorithm has to be very discerning as to what data it considers redundant.

Lossy compression is a technique that does not decompress digital data back to 100% of the original. Lossy methods can provide high degrees of compression and result in smaller compressed files but some number of the original pixels, sound waves, or video frames are removed forever. Lossy is used in an abstract sense, however, and does not mean random lost pixels, but instead means loss of a quantity such as a frequency component or perhaps loss of noise. For example, one might think that lossy text compression would be unacceptable because they are imagining missing or switched characters. However, consider the system high school students use to write college essays, in which sentences are reworded or words are replaced with synonyms so that the text is better compressed. Technically, the compression would be lossy since the text has changed, but the meaning and clarity of the message might be fully maintained or even improved. However, text, and business data in general, does not use lossy compression because this data requires perfect restoration of data. When the amount of the compression increases, the size of the resulting file decreases. However, there is a greater amount of data that cannot be restored.

Images—a high image compression loss can be observed in photos when enlarged

Music—there is a difference between an MP3 and a high-resolution audio file

Video—moving frames of video can handle a greater loss of pixels compared to an image

Lossy Compression with Images

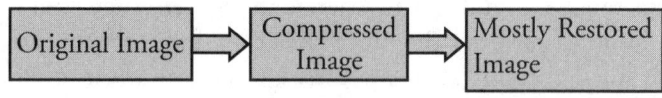

Lossless Compression with Business Data

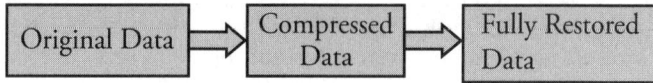

Examples:

Lossy	Lossless
Images: JPEG	Archiving formats: Zip, GZip, bZip2, 7-Zip, etc.
Audio: MP3, Windows Media	Images/diagrams: GIF, PNG, PCX
Video: MPEG, DivX, Windows Video	Audio: ALAC, FLAC, WAV

EXTRACTING INFORMATION FROM DATA

Data science deals with extracting information from and visualizing the results of manipulating large data sets. In a digital world where social media apps collect data about our posts and our likes, online stores collect data about the products we view, and advertising agencies collect data about what we click, it seems like data is all-pervasive.

Each second, millions of data points are collected. Thousands of sensors installed across cities worldwide collect data about all sorts of topics: air quality, noise, the temperature, even about which parking spots on different streets are free or when specific gardens need watering. Users also generate data: everything they do on their smartphones and every interaction they have with any business can be stored. It is possible to process any text or image published online as data in order to extract information. Therefore, companies' big challenge is to give data meaning, transforming it so that it really and faithfully tells a good story about the business, its customers, or society in general.

The difference between data and information is that organized and structured data is information. Information is obtained by extracting useful information from vast amounts of data and creating correlations using this data. Depending on the data and the patterns, sometimes we can see that pattern in a simple tabular presentation of the data. It also helps to visualize the data in a chart, like a time series, line graph, or scatterplot.

Let's explore examples of patterns that we can find in the data around us.

Data analysis involves analyzing and thinking through the various processes and the data. It is sometimes difficult to separate the processes involved in organizing geographic information from the procedures used in analyzing it; the two processes go on simultaneously in many cases. However, in other instances, analysis follows the manipulation of raw data into an easily understood and usable form. Both activities involve the use and development of students' spatial skills. Models can be analyzed to understand the correlations and to describe the relationships and patterns resulting from the overlay of multiple data sets, like describing the relationship of earthquakes taking place with specific kinds of fauna and flora under specific temperatures. Models can be used to analyze data from multiple data sets. By comparing these models, it is possible to identify patterns or relationships between data sets. Data is also analyzed to explain changes through time.

Graphs such as a scatterplot or histogram help identify possible relationships or trends in the data.

In information technology, the prefix meta- means "an underlying definition or description." Metadata is data that describes other data. Metadata describes whatever data it is connected to, whether it is video, a photograph, or Web pages, and summarizes necessary information about data such as author, date created, usage, file size, and more. Metadata is needed to classify and categorize data. Metadata is organized information that describes, locates, or otherwise makes it easier to retrieve information. When a digital product is created, information such as its origin, time, date, and format is stored. A good understanding of metadata helps identify useful data. Data is usually simply a piece of information or a collection of measurements, tables of observations, or a story. On the other hand, metadata provide the relevant information about the data, which helps in identifying the nature and feature of the data.

Summarizing

Data	Metadata
Data is simply the content that describes or reports anything such as a measurement or observation.	Metadata describes the relevant information about the data.
Some data is informative; some may not be, as data can be raw data like numbers or characters, which may not be informative.	Metadata is always informative as it is a reference to other data.
Data may or may not be processed, as raw data is always unprocessed data.	Metadata is processed data.

The problem with unstructured data is that it is hard to sort, manage, and organize. Files stored on servers could have thousands of duplicate copies of data in many different formats, some of which may be invalid or incomplete. The unstructured data is also hard to search and process. There arises a need to add some structure to the data by cleaning it up. The process of adding structure to data is called data mining or data analytics. There are two main ways of adding structure. The first is by adding a storage format to the data. A consistent format helps eliminate the invalid data, making this process a right choice for cleaning data. Another way of cleaning data is using log files that help cluster data that is easier to manipulate, such as grouping data with the same time stamps. In doing this, the data is cleaned up by parsing/extracting through the log files and finding meaningful data. This data is now called unstructured data.

Consider the fact that there is no downtime as far as the World Wide Web is concerned; therefore, there may be a need for many data stores. Sometimes the data available is much higher than the model can effectively process. In such cases, the model responses to the data fed in have a bias in them. More data does not fix this problem. It may worsen the situation by adding to the noise in the data. The World Wide Web is used by everyone, from scientists and businesses to five-year-olds exchanging emojis. As a result, there is a need for scalability, which is the potential of a system, network, or process to be enlarged to accommodate that data growth. Before we scale a system, there needs to be an analysis done on the system's capacity. It is important to understand the extreme requirements such as highest and average transactions per second, the highest number of queries, payload size, expected throughput, and backup requirements. This helps with the data store scalability design in making decisions such as how many physical servers are needed, the hardware configuration of the data storage devices, memory footprint, disk size, CPU Cores, I/O throughput, etc.

USING PROGRAMS WITH DATA

The increase in digitization of information, mixed with multiple transactions, has resulted in a flood of data. The advancement in technology has promoted the rapid growth of data volume in recent years. By analyzing large sets of data, it is possible to categorize connections from unconnected data sources and find specific patterns. Data extraction is the process of obtaining data from a database or software such as a social media website so that it can transport it to a different software (such as spreadsheets) designed to support online analytical processing. Data extraction is the first step. The next step is to transform (either through filters or programs). The final step is to analyze using graphs and other data visualization tools.

The process of extracting involves finding entities such as name, email I.D., online profile names, and other such private data belonging to someone. This data is then classified and stored in a repository such as a database. The information extraction (IE) process extracts specific, prespecified, and useful information from text, such as attributes related to objects, events, etc. The extracted information is used to prepare data for analysis, and hence there is a need for efficient and accurate transformation. Different techniques are applied based on the type of data (such as text, image, audio, and video).

An excellent example is data mining that happens within email software. Some emails have data embedded, which is added to the email software calendar. The email software knows to identify the data in these emails and add it to the calendar.

Below are the steps to extract data and analyze them:

1. **Analyze the data sources.** Data sources are found in different forms like Web pages, video files, audio files, text documents, customer emails, and chat messages.
2. **Know what will be done with the results of the analysis.** It is vital to understand what sort of outcome is required. Is it a trend, effect, cause, quantity, or something else that is needed?
3. **Decide the tools needed to read the data and the repositories, such as databases, needed to store the data.** Clean the data of whitespace, symbols, duplicates, etc.
4. **Understand the data patterns and text flow.** This should be done using visualization tools.

This process is also known as data mining. Below is an illustration that shows the process.

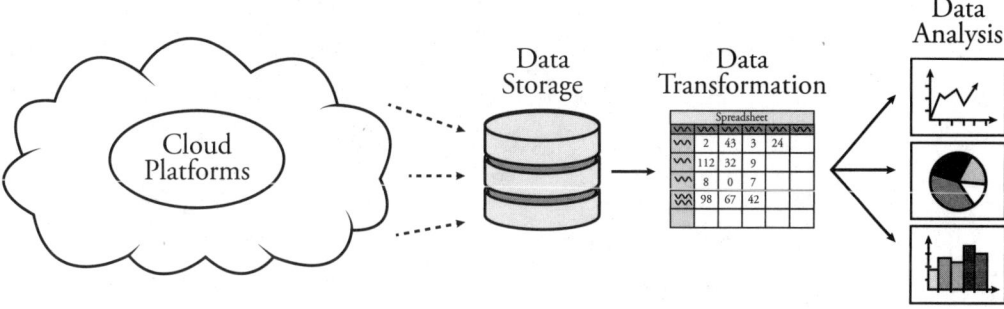

How to Read and Analyze Graphs

A graph is a pictorial representation, like a diagram used to represent data. It usually is used to depict a relationship. Graphs and charts represent data in points, lines, bars, pie charts, and scatterplots. Different types of graphs and charts display data in different ways. Some are better suited than others for different uses.

Picture graphs use pictures to represent values.
Bar graphs use either vertical or horizontal bars to represent the values.
Line graphs use lines to represent the values.
Scatterplots represent the data with points, and then a best-fit line is drawn through some of the points.

While analyzing graphs, it is essential to determine what the graph displays and why such information is pertinent to the experiment or the question's context. Read the graph first. Next, read the title and axes of the graph to determine the type of data represented. The x-axis is the independent variable, or that which can be changed. The y-axis is the dependent variable, or that which depends on the independent variable.

In a picture graph, look for the line with the highest number of pictures. For a bar graph, look for the highest bar. For a line graph or a scatterplot, look at the slope of the line. If the line is pointing to the upper right corner, then the slope is positive. If the line is pointing to the lower right corner, then the slope is negative. Use the graph to make predictions about future sets of data. Next, study the graph to understand what it shows. To interpret a graph or chart, read the title, look at the key, and read the labels. Draw conclusions based on the data. It is possible to reach conclusions faster with graphs than with a data table or a written description of the data.

CHAPTER 4 KEY TERMS

bit
binary digit
byte
data abstraction
decimal
base conversion
precision
information/data
trends
graphs
binary
hexadecimal
integer overflow
integer roundoff
metadata
patterns
cleaning data
scalability
bias
data compression
lossy compression
lossless compression

CHAPTER 4 REVIEW DRILL

1 ▢ Mark for Review

Which of the following are likely metadata collected for a music file?

Ⓐ Song name

Ⓑ Size of song

Ⓒ Type of file (MP3, AVI, etc.)

Ⓓ Time at which the song was recorded

2 ▢ Mark for Review

Binary to Decimal Conversion

Binary	Decimal
00110001_2	
11100000_2	
11000011_2	
11110010_2	
10010100_2	
10101110_2	
1101000_2	
01011100_2	
00001100_2	
10111111_2	

3 ▢ Mark for Review

Decimal to Binary Conversion

Decimal	Binary
123_{10}	
210_{10}	
75_{10}	
103_{10}	
25_{10}	
77_{10}	
235_{10}	
102_{10}	
200_{10}	
45_{10}	

4 ▢ Mark for Review

The biggest advantage of lossy compression algorithms over a lossless one is that while transmitting data

Ⓐ the loss of data is inconsequential

Ⓑ the packet transfer through the Internet is faster

Ⓒ the number of bits stored or transmitted is reduced

Ⓓ the algorithm is designed for efficient transmission

5 ☐ Mark for Review

Lossless compression is most suitable for transfer of

(A) images

(B) music files

(C) text files

(D) computer programs

Chapter 4 Summary

o   The way a computer represents data internally is different from the way the data is interpreted and displayed for the user. Programs are used to translate data into a representation more easily understood by people.

o   Data values can be stored in variables, lists of items, or stand-alone constants and can be passed as input to (or output from) procedures.

o   Abstraction is the process of reducing complexity by focusing on the main idea. By hiding details irrelevant to the question at hand and bringing together related and useful details, abstraction reduces complexity and allows one to focus on the big idea.

o   Bits are grouped to represent abstractions. These abstractions include, but are not limited to, numbers, characters, and color.
   •   *Bit* is shorthand for *binary digit* and is either 0 or 1.
   •   A *byte* is 8 bits.

o   Analog data such as pitch, color, and location can be closely approximated digitally using a *sampling technique*, which means measuring values of the analog signal at regular intervals called *samples*. The samples are measured to figure out the exact bits required to store each sample.

o   In programming languages, the fixed number of bits used to represent real numbers limits the range and mathematical operations on these values; this limitation can result in round-off, overflow, and other errors. Some real numbers are represented as approximations in computer storage. *Specific range limitations for real numbers are outside the scope of this course and the AP Exam.*

o   Number bases, including binary and decimal, are used to represent data.
   •   Binary (base 2) uses only combinations of the digits zero and one.
   •   Decimal (base 10) uses only combinations of the digits 0–9.

o   *Data compression* can reduce the size (number of bits) of data transmitted or stored.

o   *Lossless* data compression algorithms can usually reduce the number of bits stored or transmitted while guaranteeing complete reconstruction of the original data.
   •   In situations where quality or ability to reconstruct the original is maximally important, lossless compression algorithms are typically chosen.

o *Lossy* data compression algorithms can significantly reduce the number of bits stored or transmitted but only allow reconstruction of an approximation of the original data.

- Lossy data compression algorithms can usually reduce the number of bits stored or transmitted more than lossless compression algorithms.
- In situations where minimizing data size or transmission time is maximally important, lossy compression algorithms are typically chosen.

o Digitally processed data may show correlation between variables. A correlation found in data does not necessarily indicate that a causal relationship exists. Additional research is needed to understand the exact nature of the relationship.

o Often, a single source does not contain the data needed to draw a conclusion. It may be necessary to combine data from a variety of sources to formulate a conclusion.

o *Metadata* is data about data. For example, the piece of *data* may be an image, while the *metadata* may include the date of creation or the file size of the image.

o Changes and deletions made to metadata do not change the primary data.

o Metadata is used for finding, organizing, and managing information.

o Metadata can increase the effective use of data or data sets by providing additional information.

o Metadata allow data to be structured and organized.

o The ability to process data depends on the capabilities of the users and their tools.

o Data sets pose challenges regardless of size, such as:

- the need to clean data
- incomplete data
- invalid data
- the need to combine data sources

o *Cleaning data* is a process that makes the data uniform without changing its meaning (e.g., replacing all equivalent abbreviations, spellings, and capitalizations with the same word).

o   Problems of bias are often created by the type or source of data being collected. Bias is not eliminated by simply collecting more data.

o   Tables, diagrams, text, and other visual tools can be used to communicate insight and knowledge gained from data.

o   Programmers can use programs to filter and clean digital data, thereby gaining insight and knowledge.

o   Combining data sources, clustering data, and classifying data are parts of the process of using programs to gain insight and knowledge from data.

o   Patterns can emerge when data is transformed using programs.

Chapter 5
Algorithms and Programming

The AP Computer Science Principles Exam uses the Exam Reference Sheet (provided to students at exam time and found on page 313 of this book) with a specific pseudocode-like syntax for the different programming constructs. Students must get familiar with this pseudocode's syntax so that they can recognize these code snippets on the test.

The next few pages that discuss the Algorithms and Programming Big Idea use this reference sheet to explain the syntax and the concepts for each of the reference sheet constructs.

VARIABLES AND ASSIGNMENTS

The primary purpose of a computer program is to manipulate information, and information is manipulated in many forms. A variable is a name for a location in memory used to hold a data value. A variable declaration instructs the compiler to reserve a portion of the main memory space large enough to hold a value and indicate the name we use to refer to that location. Most programming languages require that programmers be explicit about what kind of information needs manipulation. In turn, it guarantees that it is easy to manipulate the data.

Data Type	Description	Examples
int	Whole numbers	5, –2,
double	Real numbers	7.5, 3.78, –1.99
char	Characters—single letters	'a', 'p'
Boolean	Logical values	true, false

Many popular programming languages (probably including whatever language you have studied in this course) use standard type names such as int and double for numbers, char and string for letters and words, respectively, and Boolean for true or false, as shown in the table above. (We will examine Strings in another section.)

The College Board provided Exam Reference Sheet, however, does not specify the type of data that is stored in memory. Characters and numbers have a generic representation to assign a value to a variable, as shown below.

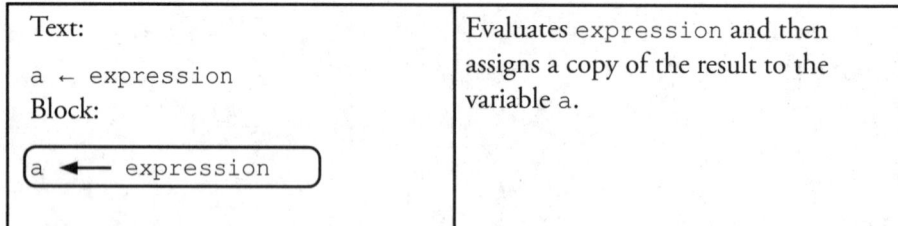

Text: a ← expression Block: `a ← expression`	Evaluates `expression` and then assigns a copy of the result to the variable a.

A variable can store only one value as a result of an assignment statement. When a new value is assigned, an assignment statement overwrites the old one. An assignment statement is named as such and is intuitive because it assigns a value to a variable. The evaluation of the expression on the right-hand side happens when the expression executes. The variable on the left-hand side then stores the result (to be more precise, in the variable's memory location on the left-hand side).

You can assign a single number or word to a variable:

```
a ← 5 or a ← "this"
```

You can also assign the result of an expression to a variable:

```
a ← 5 + 4 - 3
```

Here the value contained in a would be 6 since 5 + 4 is 9 and 9 – 3 is 6.

An input statement gets information from the user. An example below would ask the user for their name, store it in the variable name and then print out Hello and the data contained in the variable name:

```
DISPLAY("Please enter your name")
name ← INPUT()
DISPLAY("Hello" + name)
```

Text:
`DISPLAY(expression)`
Block:
`DISPLAY [expression]`
	Displays the value of `expression`, followed by a space.

Text:
`INPUT()`
Block:
`INPUT`
	Accepts a value from the user and returns the input value.

DATA ABSTRACTION

A popular way of defining abstraction is information hiding. Just as related program statements are bundled together, related program variables can be bundled together. Such abstractions allow us to think of the data within a program hierarchically. A list is an example of data abstraction. Let's dig deeper into this.

Look at this example:

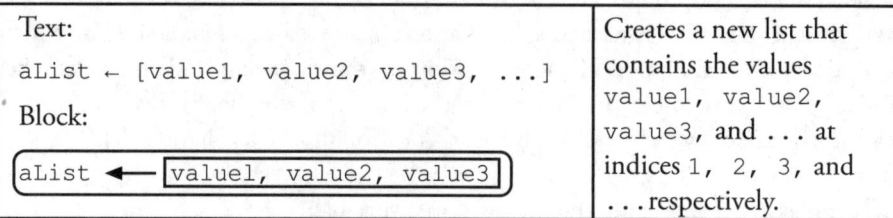

Text: aList ← [value1, value2, value3, ...] Block: aList ←─── value1, value2, value3	Creates a new list that contains the values value1, value2, value3, and ... at indices 1, 2, 3, and ...respectively.

A list is a data type that holds a collection of values. In the example shown above (as given in the exam reference sheet),

aList ← [3, 7, 11]

aList is described as a "list of integers."

Within a list, when accessing its parts using an integer index, aList[1] gives us the value 3, aList[2] = 7, and so on. Lists allow for data abstraction in that we can give a name to a set of memory cells. For instance, in a colorList, a list that holds three colors ['red', 'blue', 'green'] instead of using three separate variables, color1, color2, etc., one variable colorList holds all the three variables. Each of the contents of the list is accessed by changing the index value.

> Note: List Index in the Exam Reference Sheet starts at 1. This concept is confusing because, in many programming languages, the index values start at 0.

Because the indexing on the Exam Reference Sheet is different from the language you likely used in your course, the conditions for an error message are different. On the AP Computer Science Principles Exam, a program will terminate and display an error message whenever a list index is less than 1 or greater than the length of the list.

MATHEMATICAL EXPRESSIONS

While writing programs, it is often necessary to include calculations. These are called expressions. An expression is a combination of one or more operators and operands that perform a calculation. The operations' operands might be literals, constants, variables, or other sources of data. This process of obtaining a value is called an evaluation. Evaluation of expressions is fundamental to having a good understanding of programming. For now, we will focus on mathematical expressions that use numeric operands and produce numeric results.

Below is a list of operations provided by the College Board in the Exam Reference Sheet.

Text and Block:
 	
`a + b`
`a - b`
`a * b`
`a / b`
	The arithmetic operators +, -, *, and / are used to perform arithmetic on a and b.
	
	For example, `17 / 5` evaluates to `3.4`.
	
	The order of operations used in mathematics applies when evaluating expressions.

Text and Block: `a MOD b`	Evaluates to the remainder when a is divided by b. Assume that a is an integer greater than or equal to 0 and b is an integer greater than 0. For example, `17 MOD 5` evaluates to `2`. The MOD operator has the same precedence as the * and / operators.

The operation MOD (short for modulus) is an important operation in computer science, but one you probably don't use a lot in math class. Modulus refers to remainder after division. For example, to find 5 MOD 3:

$$3\overline{)\,5} \\ \underline{-3} \\ ②$$

Therefore 5 MOD 3 = 2. Notice that the resulting 1 isn't important. It's only the remainder that counts.

Most programming languages (as well as the AP Computer Science Principles Exam Reference Sheet) follow operations rules while establishing precedence.

- An operator with high precedence is evaluated first, followed by operators of lower precedence.
- Within a given precedence level, the operators are evaluated in one direction, usually left to right.
- There are two levels of precedence in arithmetic operations. The multiplicative operators (*, /, MOD) have a higher precedence level than the additive operators (+, -). Arithmetic operations with the same level of precedence are evaluated left to right.
- The final point to note: any operator precedence can be overridden with parentheses.

For example, let's look at the expression 3 − 5 * 4 MOD 3. The operations with first precedence in this example are multiplication and MOD. Since multiplication is to the left of MOD, begin by executing multiplication:

$$3 - 5 * 4 \text{ MOD } 3 = 3 - 20 \text{ MOD } 3$$

Now, since MOD has precedence over subtraction, execute MOD:

$$3 - 20 \text{ MOD } 3 = 3 - 2$$

Finally, execute subtraction:

$$3 - 2 = 1$$

Therefore, $3 - 5 * 4 \text{ MOD } 3 = 1$.

Selection uses a Boolean condition to evaluate which of two parts of an algorithm to use.

Iteration is the process where a part (a set of instructions, a few lines of program code, etc.) of the algorithm repeats until it meets a condition or iterates for a fixed number of times either specified within the program or by the user.

Different algorithms can solve the same problem. A good example is Google Maps on a cellphone. Once the from and to locations get filled, the software frequently provides multiple routes as options—this is the algorithm within the software providing multiple solutions to the problem.

There are many ways to express algorithms. Some of them include natural language, pseudocode, and visual and textual programming languages. Natural language and pseudocode describe algorithms so that humans can understand them. Algorithms described in a programming language are compiled and run on a computer. The programming language used to express an algorithm can affect clarity or readability. It does not determine whether an algorithmic solution exists.

STRINGS

In computer science, a character is a symbol that appears on the keyboard, such as a letter, digit, or punctuation mark. A collection of these characters is usually surrounded with double quotes: "computer!" is called a string literal. A string can be a word or a sentence or even a single letter.

For example:

```
String mySentence = "CS Principles Rock!"
String myWord = "Principles"
String myLetter = "C"
```

The syntax for Strings depends on the programming language. The Exam Reference Sheet does not have a specific syntax for Strings.

Strings can be concatenated using the + sign:

```
String wordConcatenated = "black" + "board"
```

The + sign combines the two or more Strings together in an end-to-end manner to make a single String. This is called concatenation.

Substrings are part of an existing string.

For example:

```
phrase ← "Computer Science"
```

"Science" and "Computer" are substrings of the variable phrase.

BOOLEAN EXPRESSIONS

An expression that evaluates true or false is called a Boolean expression, typically used in conditionals and iterative statements. Boolean expressions use relational operators and logical operators to make decisions.

The table below contains the list of relational operators. They are specific symbols given by the Exam Reference Sheet. While comparing two operands or expressions with a relational operator, the result is a Boolean value, a true or false.

Text and Block:	The relational operators =, ≠, >, <, ≤, and ≥ are used to test the relationship between two variables, expressions, or values. A comparison using relational operators evaluates to a Boolean value.
a = b	
a ≠ b	
a > b	For example, a = b evaluates to true if a and b are equal; otherwise it evaluates to false.
a < b	
a ≥ b	
a ≤ b	

It is important to note that the Exam Reference Sheet uses = as the equality operator to compare two operands, since the ← operator assigns a value to a variable.

Below are the logical operators, which are useful for building complex Boolean expressions.

Text: `NOT condition` Block: NOT `condition`	Evaluates to `true` if `condition` is `false`; otherwise evaluates to `false`.
Text: `condition1` AND `condition2` Block: `condition1` AND `condition2`	Evaluates to `true` if both `condition1` and `condition2` are `true`; otherwise evaluates to `false`.
Text: `condition1` OR `condition2` Block: `condition1` OR `condition2`	Evaluates to `true` if `condition1` is `true` or if `condition2` is `true` or if both `condition1` and `condition2` are `true`; otherwise evaluates to `false`.

Below are examples of Boolean expressions using logical operators.

Operator	Example	Result
AND	`(1 = 1) AND (6 < 7)`	true
OR	`(2 = 1) OR (6 < 7)`	true
NOT	`NOT (5 > 3)`	false

CONDITIONALS

An IF-ELSE statement is called a conditional statement. Sometimes while designing a program, one or more program statements will be executed when a condition is true. Some lines of code will not be executed when false. Conditional statements are also known as selection statements. The condition within an IF statement is usually a Boolean expression that returns a true or false.

The Exam Reference Sheet has the following syntax for IF-ELSE statements:

<table>
<tr>
<td>
Text:

```
IF(condition)
{
<block of statements>
}
```

Block:

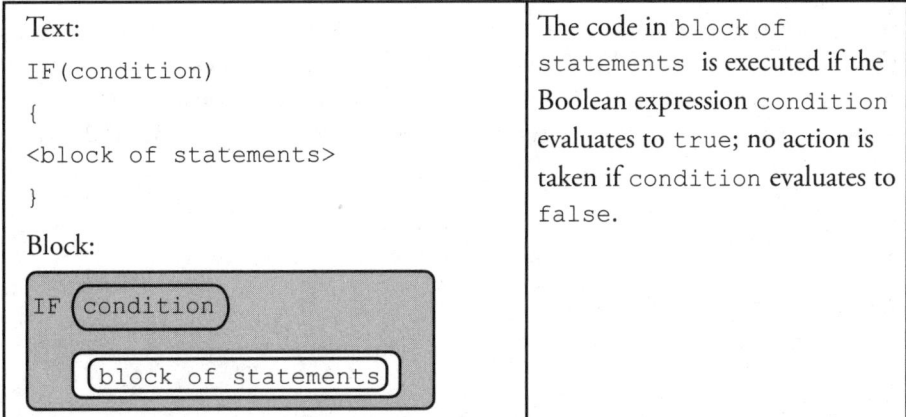
</td>
<td>
The code in `block of statements` is executed if the Boolean expression `condition` evaluates to `true`; no action is taken if `condition` evaluates to `false`.
</td>
</tr>
<tr>
<td>
Text:

```
IF(condition)
{
<first block of statements>
}
ELSE
{
<second block of statements>
}
```

Block:

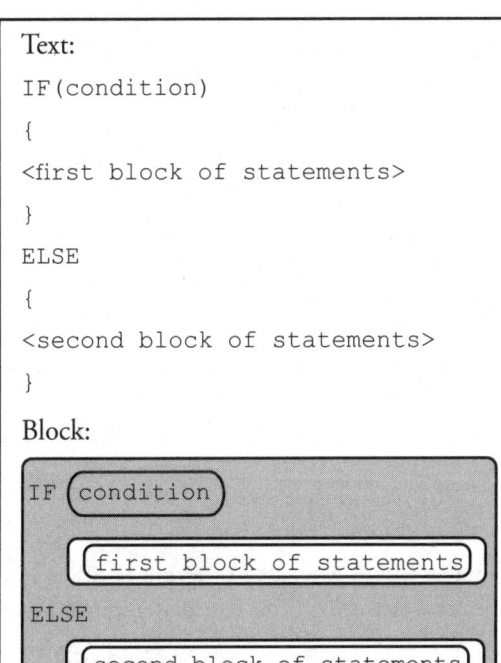
</td>
<td>
The code in `first block of statements` is executed if the Boolean expression `condition` evaluates to `true`; otherwise the code in `second block of statements` is executed.
</td>
</tr>
</table>

Below is an illustration of a simple IF Statement:

```
IF (number1 > number2)
{
    smallerNumber ← number1
}
ELSE
{
    smallerNumber ← number2
}
```

NESTED CONDITIONALS

An additional IF statement in a program or code snippet that already has an IF statement is called a nested IF statement. When the outer IF statement is executed, the inner IF statement may also get executed. This allows for the program solution to evaluate another expression after determining the results of a previous decision.

```
IF (number1 < number2)
{
    IF (number1 < number3)
    {
        smallerNumber ← number1
    }
    ELSE
    {
        smallerNumber ← number3
    }
}
ELSE
{
    IF (number1 < number3)
    {
        smallerNumber ← number2
    }
    ELSE
    {
        smallerNumber ← number3
    }

}
```

ITERATION

The loop construct is used in a computer program when the program requires specific code statements to be repeated more than once. The Exam Reference Sheet syntax is shown below.

Text:
 	
`REPEAT n TIMES`
 	
`{`
 	
`<block of statements>`
 	
`}`
 	
Block:
 	
`REPEAT n TIMES`
`  block of statements`
	The code in `block of statements` is executed n times.

Text:
 	
REPEAT UNTIL(condition)
 	
{
 	
<block of statements>
 	
}
 	
Block:
 	
REPEAT UNTIL(condition)
 	
(block of statements)
	The code in block of statements is repeated until the Boolean expression condition evaluates to true.

The "REPEAT n TIMES" is a predetermined loop; that is, the loop will execute the program statements within the loop n number of times. The "repeat until *condition*" executes if the condition is true. The loop construct requires an exact ending condition that terminates the loop and exits the loop construct.

In summary, to have a clear functioning loop, every loop designed should have:

- a clear beginning condition
- a clear ending condition

This could be a program statement that leads the code toward the ending condition (a counter, a condition that is satisfied, or an input from the user that meets the condition the loop is looking for).

For example:

```
number ← 1
REPEAT UNTIL (number ≤ 10)
{
    number ← number + 1
}
```

The above loop will execute 9 times. When number is given the value 10, the loop will terminate.

DEVELOPING ALGORITHMS

An algorithm is a clear, step-by-step, detailed computable set of instructions (which include arithmetic operations) that, when executed, returns a result in a finite amount of time. Sequencing, selection, and iteration are the fundamental blocks of algorithms.

Algorithms are building blocks for programs. There are multiple solutions to a problem. Using existing correct algorithms as building blocks for constructing a new algorithm helps ensure the new algorithm is correct. Algorithms are written in English or pseudocode so that humans can understand them. Programs are algorithms that are written in a programming language so that computers can understand them.

Linear Search

An excellent example of a general algorithm is a linear search. A linear search is one straightforward way to perform the search by starting at the beginning of the list and comparing each value, in turn, to the target element. Eventually, either the target element will be identified or will come to the end of the list and conclude that the target does not exist in the group. This approach is called a linear search.

Let's look at an example. Suppose you were to use a linear search for the location of 21 in the list [5, 16, –3, 21, 7]. Start at index 1 and move forward.

Target Value = 4

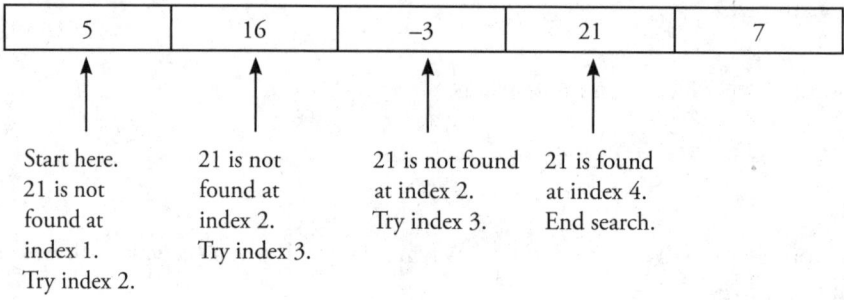

Therefore, the algorithm will indicate that the element 21 is found at index 4.

This table (from the College Board-provided Course and Exam Description) describing all the shapes in a flow chart will be provided:

Block	Explanation
Oval	The start of the algorithm
Parallelogram	An input or output step
Diamond	A conditional or decision step, where execution proceeds to the side labeled "Yes" if the answer to the question is yes and to the side labeled "No" if the answer to the question is no
Rectangle	The result of the algorithm

LISTS

We have discussed lists as a data type and how lists are good examples of data abstraction. This section will revisit lists and discuss the various operations that use lists. We will discuss how list transversal works and examine the Exam Reference Sheet syntax for list operations.

In a list, each value is stored at a specific, numbered position in the array. The number corresponding to each position is called an index or a subscript. As stated on the Exam Reference Sheet, the index value begins at 1.

Below is the list of functions that use lists. The listing is provided to students as part of the Reference Sheet.

Text:
`aList ← [value1, value2, value3, ...]`
Block:
`aList ⟵ [value1, value2, value3]`
	Creates a new list that contains the values `value1`, `value2`, `value3`, and ... at indices 1, 2, 3, and ... respectively and assigns it to `aList`.

Text:
`aList ← []`
Block:
`aList ⟵ []`
	Creates an empty list and assigns it to `aList`.

Text:
`aList ← bList`
Block:
`aList ⟵ bList`
	Assigns a copy of the list `bList` to the list `aList`. For example, if `bList` contains [20, 40, 60], then `aList` will also contain [20, 40, 60] after the assignment.

Text:
 	
`aList[i]`
 	
Block:
 	
`aList` `i`
	Accesses the element of `aList` at index i. The first element of `aList` is at index 1 and is accessed using the notation `aList[1]`.

Text:
 	
`x ← aList[i]`
 	
Block:
 	
`x ⟵ aList` `i`
	Assigns the value of `aList[i]` to the variable x.

Text:
 	
`aList[i] ← x`
 	
Block:
 	
`aList` `i` `⟵ x`
	Assigns the value of x to `aList[i]`.

Text:
 	
`aList[i] ← aList[j]`
 	
Block:
 	
`aList` `i` `⟵ aList` `j`
	Assigns the value of `aList[j]` to `aList[i]`.

Text:
 	
`INSERT(aList, i, value)`
 	
Block:
 	
`INSERT` `aList, i, value`
	Any values in `aList` at indices greater than or equal to i are shifted one position to the right. The length of the list is increased by 1, and `value` is placed at index i in `aList`.

Text:
 	
`APPEND(aList, value)`
 	
Block:
 	
`APPEND` `aList, value`
	The length of `aList` is increased by 1, and `value` is placed at the end of `aList`.

Text:
 	
`REMOVE(aList, i)`
 	
Block:
 	
`REMOVE aList, i`
	Removes the item at index i in aList and shifts to the left any values at indices greater than i. The length of aList is decreased by 1.

Text:
 	
`LENGTH(aList)`
 	
Block:
 	
`LENGTH aList`
	Evaluates to the number of elements in aList.

The Exam Reference Sheet provides a loop construct that simplifies certain array loops. You can use it whenever you want to examine each value in an array.

Text:
 	
`FOR EACH item IN aList`
 	
`{`
 	
`<block of statements>`
 	
`}`
 	
Block:
 	
`FOR EACH item IN aList`
`   block of statements`
	The variable item is assigned the value of each element of aList sequentially, in order, from the first element to the last element. The code in block of statements is executed once for each assignment of item.

An example of how the FOR-EACH loop can be used is shown in this snippet of code as follows:

```
FOR EACH n IN temp
{
   if (n > 0)
     DISPLAY ("NUMBER IS POSITIVE")
}
```

BINARY SEARCH

In a binary search, the search algorithm requires sorted elements before applying the algorithm. Binary searches look for an item by comparing the middlemost item of the collection. If a match occurs, then the index of the item is returned. If the middle item is greater than the item, then the item is searched in the sub-array to the middle item's left. Otherwise, the item is searched for in the sub-array to the right of the middle item. This process continues the sub-array as well until the size of the sub-array reduces to zero. Here's an example. The binary search in the diagram searches to the element 1 in the ordered list [1, 2, 3, 4, 5].

Target Value = 1

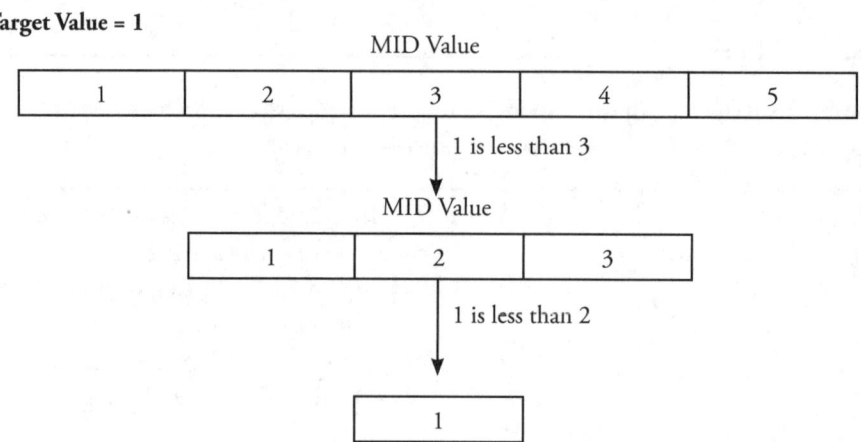

CALLING PROCEDURES, DEVELOPING PROCEDURES, AND LIBRARIES

One of the most basic building blocks of programming is procedures. Programmers break down problems into smaller and more manageable pieces. By creating procedures and leveraging parameters, programmers generalize processes that get reused. Procedures allow programmers to draw upon code that has already been tested, allowing them to write programs more quickly and more confidently. Even the simplest of programs usually use procedures that are built-in within the programs. All programming procedures have input and output. The procedure contains instructions used to create the output from its input. A procedure call is a programming statement made by stating the procedure name, listing actual parameter names or values within parentheses.

A formal definition of a procedure is as follows: A programming procedure is a named group of program code that performs a specific task. Other languages call them methods, subroutines, or procedures.

After defining a procedure, programmers write code within it just like anywhere else in the program. Giving the function a name and defining parameters it should accept is called the header. The information the function needs gets passed as parameters. Finally, the function sometimes returns some result. Procedures are reusable. Once defined, the program calls it from other places.

The following are some of the advantages of writing procedures:

1. Procedures help abstract information. They are "black" boxes. A programmer calls a function; they do not care what exactly the code inside it does; they need the result. This is called procedural abstraction. Designing procedures in a program helps implement procedural abstraction. Furthermore, designing procedures helps separate the logic from the actual data. As long as it passes the procedure's parameters, it does not care what the data is. Each run of the procedure executes the code and returns a result.

2. Procedures help reuse code. Copying and pasting the same lines of code in multiple places adds complexity to the program. It introduces more places for something to go wrong. It becomes harder to maintain as well as isolate errors in the program. Creating a procedure eliminates these problems. They make it easy to reuse code anywhere else in the program. Once a procedure is defined, a programmer can call it anywhere in the program and know that it will behave the same way. All programming languages include procedures that a programmer can use without having to create them. These are called built-in functions or libraries. Consider the example: All programming languages have the built-in functions for displaying information on the screen. The built-in function for this as shown in the Reference Sheet is `DISPLAY()`. Application program interfaces (APIs) are specifications for using the library's procedures and understanding how they behave. Documentation for an API/library is necessary for understanding the library of procedures' behaviors.

Below is the syntax that the Exam Reference Sheet uses:

Text:
 	
`PROCEDURE procName(parameter1,`
`                parameter2, ...)`
 	
`{`
 	
`<block of statements>`
 	
`}`
 	
Block:
 	
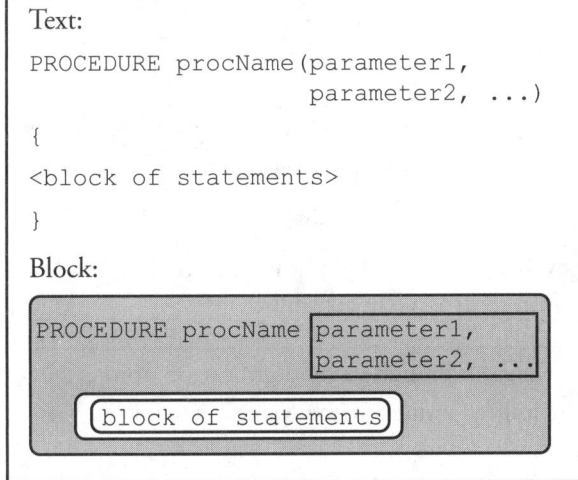
	Defines `procName` as a procedure that takes zero or more arguments. The procedure contains `block of statements`.
	The procedure `proc-Name` can be called using the following notation, where `arg1` is assigned to `parameter1`, `arg2` is assigned to `parameter2`, etc.: `procName(arg1, arg2, ...)`

Text:
 	
``
PROCEDURE procName(parameter1,
                   parameter2, ...)
{
<block of statements>
RETURN(expression)
}
``
 	
Block:
 	
``
PROCEDURE procName parameter1,
                    parameter2, ...
 	
    block of statements
    RETURN expression
``
	Defines `procName` as a procedure that takes zero or more arguments. The procedure contains `block of statements` and returns the value of `expression`. The `RETURN` statement may appear at any point inside the procedure and causes an immediate return from the procedure back to the calling statement.
	
	The value returned by the procedure `procName` can be assigned to the variable `result` using the following notation: `result ← procName(arg1, arg2, ...)`

Text:
 	
`RETURN(expression)`
 	
Block:
 	
`RETURN expression`
	Returns the flow of control to the point where the procedure was called and returns the value of `expression`.

RANDOM VALUES

Random number generator programs are useful tools for writing software, mainly in designing games. A random number generator picks a number at random out of a range of values.

The Exam Reference Sheet shows the syntax for the random number generator. Note that the RANDOM function returns a whole number.

Text:
 	
`RANDOM(a, b)`
 	
Block:
 	
`RANDOM  a, b`
	Generates and returns a random integer from `a` to `b`, including `a` and `b`. Each result is equally likely to occur.
	
	For example, `RANDOM(1, 3)` could return `1`, `2`, or `3`.

Example:

```
value ← Random (2, 5)
//value could hold any value from 2 to 5, inclusive
```

SIMULATIONS

When real-world experiments would be dangerous to humans or to animals or would simply be too slow, computer simulations can be a very useful tool. Simulations are just a collection of computer software that responds to real-time input data to simulate a response that would resemble the real world. Often, it is impractical to test the software in the real world. It is either too expensive or too inconvenient, and sometimes can be a real danger to life.

Scientists build simulations for almost everything. Street Traffic Models and Solar Activity Models are two examples of simulations that we will take a closer look at in this section.

Street Traffic Models

Simulation, as a tool, is used when studying traffic systems when the system is too complicated. The advantage of simulation tools is that they provide visual demonstrations for different scenarios, both present and future. These models are necessary tools for planning and operating traffic systems, as they help to predict the behavior of vehicles in the traffic system.

The output from traffic simulation can be used to evaluate new infrastructure and to test forms of traffic control, e.g., maximum and minimum speed limits. Another advantage is the ability to use new technology that may not be available in real life, such as use of autonomous cars. It is predicted that future traffic systems will include a mix of partly and fully automated vehicles and human-driven vehicles. Traffic simulation models have been found to be very useful in understanding traffic patterns and human behavior.

Solar Activity Models

All engineering disciplines use simulation tools that help them study phenomena specific to their field of expertise. Simulations are now part of the design process. Models require considerable time and effort to develop. Simulation models are used to study the solar system. The use of modeling and simulation is a powerful method to evaluate the design of a space system. Simulation models represent valuable knowledge that scientists use to build systems to explore space. New supercomputer simulations have successfully modeled a mysterious process believed to produce some of the hottest and most dangerous solar flares. The computer simulations demonstrate how certain phenomena could have occurred. All this is because of the development of sophisticated simulation models that are possible because of the availability of powerful computer systems that were previously not available.

ALGORITHMIC EFFICIENCY

Algorithmic efficiency is about determining how an algorithm performs with regards to both time and space. Often, there are multiple solutions to a problem, and it is essential to understand that not all algorithmic solutions are optimal. Depending on the hardware used, the choice of algorithm can be different. Determining an algorithm's efficiency is mathematically done by implementing the algorithm and running it on different inputs. The correctness of an algorithm is determined by formal reasoning, not by writing an algorithm to implement a program. An algorithm may be correct but have a different efficiency from another algorithm. A more efficient algorithm could be more complicated by implementing, i.e., writing the algorithm's actual program.

One approach is what is called a heuristic technique, which is one that approximates a solution when typical methods fail to find an exact solution. Heuristics may help find an approximate solution more quickly when exact methods are too slow.

UNDECIDABLE PROBLEMS

In addition to problems that take a long time to compute, there are some problems that a computer can never solve, even the world's most powerful computer with infinite time: the undecidable problems. An undecidable problem may have instances that have an algorithmic solution. However, there is no algorithmic solution that solves all instances of the problem. A decidable problem is when the constructed algorithm answers "yes" or "no" for all inputs, such as "is the number even?" A problem where it is not possible to construct an algorithm is called an undecidable problem.

An example of this is the halting problem (Alan Turing). Algorithms exist that can correctly predict when some programs halt. These are simple programs that do not change based on different inputs. However, no algorithm exists that can analyze *any* program's code and determine whether it halts or not. Hence, a halting problem is an undecidable problem.

CHAPTER 5 KEY TERMS

Variables
Selection
Iteration
Boolean Expression
List
Strings
Abstraction
Application Program Interface (API)
Simulation Models
Algorithm Efficiency
Assignment
Sequencing
Loops
Data Types
Procedures
Pseudocode
Procedural Abstraction
Random Number Generator
Algorithm
Undecidable Problem
Heuristic
Libraries
Binary Search

CHAPTER 5 REVIEW DRILL

1 ⬚ Mark for Review

A Boolean is a data type that

Ⓐ holds numbers, including integers, floats, and doubles

Ⓑ holds characters, including special characters

Ⓒ holds only two values, true or false

Ⓓ holds letters, characters, and numbers

2 ⬚ Mark for Review

A variable (such as numbers, a list, etc.) is a good example of

Ⓐ data abstraction

Ⓑ modularity

Ⓒ procedural abstraction

Ⓓ algorithm

3 ⬚ Mark for Review

In the Exam Reference Sheet, the index value of a list starts at

Ⓐ 1

Ⓑ the length of the list

Ⓒ *n*

Ⓓ 0

4 ⬚ Mark for Review

An important property of an algorithm is that

Ⓐ it is a step-by-step process

Ⓑ it has abstraction built in

Ⓒ it is important to calculate efficiency

Ⓓ it is written using pseudocode

5 ⬚ Mark for Review

Combining two strings to make a new string is called

Ⓐ abstraction

Ⓑ adding

Ⓒ concatenation

Ⓓ manipulation

6 ⬚ Mark for Review

An example of a logical operator is

Ⓐ ←

Ⓑ OR

Ⓒ =

Ⓓ ≥

7 ☐ Mark for Review

Which of the following are building blocks of an algorithm?

(A) Sequencing, selection, and iteration

(B) Variables, lists, and strings

(C) Procedures, blocks, and modules

(D) Recursion, selection, and iteration

8 ☐ Mark for Review

While designing algorithms it is important to remember

(A) all algorithms are efficient

(B) it is possible to calculate the amount of memory an algorithm will use

(C) there is more than one algorithmic solution to a problem

(D) all algorithms have to be expressed in a specific format

9 ☐ Mark for Review

Procedural abstraction is MOST useful because

(A) of the ability to reuse code

(B) it provides APIs

(C) it helps with readability

(D) it reduces complexity

10 ☐ Mark for Review

Which of the following are true statements about simulations?

(A) A simulation allows investigation of a real-world phenomenon without the constraints of the real world.

(B) A simulation is an abstraction of a real-world object or phenomena.

(C) The process of developing a simulation involves simplifying the functionality.

(D) All of the above.

Chapter 5 Summary

- To find specific solutions to generalizable problems, programmers represent and organize data in multiple ways.

- A variable is an abstraction inside a program that can hold a value. Each variable has associated data storage that represents one value at a time, but that value can be a list or other collection that, in turn, contains multiple values.

- Using meaningful variable names helps with the readability of program code and the understanding of what values are represented by the variables.

- The assignment operator allows a program to change the value represented by a variable. The exam reference sheet provides the ← operator to use for assignment. For example, Text: a ← expression evaluates `expression` and then assigns a copy of the result to the variable a.

- A list is an ordered sequence of elements. For example, [value1, value2, value3, ...] describes a list where `value1` is the first element, `value2` is the second element, `value3` is the third element, and so on.

- An element is an individual value in a list that is assigned a unique index.

- An index is a common method for referencing the elements in a list or string using natural numbers.

- A string is an ordered sequence of characters.

- Data abstractions manage complexity in programs by giving a collection of data a name without referencing the specific details of the representation.

- Developing a data abstraction to implement in a program can result in a program that is easier to develop and maintain.

○ The exam reference sheet provides the notation [value1, value2, value3, ...] to create a list with those values as the first, second, third, and so on, items. For example, aList ← [value1, value2, value3, ...] creates a new list that contains the values value1, value2, value3, etc., at indices 1, 2, 3, etc., respectively, and assigns them to aList.

○ The command aList ← [] creates a new empty list and assigns it to aList.

○ The Exam Reference Sheet describes a list structure whose index values are 1 through the number of elements in the list, inclusive. For all list operations, if a list index is less than 1 or greater than the length of the list, an error message is produced, and the program will terminate.

○ The way statements are sequenced and combined in a program determines the computed result. Programs incorporate iteration and selection constructs to represent repetition and make decisions to handle varied input values.

○ To make a selection algorithm:
  • Write conditional statements.
  • Determine the result of conditional statements.
  • Write nested conditional statements.
  • Determine the result of nested conditional statements.

○ To make an iterative algorithm:
  • Write iteration statements.
  • Determine the result or side effect of iteration statements.
  • Compare multiple algorithms to determine whether they yield the same side effect or result.

○ To use list operations:
  • Write expressions that use list indexing and list procedures.
  • Evaluate expressions that use list indexing and list procedures.

○ To create algorithms involving elements of a list:
  • Write iteration statements to traverse a list.
  • Determine the result of an algorithm that includes list traversal.

- o To create binary search algorithms:
  - Determine the number of iterations required to find a value in a data set.
  - Explain the requirements necessary to complete a binary search.

- o To use procedure calls:
  - Write a statement to call a procedure.
  - Determine the result or effect of a procedure call.
  - Select appropriate libraries or existing code segments to use in creating new programs.

- o To generate random values:
  - Write expressions to generate possible values.
  - Evaluate expressions to determine the possible values.

- o Computers can use simulations to represent real-life phenomena or outcomes.

- o To determine the efficiency of an algorithm:
  - Explain the difference between algorithms that run in reasonable time and those that do not.
  - Identify situations where a heuristic solution may be more appropriate.

- o There exist problems that computers cannot solve, and even when a computer can solve a problem, it may not be able to do so in a reasonable amount of time.

Chapter 6
Computer Systems and Networks

THE INTERNET

The word "networking" almost immediately brings the word "Internet" to mind. While this idea is conceptually correct, the Internet is an example of a massive computer network. Computer networks make it possible for one device to communicate with another device. Another example of a computer network is the local area network, or LAN. The technology that lets us access all the desktops, laptops, wireless devices, and printers within a school, college, or home is called a LAN.

Every computer in a network is called a "host." A network layer address identifies each host. To send information to a remote host, a host creates a packet that includes

- the network layer address of the destination host
- its network layer address
- the information to be sent to the network layer, which limits the maximum packet size. The information is divided into packets by the transport layer before being passed to the network layer.

Each computer in the network follows a protocol to exchange information between computers. The path that the data packets take from the host computer to the destination computer is called a route.

> **Routing** is the process of finding a path from sender to receiver.

> **Bandwidth** is the maximum amount of data that can be sent in a fixed amount of time (for digital data, it is measured in bits per second). Higher bandwidth is better because the data will travel more quickly.

The Internet and the World Wide Web are two terms that are often used interchangeably in casual conversation. Although they are certainly related, the terms refer to different ideas. The World Wide Web is a collection of interlinked website documents viewed with a Web browser by typing in an address. Most Web pages use HTML (HyperText Markup Language) to run on the browser. The web browser uses HTTP (HyperText Transfer Protocol) to interpret the Web page.

The Internet is different, more general, and includes email, file transfers, and many other ways that computers communicate. The Internet has an enormous number of devices hooked to it. Realizing that the reality was that the system was likely to fail at unexpected times, designers and engineers designed the system to be reliable.

By building redundant connections into the Internet's physical systems, the designers ensured that data could be rerouted via a different path if part of the Internet fails. Furthermore, such changes to the path can happen in transit because routing on the Internet is dynamic. Creating such redundancy can require additional resources (such as additional computers and cables).

However, it also increases the Internet's fault tolerance (ability to work around problems) and helps the Internet scale (expand) to more devices and people.

While streaming data over the Internet, the stream is divided into *packets* that the IP sends individually. This process is what makes the Internet a *packet switching* network. Though the Internet is reliable, once in a while a packet will be lost. Devices on the Internet need to tolerate these faults. Sometimes the best solution is to decide that these faults aren't important. For example, if you lose one video frame, that lost frame will be imperceptible to the viewer, so that loss can be disregarded.

When the faults are more important, these faults can be tolerated using Transmission Control Protocol, better known as TCP. This protocol works by continuously sending packets until an acknowledgment of proper receipt is sent back. For applications that use TCP, it is TCP that divides the data into packets. Since packets can travel by different paths, they may arrive out of order. Despite the redundancy of the Internet, some data packets may not reach their destination. TCP guarantees reliable data transmission. It keeps track of which packets it receives successfully and resends any that have been lost or damaged. It also specifies the order for reassembling the data on the other end. The Internet is reliable, but data packets transmitted between computers within the network will sometimes be lost. Devices on the Internet need to tolerate these faults. The TCP protocol is used by computers on the Internet. The protocol's design is to keep sending packets while transmitting until a message is sent to the sending computers that the data was received successfully. The data split into packets travels by different paths. The packets may arrive out of order. Alternatively, some will not arrive at all. The receiving computer keeps track of the packets sent. It resends the lost or damaged data back (indicating that the damaged data packet needs resending). It also specifies the order for reassembling the data on the other end. All this happens to guarantee a reliable data transmission.

Internet Networking Layer	Protocol Name
Application Layer	HTTP, IMAP, SMTP
Transport Layer	TCP, UDP
Internet Layer	IP
Network Interface Hardware	Ethernet cable, Wi-Fi (Link Layer Protocols)

Scalability

Another critical design aspect of the Internet is that it is scalable. The scalability of a system is the system's capacity to change in size to meet new demands. A system is scalable when it can handle a significant amount of usage. A system may be scalable to handle only twice its designed amount, and some may handle a thousand times more. Because the Internet has global outreach, scalability will always need to be given attention.

FAULT TOLERANCE

One of the most significant features of the Internet is its fault-tolerant design. The engineers who designed the Internet made sure that it could continue to function even if some router within the system failed. The Internet has redundancy built in as part of its core design. As shown in the figure below, this allows more than one path between any two connected devices if some part of the network fails.

If a device or connection on the Internet fails, it picks a different route to send the data. The problem that occurs with redundancy is that it often requires additional resources. However, it provides the benefit of fault tolerance. The redundancy of routing options between two points increases the Internet's reliability. It helps the system scale to more devices and more people.

Having understood the fault-tolerant nature of the Internet, we now examine the causes of network failure, particularly with respect to the Internet.

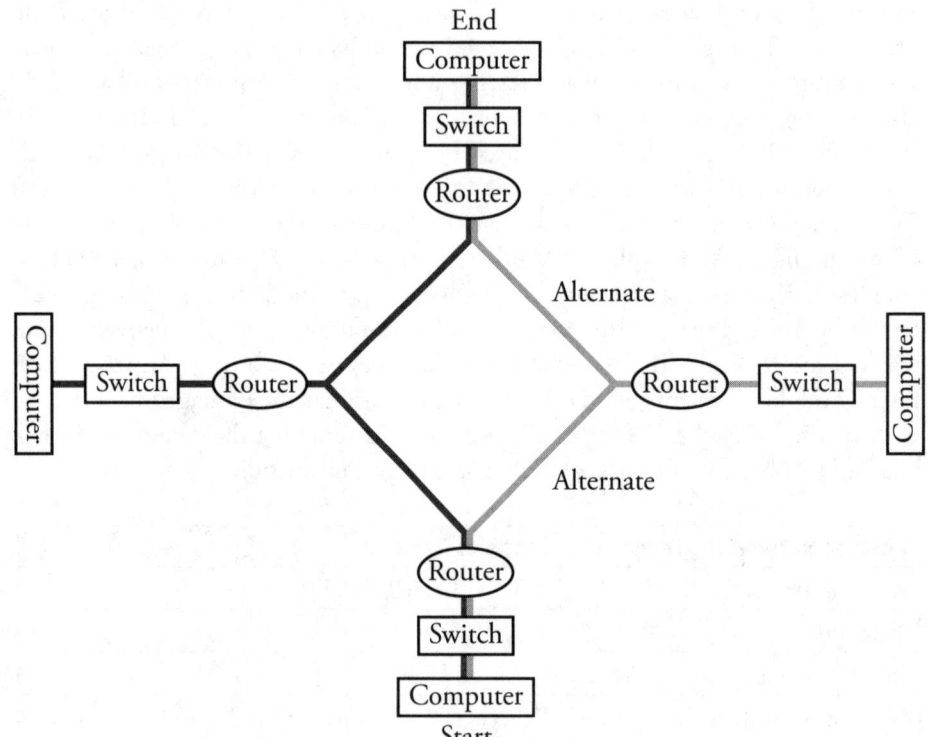

There are four broad categories of failure:

1. **Hardware Failure**
   This includes failure such as computers failing due to general wear and tear, misuse, etc., link failure due to cables getting worn out, power outages, incompatibility between devices, etc. Many network failures are attributed to router failure. Since there are many interconnected hardware elements in the network, if even one critical component fails, the network could crash. Failure could be due to complete or partial failure of any one of these devices.

2. **Operational Failures**

   Human errors in operating networking systems, mismanagement of equipment, device configuration changes, and firmware/software upgrades all are causes that lead to failure within a network system.

3. **Weather**

   The Internet has cables and wires spanning the world that connect computers. Natural disasters could cause the hardware to be destroyed, bringing the network activity to a halt. An example of this is a solar flare. A solar flare is an intense radiation that is released from the Sun. This happens because of the release of the magnetic energy from the sunspots. If something like this were to happen, it would melt down all the computer systems. This is a good example of how the Internet is subject to natural disasters that its fault-tolerant design cannot protect.

4. **Cyberattacks**

   There are many malicious attacks that could cause the network to crash. One such example is a Distributed Denial of Service (DDoS). Unfortunately, a DDoS, along with other such cyberattacks, are quite easy to create and cause a lot of damage. Cybercriminals cause harm by bringing down networks hooked to the Internet. These bad actors can be surprisingly creative.

PARALLEL AND DISTRIBUTED COMPUTING

A computer program is a step-by-step, detailed set of sequential instructions. Traditionally, program instructions are processed one at a time, using a process called sequential computing. However, with increased demands of high processing speeds, engineers have had to rethink this process. At the heart of every computer that executes instructions is the microprocessor. These processors can run only so fast before the amount of heat generated results in the devices' malfunctioning.

Parallel computing is an alternate design of computers. Here, a program is broken into smaller sequential computing operations. Some of the small pieces (identified by the parallel computing software) use multiple processors. The design of both the hardware and software changes parallel computing when compared to sequential computing. Most modern computers use parallel computing systems, with anywhere from 4 to 24 processors running simultaneously.

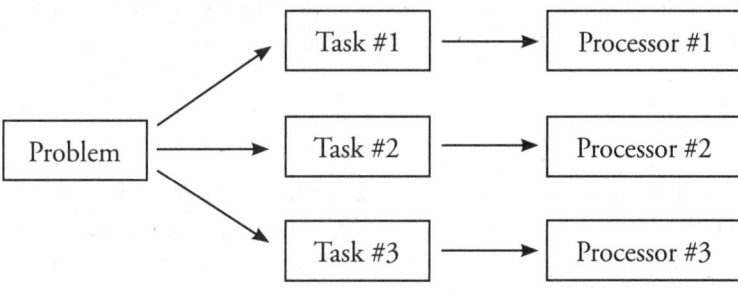

There are several advantages to parallel computing.

- Performing tasks simultaneously saves time and money.
- Parallel computing solutions scale well because they can handle more instructions.
- Parallel computing may help save time and reduce heat and malfunctioning.

A problem in parallel computing is that the total time taken is as long as its longest parallel tasks.

Distributed computing is a model in which multiple devices run a program. Distributed computing can be within the same computer or different computers. They communicate by sending messages to each other. With distributed computing, the power of multiple computers working on the same problem is made available. Distributed computing allows different users or computers to share information. The system can allow an application on one machine to leverage processing power, memory, or storage on another machine. Distributed computing solves problems that otherwise would be hard to solve because of too little available storage or too much processing time.

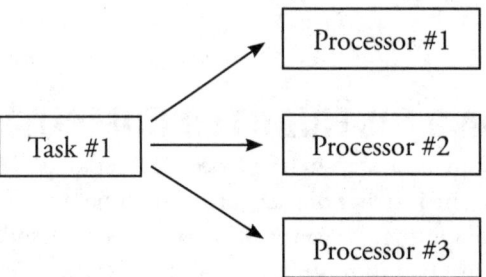

The most significant difference between distributed computing and parallel computing is that all processors may have access to shared memory to exchange information between processors in parallel computing. In distributed computing, each processor has its private memory and exchanges messages by passing them between the processors.

Compared to sequential computing, parallel and distributed computing systems have increased capacities. Consequently, these systems can process large data sets or solve complex problems faster. Remember that a sequential solution takes as long as the sum of all steps in the program. A parallel computing solution depends on the number of processors used: the more cores used, the faster the processing is likely to be.

Here's an example.

Consider a program with four steps to execute, each taking 20, 30, 10, 50 seconds. The system has two processors to use to execute the software. Assume that all steps are independent. Processor 1 would execute the first and second steps, taking 50 seconds for execution. In comparison, processor 2 would execute the third and fourth steps, taking 60 seconds for execution.

If the processes execute sequentially, executing all four processes would take 110 seconds. An important fact is that even though processor 1 only took 50 seconds, it still has to wait for processor 2 before the solution is complete. Moreover, the total execution time is 60 seconds.

This has two important conclusions.

- A parallel computing model is only as fast as the speed of its sequential portions.
- Adding parallel processors will not increase the efficiency of a solution by much. The speedup effect of adding more parallel processors gets impacted by either waiting for sequential steps to complete or other factors such as communication time.

An excellent example of this is when two students are working on a project. One team member is responsible for the drawings and sketches, and the other person does the writing. Even if the writing is complete, the project cannot be sent for publishing if the sketches are not complete. Adding another person to the team may not speed up the time it takes to complete the project. There is a limit to how many members to add and how additional members are to be utilized. Furthermore, the time needed to bring the new member up to speed must be taken into account.

CHAPTER 6 KEY TERMS

Protocol
World Wide Web
Internet Protocol
Bandwidth
Redundancy
Distributed Computing
Route
HTTP
Transmission Control Protocol (TCP/IP)
Routing
Fault Tolerance
Parallel Computing
Sequential Computing

CHAPTER 6 REVIEW DRILL

1 ▢ Mark for Review

Bandwidth is usually measured in

Ⓐ bits per second

Ⓑ bytes per second

Ⓒ KB per second

Ⓓ MB per second

2 ▢ Mark for Review

A path in a computer network that can be found between a sender computer and receiver computer is called

Ⓐ network trace

Ⓑ a route

Ⓒ network configuration

Ⓓ packet trace

3 ▢ Mark for Review

What does it mean when the protocols on the Internet are open?

Ⓐ The protocols are not owned by any company.

Ⓑ The protocols are not operating system dependent.

Ⓒ The protocols are designed using open source programming languages.

Ⓓ The protocols are not dependent on a specific hardware device.

4 ▢ Mark for Review

One significant feature of the Internet that makes it reliable is

Ⓐ protocols

Ⓑ routing

Ⓒ redundancy

Ⓓ scalability

5 ▢ Mark for Review

Which of the following is NOT a critical design aspect of the Internet?

Ⓐ Redundancy

Ⓑ Scalability

Ⓒ Fault tolerance design

Ⓓ Design of the World Wide Web

Chapter 6 Summary

o Computer systems and networks facilitate the transfer of data. Some examples include computers, tablets, servers, routers, and smart sensors.

o A *computing system* is a group of computing devices and programs working together for a common purpose.

o A *computer network* is a group of interconnected computing devices capable of sending or receiving data.

o A computer network is a type of computing system.

o A *path* between two computing devices on a computer network (a sender and a receiver) is a sequence of directly connected computing devices that begins at the sender and ends at the receiver.

o *Routing* is the process of finding a path from sender to receiver.

o The *bandwidth* of a computer network is the maximum amount of data that can be sent in a fixed amount of time.

o Bandwidth is usually measured in bits per second.

o The Internet is a computer network consisting of interconnected networks that use standardized, open (nonproprietary) communication protocols.

o Access to the Internet depends on the ability to connect a computing device to an Internet-connected device.

o A *protocol* is an agreed upon set of rules that specify the behavior of a system.

o The protocols used in the Internet are *open*, which allows users to easily connect additional computing devices to the Internet.

o IP, TCP, and UDP are common protocols used on the Internet.

o Routing on the Internet is usually dynamic; it is not specified in advance.

o   The *scalability* of a system is the capacity for the system to change in size and scale to meet new demands. The Internet was designed to be scalable.

o   Information is passed through the Internet as a *data stream*. Data streams contain chunks of data that are encapsulated in *packets*.

o   Packets contain a chunk of data and metadata used for routing the packet between the origin and the destination on the Internet, as well as for data reassembly.

o   Packets may arrive at the destination in order, out of order, or not at all.

o   The World Wide Web is a system of linked pages, programs, and files.

o   HTTP is a protocol used by the World Wide Web.

o   The World Wide Web uses the Internet.

o   Parallel and distributed computing leverage multiple computers to more quickly solve complex problems or process large data sets.

Chapter 7
Impact of
Computing

BENEFICIAL AND HARMFUL EFFECTS

Many people take up tasks and engineer products so that they can have an impact on society. Nevertheless, the reality is many ideas that people have never make it past the drawing board stage. Most modern-day ideas involve software, which requires programming to bring the concept to life. Technology has revolutionized society in the 21st century through computing innovations. Programming is a skill that is very important to know today; we recognize that algorithms rule the world.

> Know and understand that a computing innovation includes a program as an integral part of its function. A computing innovation takes in data, transforms data, and outputs data in order to solve problems and/or show creative expression. A program is a collection of program statements that performs a specific task when run by a computer. A program is often referred to as "software."

Computing Has Global Impacts

A world filled with computing innovations has changed the way people think, work, live, and play. Methods for communicating, collaborating, problem-solving, and doing business have changed. The primary reason they are changing is because of innovations enabled by computing. Advances in computing lead to innovations in other areas. Computational approaches lead to new understandings, discoveries, and a sea of change across disciplines. Students will become familiar with how computing enables innovation and analyze the potential benefits and harmful effects of computing in several contexts.

It is essential to recognize that computing and computing innovations have global effects—both beneficial and harmful—and are all-pervasive. Innovations enabled by computing raise legal and ethical concerns, such as commercial access to music and movie downloads and streaming. Access to digital content via peer-to-peer networks raises legal and ethical concerns. Both authenticated as well as anonymous access to digital information, open source and licensing of software, and censorship issues raise legal and ethical considerations.

Some other concerns that emerge from the development and use of computational systems and artifacts are privacy and security concerns. People now have instant access to vast amounts of information online. As a result of the Internet, data collection such as geolocation, cookies, and browsing history raises privacy and security concerns. Internet-based technology such as proxy servers and online anonymity software enable anonymity in online interactions. The curating of data can allow bad actors to possibly exploit the information available. The idea behind targeted advertising is to help individuals, but it can be misused. Digitized information being widely available has raised questions about intellectual property. The creation of digital audio, video, and textual content by combining existing content has given rise to copyright concerns.

DIGITAL DIVIDE

The digital divide describes the disparity between those who have access to technology and those who do not, including, but not limited to, access to a computer, the Internet, or other hardware and software. More broadly, it describes the uneven distribution of usage between groups by socioeconomic status, race, gender, and geographical location. However, the digital divide is not only seen in differences among such large-scale groups. Even within these groups, there can be massive difference between individuals in terms of access to technology. The reasons for the lack of access could be physical (geographical location), financial, or the existence of a disability. All these factors contribute to the digital divide.

Unfortunately, solutions for these problems are rarely addressed at scale because there are often more significant problems to be dealt with. Human needs, such as food and health care, take precedence over digital inclusion.

When we consider technological resources and solutions, we need to consider who has access. Who benefits from this technology? Furthermore, are these concerns that are occurring locally for a particular solution or globally? Ultimately, we as individuals, organizations, and governments have the power to improve or worsen this divide.

Research studies have found that people from the African American and Hispanic communities are less likely to say they own a computer or have high-speed Internet access. It is an encouraging trend to note that smartphones play a role in bridging these differences. People who are disabled in America are about three times as likely as those without a disability to say they never go online (15% vs. 5%), according to a 2021 Pew Research Center survey. When compared with those who do not have a disability, adults with disabilities are roughly 18 percentage points less likely to say they subscribe to home broadband and own a traditional computer, a smartphone, or a tablet. Adults who report having a disability are also less likely to have multiple devices that enable them to go online. One in four adults with disabilities say they have high-speed Internet at home, a smartphone, a desktop or laptop computer, and a tablet.

During COVID-19, millions of people in the United States felt isolated because of the lack of reliable broadband Internet at home. This problem was primarily because they could not afford it or because it simply was not available where they live. The digital divide has always left many children and adults with fewer educational and economic opportunities. Especially during the coronavirus pandemic, with schools, libraries, and workplaces closed, those without broadband struggled. Access to schoolwork, job listings, unemployment benefit applications, and video chat services that others use to keep in touch with friends and family were not available. For those on the wrong side of the digital divide, working from home is not an option.

A sobering fact is that the disabled population has a larger portion of seniors. In general, the senior members of our society (those 70 or more years of age) generally have lower digital adoption rates than the rest of the nation. Disabled Americans younger than 65 have much higher rates of home broadband services and owning digital devices. The prominence of Internet use, broadband adoption, and smartphone ownership has snowballed for all Americans—including those who are less well-off financially. Nevertheless, even as various factors that impact the digital divide have narrowed over time, lower- and higher-income Americans' digital lives remain markedly different. Rural Americans have made considerable gains in adopting digital technology over the past decade.

COMPUTING BIAS

When humans collect data to analyze, it is natural to assume some degree of bias. However, most people believe computers, specifically the software that runs these computers, are objective. It is essential to recognize that computers are only as objective as the algorithms they are running.

We will use a common scenario to describe how bias occurs in software systems. Say we want to design a machine-learning algorithm that recommends candidates to employers. The first step is to have the algorithm learn what is desired from a candidate using a training set, which typically collects data based on what résumés resulted in getting hired for similar jobs. Unfortunately, this can lead to biases. If employers exhibited prejudice towards a particular gender, ethnicity, or group in the past positions, the algorithm would likely reflect a similar prejudice. This is only one way that bias can be embedded in an algorithm: bias can exist at every software development level. During phases of the software development cycle, such as gathering requirements for the software product, the system's design, or during testing and deployment, unconscious bias can creep in. This type of bias is commonly known as algorithmic bias. Often, even the simplest of the algorithms cannot explain exactly how systems might be susceptible to algorithmic bias. Frequently, the programmers themselves do not know how a particular artificial intelligence-based algorithm responds to data fed into the algorithm. Machine learning-based systems train on data fed into software systems.

When thinking about "machine learning" tools, one idea is training the software. This involves exposing a computer to relevant data collections, and then that computer learns to make judgments, or predictions, about the information it processes based on the patterns it detects. While discussing data, we typically think of formal studies where researchers deliberate about the data's limitations and consider the demographics and representation details. The results are then peer-reviewed. This is not true with AI-based systems. Consider the Internet. It is possible to teach an artificial intelligence system to crawl through the web and read what has been written. Several studies have found that building a system of this kind could produce prejudices against under-represented minorities and women.

Another possibility is that the foundational assumptions of engineers can also be biased. While the data used to build an algorithm influences the decisions it makes, the programmers who design it and decide upon a deployment strategy are responsible for implicit bias that can creep into the systems. Moreover, even though this is clear, what is not clear is who is ultimately responsible for what is judged to be acceptable and ethical and what is not.

Algorithmic bias occurs in two primary ways: accuracy and impact. An AI can have different accuracy rates for different demographic groups. Similarly, an algorithm can make vastly different decisions when applied to different populations. This can potentially have a significant impact on the affected groups of people.

With that in mind, some people argue that such AI probably should not exist, or at least they should not come with such a high risk of abuse. Just because a technology makes accurate decisions, it does not mean that the decisions are fair or ethical. Several research institutes have made technical efforts to "de-bias" flawed artificial intelligence. It is also vital to keep in mind that technology alone does not have the entire solution. Ultimately, society and traditional systems that determine how society functions will need to be part of the process of addressing the fundamental challenges of fairness and discrimination presented by artificial intelligence-based algorithms.

CROWDSOURCING

> **Crowdsourcing** is the practice of obtaining input or information from a large number of people via the Internet.

Crowdsourcing is a common practice that utilizes the collective knowledge of a group to accomplish something or achieve a common goal. The Internet is the most commonly used medium to achieve these goals. It is the process of obtaining needed services, ideas, or content by soliciting contributions from a large group of people, and especially from an online community, rather than from traditional employees or suppliers. The crowdsourcing process breaks up tedious work by combining numerous people (volunteers, part-time workers) where each contributor adds a small portion to a larger goal.

Crowdsourcing has become an essential tool for businesses in various areas, such as data collection and general problem-solving. The practice of crowdsourcing has been so revolutionary that companies have scaled quickly and, in some cases, revolutionized entire industries.

In crowdsourcing, a business breaks up a more extensive project into individual micro-tasks. The business picks workers who have the skill sets to complete the business's work. A business may use a digital space called a crowdsourcing platform to unite these workers into one place and allocate their micro-tasks. Some of these businesses require workers to have specific skill sets or knowledge of specialized platforms. For example, many software developers utilize GitHub for this purpose.

Some of the advantages of crowdsourcing are:

Scalability: Scaling is a difficult problem since often, while working on massive projects, businesses have inadequate resources. Crowdsourcing provides an easy solution for scaling out any workforce by allocating small portions of a project to be completed by workers anywhere and providing greater flexibility.

Faster Completion: When a project is split into a collection of smaller pieces, providing those pieces to a larger group of workers expedites project completion. As a result, crowdsourcing allows businesses to perform tasks.

Lower Costs: Crowdsourcing is an inexpensive way to complete projects. Since most crowdsourcing is online, the operational costs are minimal when people meet to complete a task. Moreover, when the projects get completed faster, the profit margins may be higher as well.

Customer Involvement: Some crowdsourcing efforts get the customer involved in the effort. This results in an extraordinary level of consumer engagement. By asking consumers to solve a specific problem, the business gains valuable information from their customers.

Below are two examples of projects that have significantly benefited from crowdsourcing.

Open Source Software: Open source development allows programmers and developers to access the source code and to modify and improve the code as they see fit. The most significant advantage of this is that it allows many eyes to analyze the code and utilize unique skill sets to make it better. Several different companies have used crowdsourcing in this way to create stellar software that is highly popular. Some examples of open source software include the Linux operating system, Firefox browsers, and others.

Amazon's Mechanical Turk: MTurk is a crowdsourcing model followed by businesses that aim for work to be done by qualified workers who look for work on the Mechanical Turk platform. Businesses get a diverse number of workers, and workers select what they want to work on. The skills of distributed workers are made available on a pay-per-task model. Businesses can lower costs while achieving significant results.

Citizen Science: Citizen science uses the collective strength of communities and the public to identify research questions, collect and analyze data, interpret results, make discoveries, and develop technologies and applications—all to understand and solve environmental problems. Citizen science is a specialized form of crowdsourcing. In crowdsourcing, organizations put out an open call for voluntary assistance from large groups of individuals for online, distributed problem-solving. In citizen science, the public participates voluntarily in the scientific process, addressing real-world problems that may include conducting scientific experiments, collecting and analyzing data, and solving complex problems. Citizen-science proponents have grand visions. They hope that citizen science, if done correctly, can be a significant source of high-quality data and analysis in areas relevant to government officials as well as research institutions.

LEGAL AND ETHICAL CONCERNS

Intellectual property is a product created by a person—an artist, writer, scientist, or engineer. The law protects this product from being used in an unauthorized fashion. Many of these products include creative artistic work such as writing, music, drawing, photography, and film. Laws protecting intellectual property are of four different categories. These include copyright, patent, trademark, and trade secrets.

Digital content is also subject to intellectual property laws. Products such as computer software and other content that is developed on a computer are considered the intellectual property of either the person or the organization that created it. In a digital world, access to digital artifacts such as music and movies is very easy. Consequently, distribution becomes vulnerable to unauthorized use. These activities are illegal and have consequences.

Plagiarism is copying someone's work and passing it off as one's own. There are serious consequences to plagiarism. Some of the ways to avoid plagiarism include giving credit to the source of the information. Even if it is only a summary or paraphrasing, it is ethical to give credit to the sources used to provide the information.

There are many ways to add a license to the work created. Creative Commons is a not-for-profit organization that has various forms of licenses that can be used to protect original work from being plagiarized.

All Creative Common licenses have this symbol and this button that can be added.

Below is a full list of all Creative Common licenses that are available.

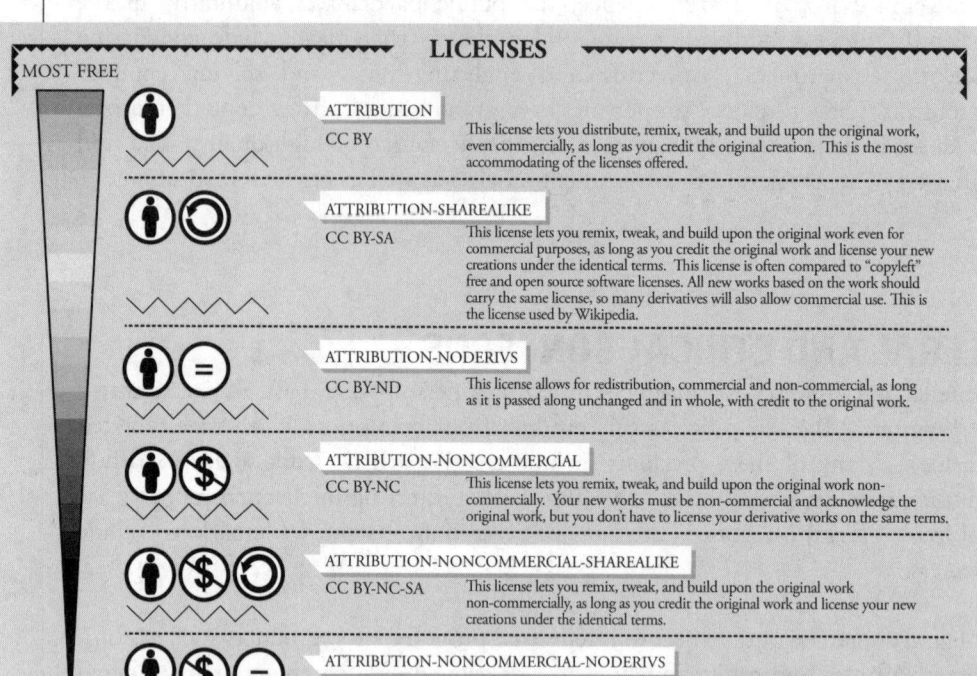

Many software products, especially crowdsourced ones, are open source. Open source primarily refers to open software products. Anyone can use, modify, and share them, since they are available on public domains. This contrasts with proprietary software, where the team that created the software are the only people who can modify it. To use the software, the consumer would need to get explicit permission and comply with the conditions placed by the software creators. With open source software, the authors make the source code available to others who would like to view that code, learn from it, or share it. An excellent example of this is the GNU Image Manipulation Program.

The term open source originated in software development. However, the term "open source" in today's environment implies that the initiative embraces the ideas of collaboration, transparency, and community-oriented development.

Open access literature refers to digital artifacts. The Internet has made many articles available online and free of charge. Open access aims to make many academic publications free of most copyright and licensing restrictions. These research articles are available through open access archives and repositories as well as open access journals.

"Open access is a broad international movement that seeks to grant free and open online access to academic information, such as publications and data. A publication is defined 'open access' when there are no financial, legal or technical barriers to accessing it—that is to say, when anyone can read, download, copy, distribute, print, search for and search within the information, or use it in education or in any other way within the legal agreements." (*Source: openaccess.nl/en/what-is-open-access*)

SAFE COMPUTING

Information about a person that can uniquely identify them, such as their educational, medical, financial, or employment information, is known as Personally Identifiable Information (PII). PII can be used to identify, contact, or locate an individual. Examples of data elements that can identify an individual include name, email address, fingerprint, etc. It is every individual's responsibility to safeguard their PII. Because of advances in technology such as the Internet, the PII has become a component of personal privacy. Websites, search engines, and other social media sites store user information using cookies, history of mouse-clicks, and browsing history to target consumers with relevant ads. All this comes at the expense of user privacy.

There are several possible ways to misuse PII because of the data available online.

- Placement of PII online to enhance a user's online experiences
- Storage of PII online to simplify online purchases
- Exploitation of commercial and governmental curation of information by ignoring privacy and other protections, leading to the unintended use of information placed online that may have a harmful impact
- Use of PII for stalking or for identity theft or for other criminal acts
- The difficulty of deletion of information placed online
- Collection of your current location and time spent at previous locations
- Acquisition of information about a person from what is posted on social media and other sources

Many online accounts can be made a great deal safer from malicious attacks just by using better passwords. The best way to improve cybersecurity is by creating a strong password.

The weakest passwords are ones that use the following:

- names of family and friends
- birthday or those of family/friends
- places where living or have lived including cities or street names

Because the Internet is full of information about people's personal lives, a password is most likely easily guessed if it contains that person's information. Many websites, applications, and mobile devices now offer Multifactor Authentication (MFA), a feature that improves account security. Suppose an MFA is set up for a given account (website, application, or device) while logging in with the username and password. In that case, the account server asks for a second, independent form of authentication. It authenticates both before granting access into the system. A comparison to this process is similar to real-life systems; to prove one's identity, systems ask for an ID and one more proof of identification (such as a passport).

Cybersecurity

Cybersecurity is also known as information security. It is the protection of a system against unauthorized or criminal use. It is the practice of ensuring integrity, confidentiality, and availability of information against unauthorized access. Cybersecurity's primary purpose is to protect networks, devices, programs, and data from external and internal threats.

The threat of cyberattacks requires vigilant security measures. These require implementation across information systems such as application security, identity management and data security, and network security. Because the technological landscape keeps evolving and the adoption of software is ever-increasing, more and more information is becoming digital and accessible through networks and across the Internet. Cyberattackers use illegal approaches to gain unauthorized access to computers, devices, networks, applications, and databases.

Below is a list of cyberattacks that criminals and attackers use to exploit software:

Malware	Ransomware
Phishing	Distributed Denial of Service (DDoS)
Vulnerable software	Remote code execution
Brute force	SQL injection
Insider threat	Password attacks

The following are useful definitions on the various ways cyberattacks occur:

Phishing	Deceiving a user into providing personal information that can then be used to access sensitive online resources, such as bank accounts and emails
Computer Virus	Programs that can repeatedly duplicate themselves and gain authorized access to a computer, often after attaching themselves to legitimate programs
Malware	Software that is capable of taking control over or harming a computing system
Keylogging	Recoding every keystroke made by a computer user hoping to gain fraudulent access to usernames, passwords, and other sensitive and confidential information
Rogue access point	Data sent over public networks can be intercepted, analyzed, and modified. One way that this can happen is through a rogue access point: a wireless access point that can intercept, analyze, and modify data sent over public networks.

Encryption and Decryption

Data encryption is the process in which data is encoded into another form, then is converted to its original readable form with the help of a secret key (this is called a decryption key). Data, or plaintext, is encrypted with an encryption algorithm and an encryption key. Data encryption aims to protect digital data confidentiality as it is stored on computer systems and transmitted using the Internet or other computer networks. Encrypted data is commonly referred to as ciphertext, while unencrypted data is called plaintext. The conversion of encrypted data into its original form is called decryption. It is the reverse process of encryption. It decodes the encrypted information so that only an authorized user can decrypt the data because decryption requires a secret key or password.

A strong encryption-decryption system ensures privacy. As information travels over the Internet, it is necessary to scrutinize the access requests from various sources. Data that is encrypted before being sent through the Internet include text files, images, email, etc. At the receiving end, decryption software needs to enter a key to access the encrypted data. The decryption software extracts and converts the garbled data and transforms it into words and images easily understandable by a system. The decryption process is either manual or automatic.

There are two main types of encryption:

- asymmetric encryption (also known as public-key encryption)
- symmetric encryption

These encryption algorithms help with authentication and ensure the integrity of systems. The process results in ciphertext, which can only be viewed in its original form if decrypted with the correct key.

Symmetric-key ciphers use the same secret key for encrypting and decrypting a message or file. While symmetric-key encryption is much faster than asymmetric encryption, the sender must exchange the encryption key with the recipient before the message can be decrypted. Asymmetric cryptography is also known as public-key cryptography. This form of cryptography uses two different keys, one public and one private. As it is named, the public key is one that everyone has access to, but the private key must be protected.

To summarize, cyberattacks occur everywhere. Cybersecurity tools must work in harmony to combat cybercriminals. It is important to understand what is at stake, and society needs to take action to protect our most vital information and digital data.

CHAPTER 7 KEY TERMS

Computing Innovations
Legal and Ethical Concerns
Beneficial and Harmful Effects of Computing
Digital Divide
Artificial Intelligence
Machine Learning
Personally Identifiable Information (PII)
Encryption
Crowdsourcing
Citizen Science
Intellectual Property
Creative Commons
Plagiarism
Open Source
Cybersecurity (Information Security)
Decryption

CHAPTER 7 REVIEW DRILL

1 ☐ Mark for Review

Computing innovation is not always met with approval from the lawmakers in society. This is because

- (A) all computing innovations cause problems

- (B) computing innovations once deployed can sometimes cause unexpected problems

- (C) all computing innovations have predictable behavior

- (D) the impact a computing innovation has on society does not last forever

2 ☐ Mark for Review

The digital divide in the time of Coronavirus became more evident because

- (A) the people who could afford the technology had better access to the vaccines

- (B) the people who could afford the technology had access to education and the news

- (C) the people who could afford the technology could pay for high-speed Internet

- (D) the people who could afford the technology knew how to hook up computers and other digital devices

3

In order to remove bias from software, which of the following steps must be taken?

   I. The data that is collected and provided to the AI algorithms should be gathered from diverse sources.
   II. There should be efforts taken to technically remove bias from the algorithms.
   III. The algorithms should be removed from use in society.

- (A) I, II, and III

- (B) I and II only

- (C) I and III only

- (D) II and III only

4 ☐ Mark for Review

Citizen science is a form of crowdsourcing. Which of the following answer choices justify this statement?

- (A) Citizen science is scientific research conducted by distributed individuals who contribute relevant data to research using their own computing devices. This is a form of crowdsourcing.

- (B) Citizen science is distributed in how it is conducted. This is a form of crowdsourcing.

- (C) Citizen science is all about research. Crowdsourcing is very helpful in conducting research.

- (D) Citizen science helps collect data. Crowdsourcing is very useful in facilitating collection of large volumes of data.

5 ◻ Mark for Review

One of the most important technologies needed for crowdsourcing is

(A) knowing how to write computer programs

(B) access to the Internet

(C) the ability to attend online classes

(D) having a webcam, microphone, and speaker

6 ◻ Mark for Review

Intellectual property is defined as

(A) something that a person owns (that is, they have paid to use the product)

(B) something that, while free, cannot be distributed

(C) something that, because it is created by a person, cannot be sold or distributed

(D) something that a person has created, like a song, story, movie, and can be sold or distributed with permission

7 ◻ Mark for Review

The best way to avoid plagiarism is

(A) to get the permission of the author before using their work

(B) to give credit by citing the sources

(C) to pay for the work that is being used

(D) to not use the resource and make all work original

8 ◻ Mark for Review

Information about a person such as name, age, and email identification is called

(A) personalized data

(B) metadata

(C) cookie data

(D) Personally Identifiable Information

9 ◻ Mark for Review

Which of the following list can be described as a cyberattack?

Select <u>two</u> answers.

☐ Operating System failure

☐ Hard disk crash

☐ Distributed Denial of Service

☐ Ransomware

10 ◻ Mark for Review

The process of converting data into its original readable form is called

(A) encryption

(B) decryption

(C) asymmetric key

(D) packet transfer

Chapter 7 Summary

○ While computing innovations are typically designed to achieve a specific purpose, they may have unintended consequences.

○ A single computer innovation-based effect can be viewed as both beneficial and harmful by different people or even by the same person.

○ Computing innovations can be used in ways that their creators had not originally intended:
  • The World Wide Web was originally intended only for rapid and easy exchange of information within the scientific community.
  • Targeted advertising is used to help businesses, but it can be misused at both individual and aggregate levels.
  • Machine learning and data mining have enabled innovation in medicine, business, and science, but information discovered in this way has also been used to discriminate against groups of individuals.

○ Some of the ways computing innovations can be used may have a harmful impact on society, the economy, or culture.

○ Responsible programmers try to consider the unintended ways their computing innovations can be used and the potential beneficial and harmful effects of these new uses, but it is not possible for a programmer to consider all the ways a computing innovation can be used.

○ The *digital divide* refers to differing access to computing devices and the Internet, based on socioeconomic, geographic, or demographic characteristics.
  • The digital divide can affect both groups and individuals.
  • The digital divide raises issues of equity, access, and influence, both globally and locally.
  • The digital divide is affected by the actions of individuals, organizations, and governments.

○ Computing innovations can reflect existing human biases because of biases written into the algorithms or biases in the data used by the innovation.

○ Programmers should take action to reduce bias in algorithms used for computing innovations as a way of combating existing human biases.

o Widespread access to information and public data facilitates the identification of problems, development of solutions, and dissemination of results.

o Citizen science is scientific research conducted in whole or part by distributed individuals, many of whom may not be scientists, who contribute relevant data to research using their own computing devices.

o *Crowdsourcing* is the practice of obtaining input or information from a large number of people via the Internet.

o Material created on a computer is the intellectual property of the creator or an organization. The use of material created by someone else without permission and presented as one's own is plagiarism and may have legal consequences.

o Some examples of legal ways to use materials created by someone else include:
  • Creative Commons—a public copyright license that enables the free distribution of an otherwise copyrighted work. This is used when the content creator wants to give others the right to share, use, and build upon the work they have created.
  • open source—programs that are made freely available and may be redistributed and modified
  • open access—online research output free of any and all restrictions on access and free of many restrictions on use, such as copyright or license restrictions

o The use of material created by someone other than you should always be cited.

o As with any technology or medium, the potential of using computing to harm individuals or groups of people raises legal and ethical concerns.

o Computing can play a role in social and political issues, which in turn often raises legal and ethical concerns. Some examples of these include:
  • the development of software that allows access to digital media downloads and streaming
  • the existence of computing devices that collect and analyze data by continuously monitoring activities

o   Personally Identifiable Information (PII) is information about an individual that identifies, links, relates, or describes them. Examples of PII include:
  • Social Security number
  • age
  • race
  • phone number(s)
  • medical information
  • financial information
  • biometric data
  • PII and other information placed online can be used to enhance a user's online experiences.

o   PII can be used to stalk or steal the identity of a person or to aid in the planning of other criminal acts.

o   PII stored online can be used to simplify making online purchases.

o   Commercial and governmental curation of information may be exploited if privacy and other protections are ignored. Information placed online can be used in ways that were not intended and that may have a harmful impact. For example, an email message may be forwarded, tweets can be retweeted, and social media posts can be viewed by potential employers.

o   Once information is placed online, it is difficult to delete.

o   Authentication measures protect devices and information from unauthorized access. Examples of authentication measures include strong passwords and multifactor authentication.

o   *Encryption* is the process of encoding data to prevent unauthorized access. *Decryption* is the process of decoding the data. Two common encryption approaches are:
  • Symmetric key encryption, involving one key for both encryption and decryption.
  • Public key encryption, pairing a public key for encryption and a private key for decryption.

o   *Phishing* is a technique that attempts to trick a user into providing personal information. That personal information can then be used to access sensitive online resources, such as bank accounts and emails.

o   *Keylogging* is the use of a program to record every keystroke made by a computer user in order to gain fraudulent access to passwords and other confidential information.

o   *Malware* is software intended to damage a computing system or to take partial control over its operation. This is often found on suspicious or free programs.

o   A *computer virus* is a malicious program that can copy itself and gain access to a computer in an unauthorized way. Computer viruses often attach themselves to legitimate programs and start running independently on a computer.

o   Data sent over public networks can be intercepted, analyzed, and modified. One way that this can happen is through a rogue access point.

o   A *rogue access point* is a wireless access point that gives unauthorized access to secure networks.

o   A malicious link can be disguised on a Web page or in an email message.

Chapter 8
End of Chapter
Drill Answers and
Explanations

CHAPTER 4

1. **D** Metadata is a data about data, information that gives more details about the data itself. In this case, the time at which the song was recorded, while useful information, is not information about the song itself.

2.

00110001_2	49_{10}
11100000_2	224_{10}
11000011_2	195_{10}
11110010_2	242_{10}
10010100_2	148_{10}
10101110_2	174_{10}
1101000_2	104_{10}
01011100_2	92_{10}
00001100_2	12_{10}
10111111_2	191_{10}

3.

123_{10}	01111011_2
210_{10}	11010010_2
75_{10}	01001011_2
103_{10}	01100111_2
25_{10}	00011001_2
77_{10}	01001101_2
235_{10}	11101011_2
102_{10}	01100110_2
200_{10}	11001000_2
45_{10}	00101101_2

4. **C** Choice (D), while true, is not really an advantage. Choice (C) is the advantage of lossy compression. Choices (A) and (B) are not valid responses.

5. **D** This is true because even the slightest loss of information may cause the program to not run. Images, video, and music files can withstand some loss of data and retain the quality of data after transmission and decompression.

CHAPTER 5

1. **C**   In most programming languages, variables are assigned data using the assignment statement. Boolean is a special data type that holds only two values, true or false. The other data types are int, double, string, etc.

2. **A**   A variable or a list is a data abstraction; when the programmer creates a variable, it is a collection of characters, numbers, or strings. The value of the variable is stored in the computer's memory as a bunch of bits. This is data abstraction or information hiding. Choice (D) is a process used to solve a problem. Choices (B) and (C) deal with procedures and not with variables, which is what the question is about.

3. **A**   In most programming languages, when dealing with the arrays, the first element in an array starts with a 0. However, in the Exam Reference Sheet, the index value starts with 1, and it is important to pay attention to this detail.

4. **A**   An algorithm is a detailed, step-by-step process used to solve a problem. While (B) and (C) may be true, they are not part of the definition of an algorithm. An algorithm can be written in English, pseudocode, or any other programming language.

5. **C**   Strings are formed by a list (or an array) of characters. Most programming languages "add" strings together, which really means concatenation.

6. **B**   The logical operators are OR and AND. In most programming languages, (A) is the symbol usually used for assignment statements, and (C) and (D) are symbols for arithmetic operators.

7. **A**   Sequencing (where one action leads to the next in a predetermined order), selection (also called decision statements, or IF statements), and iteration (repetition) are considered building blocks of algorithms. Sequencing has to be a part of every algorithm. Selection and Repetition are very important, and most algorithms need these blocks to solve harder problems.

8. **C**   Different algorithms for the same problem have different levels of efficiency, including ones that are so inefficient they become impractical to use, so eliminate (A). Although it may be possible to calculate the memory the algorithm will use for variable storage, memory used for executing the instructions can vary in different executions, so eliminate (B). Algorithms are informal descriptions of a program, so they don't have to follow a set format. Eliminate (D). Any problem can be solved in multiple ways, perhaps using slight tweaks of another method or more drastic changes. The answer is (C).

9. **A**   Procedural abstraction is, by definition, the use of a function to perform a particular repeated task so that the programmer only needs to be concerned with the end result of the function call. Thus, by using abstraction, the programmer can call a function anytime a particular task is required rather than recreating the individual steps of the task on every instance. The answer is (A).

10. **D**   All of the answer choices are valid statements about simulations. Choice (B) is a formal definition of simulations. Choices (A) and (C) are advantages of simulations.

CHAPTER 6

1. **A**   Bandwidth is measured as bits per second (bps).

2. **B**   The path that the data takes when it is sent from one computer to another is called a route.

3. **A**   Open Internet protocol standards allow anyone to set up a service online using the appropriate and established protocol; no permission is required from anyone else to make it available to everyone on the Internet. While (B), (C), and (D) may be true, that is not why they are called open standards.

4. **C**   The fact that there is more than one way to send data between two points on the Internet increases the reliability of the Internet. This idea of there being more than one route is called redundancy. The Internet system was designed with built-in redundancy. While (A), (B), and (D) are significant features of the Internet, they are not the reason the Internet is reliable.

5. **D**   The World Wide Web is different from the Internet. The Internet, which is a network of computers, is scalable and reliable with a fault-tolerant design built into the system. The WWW is one system (more user-friendly and popular) with which to access the Internet.

CHAPTER 7

1. **B**   Choices (A) and (C) are not true. Choice (D), while true, is not a good reason to not approve a computing innovation.

2. **B**   Choice (A) is not related to the digital divide or technology. Choices (C) and (D) existed in non-pandemic times.

3. **B**   Statement III will not remove bias from the algorithm. Statements I and II are steps taken to solve the problem.

4. **A**   The three key features of citizen science are that it is distributed, conducted by people using their own devices, and is scientific research. The other answer choices do not cover all three features.

5. **B**   The other features will help with crowdsourcing but are not needed for the process to be successful.

6. **D**   The most important aspect of intellectual property is that users have to seek explicit permission or need to understand how to clearly acknowledge the contribution of the creator of the movie, song, photo, etc. The other answer choices may or may not be true in all cases.

7. **B** Choice (B) is the practical solution. Choices (A) and (D) may not always be possible. Choice (C) may not be needed in all cases.

8. **D** Personally Identifiable Information is data that can be used to uniquely identify an individual. Name, age, and email can potentially be used for this purpose.

9. **C, D** Choices (A) and (B) are computer hardware failures. Choices (C) and (D) are cyberattacks.

10. **B** Encryption is the conversion of data from a readable format to an unreadable one. This is reversible. The reverse process is called decryption. Choice (C) can be used for encryption but does not support the definition stated in the question. Choice (D) is not related to the encryption and decryption process.

Part VI
Additional Practice Tests

- Practice Test 2
- Practice Test 2: Answers and Explanations
- How to Score Practice Test 2
- Practice Test 3
- Practice Test 3: Answers and Explanations
- How to Score Practice Test 3

Practice Test 2

AP® Computer Science Principles Exam

SECTION I: Multiple-Choice Questions

DO NOT BEGIN THE EXAM UNTIL YOU ARE TOLD TO DO SO.

At a Glance

Total Time
2 hours
Number of Questions
70
Percent of Total Score
70%

DISCLAIMER: The official AP Computer Science Principles will be administered digitally. Instructions for the digital exam may differ from this practice test.

Instructions

Section I has 70 multiple-choice questions and lasts 2 hours.

Each question is followed by four suggested answers.

For questions 1–62, select the single best answer choice for each question.

For questions 63–70, **two** of the suggested answers are correct. **For each of these questions, you must select both correct choices to earn credit.** No partial credit will be earned if only one correct choice is selected. Select the two that are best in each case.

Reference information for programming questions is available in this application and can be accessed throughout Section I.

GO ON TO THE NEXT PAGE.

Quick Reference

Instruction	Explanation
Assignment, Display, and Input	

Text:
 	
`a ← expression`
 	
Block:
 	
`a ◄── expression`
	Evaluates `expression` and then assigns a copy of the result to the variable a.

Text:
 	
`DISPLAY(expression)`
 	
Block:
 	
`DISPLAY expression`
	Displays the value of `expression`, followed by a space.

Text:
 	
`INPUT()`
 	
Block:
 	
`INPUT`
	Accepts a value from the user and returns the input value.

Arithmetic Operators and Numeric Procedures	

Text and Block:
 	
`a + b`
`a - b`
`a * b`
`a / b`
	The arithmetic operators `+`, `-`, `*`, and `/` are used to perform arithmetic on a and b.
	
	For example, `17 / 5` evaluates to `3.4`.
	
	The order of operations used in mathematics applies when evaluating expressions.

Text and Block: `a MOD b`	Evaluates to the remainder when a is divided by b. Assume that a is an integer greater than or equal to 0 and b is an integer greater than 0. For example, `17 MOD 5` evaluates to 2. The `MOD` operator has the same precedence as the `*` and `/` operators.

Text:
 	
`RANDOM(a, b)`
 	
Block:
 	
`RANDOM a, b`
	Generates and returns a random integer from a to b, including a and b. Each result is equally likely to occur.
	
	For example, `RANDOM(1, 3)` could return `1`, `2`, or `3`.

Instruction	Explanation
Relational and Boolean Operators	
Text and Block: a = b a ≠ b a > b a < b a ≥ b a ≤ b	The relational operators =, ≠, >, <, ≤, and ≥ are used to test the relationship between two variables, expressions, or values. A comparison using relational operators evaluates to a Boolean value. For example, a = b evaluates to true if a and b are equal; otherwise it evaluates to false.
Text: NOT condition Block: NOT (condition)	Evaluates to true if condition is false; otherwise evaluates to false.
Text: condition1 AND condition2 Block: (condition1) AND (condition2)	Evaluates to true if both condition1 and condition2 are true; otherwise evaluates to false.
Text: condition1 OR condition2 Block: (condition1) OR (condition2)	Evaluates to true if condition1 is true or if condition2 is true or if both condition1 and condition2 are true; otherwise evaluates to false.
Selection	

Text:
 	
IF(condition)
 	
{
 	
<block of statements>
 	
}
 	
Block:
 	
IF (condition)
(block of statements)
	The code in block of statements is executed if the Boolean expression condition evaluates to true; no action is taken if condition evaluates to false.

Instruction	Explanation
Selection—Continued	

Text:
 	
IF(condition)
{
<first block of statements>
}
ELSE
{
<second block of statements>
}
 	
Block:
 	
IF (condition)
    first block of statements
ELSE
    second block of statements
	The code in first block of statements is executed if the Boolean expression condition evaluates to true; otherwise the code in second block of statements is executed.

Iteration	

Text:
 	
REPEAT n TIMES
{
<block of statements>
}
 	
Block:
 	
REPEAT n TIMES
    block of statements
	The code in block of statements is executed n times.

Text:
 	
REPEAT UNTIL(condition)
{
<block of statements>
}
 	
Block:
 	
REPEAT UNTIL condition
    block of statements
	The code in block of statements is repeated until the Boolean expression condition evaluates to true.

Instruction	**Explanation**
List Operations	
For all list operations, if a list index is less than 1 or greater than the length of the list, an error message is produced and the program terminates.	
Text: aList ← [value1, value2, value3, ...] Block: [aList ⟵ [value1, value2, value3]]	Creates a new list that contains the values value1, value2, value3, and ... at indices 1, 2, 3, and ... respectively and assigns it to aList.
Text: aList ← [] Block: [aList ⟵ []]	Creates an empty list and assigns it to aList.
Text: aList ← bList Block: [aList ⟵ bList]	Assigns a copy of the list bList to the list aList. For example, if bList contains [20, 40, 60], then aList will also contain [20, 40, 60] after the assignment.
Text: aList[i] Block: aList [i]	Accesses the element of aList at index i. The first element of aList is at index 1 and is accessed using the notation aList[1].
Text: x ← aList[i] Block: x ⟵ aList [i]	Assigns the value of aList[i] to the variable x.
Text: aList[i] ← x Block: [aList [i] ⟵ x]	Assigns the value of x to aList[i].
Text: aList[i] ← aList[j] Block: [aList [i] ⟵ aList [j]]	Assigns the value of aList[j] to aList[i].
Text: INSERT(aList, i, value) Block: [INSERT aList, i, value]	Any values in aList at indices greater than or equal to i are shifted one position to the right. The length of the list is increased by 1, and value is placed at index i in aList.

Instruction	Explanation
List Operations—Continued	

Text:
 	
`APPEND(aList, value)`
 	
Block:
 	
`APPEND aList, value`
	The length of `aList` is increased by 1, and `value` is placed at the end of `aList`.

Text:
 	
`REMOVE(aList, i)`
 	
Block:
 	
`REMOVE aList, i`
	Removes the item at index `i` in `aList` and shifts to the left any values at indices greater than `i`. The length of `aList` is decreased by 1.

Text:
 	
`LENGTH(aList)`
 	
Block:
 	
`LENGTH aList`
	Evaluates to the number of elements in `aList`.

Text:
 	
`FOR EACH item IN aList`
 	
`{`
 	
`<block of statements>`
 	
`}`
 	
Block:
 	
`FOR EACH item IN aList`
`block of statements`
	The variable `item` is assigned the value of each element of `aList` sequentially, in order, from the first element to the last element. The code in `block of statements` is executed once for each assignment of `item`.

Procedures and Procedure Calls	

Text:
 	
`PROCEDURE procName(parameter1,`
`            parameter2, ...)`
 	
`{`
 	
`<block of statements>`
 	
`}`
 	
Block:
 	
`PROCEDURE procName parameter1,`
`            parameter2, ...`
`block of statements`
	Defines `procName` as a procedure that takes zero or more arguments. The procedure contains `block of statements`.
	
	The procedure `procName` can be called using the following notation, where `arg1` is assigned to `parameter1`, `arg2` is assigned to `parameter2`, etc.:
	`procName(arg1, arg2, ...)`

Instruction	Explanation
Procedures and Procedure Calls—Continued	

Text:
 	
`PROCEDURE procName(parameter1,`
`              parameter2, ...)`
 	
`{`
 	
`<block of statements>`
 	
`RETURN(expression)`
 	
`}`
 	
Block:
 	
PROCEDURE procName parameter1, parameter2, ...
block of statements
RETURN expression
	Defines `procName` as a procedure that takes zero or more arguments. The procedure contains `block of statements` and returns the value of `expression`. The RETURN statement may appear at any point inside the procedure and causes an immediate return from the procedure back to the calling statement.
	
	The value returned by the procedure `procName` can be assigned to the variable `result` using the following notation:
	`result ← procName(arg1, arg2, ...)`

Text: `RETURN(expression)` Block: RETURN expression	Returns the flow of control to the point where the procedure was called and returns the value of `expression`.
Robot	
If the robot attempts to move to a square that is not open or is beyond the edge of the grid, the robot will stay in its current location and the program will terminate.	
Text: `MOVE_FORWARD()` Block: MOVE_FORWARD	The robot moves one square forward in the direction it is facing.
Text: `ROTATE_LEFT()` Block: ROTATE_LEFT	The robot rotates in place 90 degrees counterclockwise (i.e., makes an in-place left turn).
Text: `ROTATE_RIGHT()` Block: ROTATE_RIGHT	The robot rotates in place 90 degrees clockwise (i.e., makes an in-place right turn).
Text: `CAN_MOVE(direction)` Block: CAN_MOVE direction	Evaluates to `true` if there is an open square one square in the direction relative to where the robot is facing; otherwise evaluates to `false`. The value of `direction` can be `left`, `right`, `forward`, or `backward`.

This page intentionally left blank.

GO ON TO THE NEXT PAGE.

AP COMPUTER SCIENCE PRINCIPLES

SECTION I

Time—2 hours

Number of Questions—70

Percent of total exam grade—70%

Directions: Choose one best answer for each question. Some questions at the end of the test will have more than one correct answer; for these, you will be instructed to choose two answer choices.

---

1 ▢ Mark for Review

The metadata from an image you took was released. Which of the following information could not be determined from the metadata?

(A) The names of the people in the picture

(B) Where you took the picture

(C) When you took the picture

(D) Size of the image

---

2 ▢ Mark for Review

A student is designing a new classroom library record system. She has based it on 9 bits. How many possible books can she store in the library?

(A) 18

(B) 81

(C) 511

(D) 512

GO ON TO THE NEXT PAGE.

3 ☐ Mark for Review

Which of the following would be an example of multifactor authentication?

Ⓐ Requiring a password to log in to the main website and an additional password to enter a chatroom feature of the website

Ⓑ Requiring an email to verify joining a website

Ⓒ Requiring both a text message code and password to log in to a website

Ⓓ Allowing users to set up a password or use their fingerprint to log in to an application

4 ☐ Mark for Review

A technology company plans to launch satellites that will be able to offer high-speed Internet anywhere on the planet. The plan is to ultimately create an interconnected network of about 12,000 small satellites in low orbit around Earth. Which of the following descriptions best describes the company's actions?

Ⓐ Launching these satellites will increase the chance of crowdsourcing.

Ⓑ The availability of high-speed Internet will most likely reduce the digital divide.

Ⓒ This project is an example of citizen science.

Ⓓ These satellites will most likely become a rogue access point.

GO ON TO THE NEXT PAGE.

5 ▢ Mark for Review

The following grid contains a robot represented as a triangle. The robot is initially facing right. Which of the following code lines can replace the missing code to move the robot to the grey square?

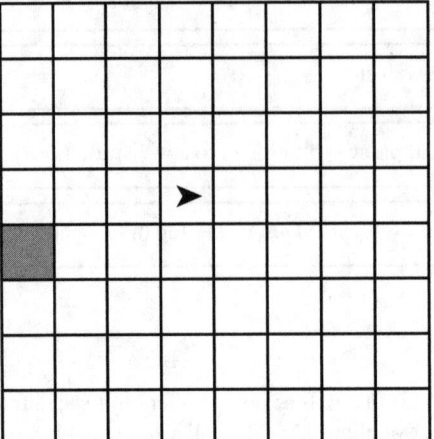

```
REPEAT 3 TIMES
{
        <missing code>
}
MOVE_FORWARD()
REPEAT 2 TIMES
{
        ROTATE_LEFT()
        MOVE_FORWARD()
}
ROTATE_RIGHT()
MOVE_FORWARD()
MOVE_FORWARD()
```

(A) MOVE_FORWARD()
     ROTATE_RIGHT()

(B) ROTATE_RIGHT()
     MOVE_FORWARD()

(C) MOVE_FORWARD()
     ROTATE_LEFT()

(D) ROTATE_LEFT()
     MOVE_FORWARD()

GO ON TO THE NEXT PAGE.

6 ☐ Mark for Review

A teacher is dividing her students in groups of 3 for an in-class project. She has created a computer program that will tell her whether or not she is able to equally distribute her students into groups of 3. Which of the following can replace the missing code to evaluate whether her classes can be divided into groups of 3 students evenly?

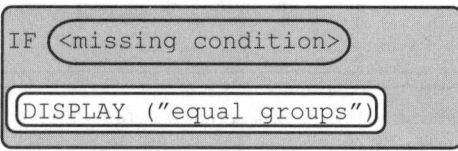

IF (<missing condition>)

DISPLAY ("equal groups")

- (A) numStudents MOD 2 + 1 = 3

- (B) numStudents MOD 3 = 0

- (C) numStudents / 3 = 0

- (D) numStudents / 3 - 3 = 0

7 ☐ Mark for Review

Which of the following best describes an example of crowdsourcing?

- (A) In 2020, similar to the past 12 years, Google released the Google Doodle challenge, which asked students to design a doodle that expressed kindness. This challenge allowed Google to deepen their engagement with users.

- (B) Code.org presents Hour of Code each year for students to engage in different types of coding to promote the idea that anyone can code.

- (C) FoxSports.com streams the Super Bowl to allow anyone with Internet access to watch the game free. This increased the availability of the Super Bowl to many people.

- (D) In July 2020, Loon, a part of Google's parent company Alphabet, launched high-altitude balloons in Kenya to deliver the Internet to rural and remote areas. These balloons would allow more people access to the Internet.

GO ON TO THE NEXT PAGE.

8 ⬛ Mark for Review

Which of the following provides an example of identity theft in relation to Personally Identifiable Information?

(A) You receive an email from your bank stating that your savings and checking accounts have been locked because of suspicious withdrawals. The email instructs you to click on the link in order to reset your passwords and receive more details about the suspicious activity.

(B) A friend sends you an email with an attachment. You expect that it's something important and download it. Your computer then starts acting strange and is slow responding.

(C) Your credit report shows a fraudulent identity, where your social security number has been combined with fake details. This identity was used to file a tax return and open several credit card accounts.

(D) A friend posts on social media from your account, pretending to be you.

9 ⬛ Mark for Review

A picture has been compressed and each pixel value was averaged and converted to greyscale. Which of the following statements best describes the compression?

(A) The original image cannot be restored since the above compression was lossy compression.

(B) The original image cannot be restored since the above compression was lossless compression.

(C) The original image can be restored since the above compression was lossy compression.

(D) The original image can be restored since the above compression was lossless compression.

GO ON TO THE NEXT PAGE.

10 ⬚ Mark for Review

The following data table below shows how long each of the processes take depending on the number of binary bits.

Task	8 bits	80 bits	800 bits
Backing up an audio file	0.5 seconds	2.0 seconds	8 seconds
Creating a copy of an audio file	1 second	2 second	3 second
Searching an audio file	0.5 seconds	5 seconds	50 seconds
Deleting an audio file	0.25 seconds	0.75 seconds	2.25 seconds

Using this information, which of the following would take the shortest amount of time for 1000 bytes?

(A) Deleting an audio file

(B) Backing up an audio file

(C) Searching an audio file

(D) Creating a copy of an audio file

11 ⬚ Mark for Review

Which of the following descriptions shows computing bias for the facial recognition system?

(A) Sylvia uses facial recognition in order to open the doors of her apartment when she is carrying heavy bags, but it doesn't allow the delivery driver access.

(B) The facial recognition system is being used in the subway to reduce crime but not for fare collection and subway access.

(C) In China, interlocking facial recognition cameras track where people are, what they are up to, and who they associate with—and are ultimately used to help assign people a single score based on whether the government considers them trustworthy.

(D) Rekognition, Amazon's face-ID system, once identified Oprah Winfrey as male and is why many companies are abandoning facial recognition research.

GO ON TO THE NEXT PAGE.

12 ☐ Mark for Review

Currently, the list of processes below is being completed sequentially. Since there are 2 processors available, what two processes could be done in parallel to best improve execution time?

Task	Processing Time
X	110 sec
Y	85 sec
Z	20 sec

(A) Y and Z would be done sequentially and X would be run parallel.

(B) X and Y would be done sequentially and Z would be run parallel.

(C) Z and Y would be done sequentially and X would be run parallel.

(D) Execution time would not be improved by running a parallel process.

13 ☐ Mark for Review

What type of data is returned by the following procedure, equalNums?

```
PROCEDURE equalNums(num)
{
    counter ← 1
    done ← true
    REPEAT UNTIL(counter ≥ num)
    {
        counter ← counter + 1
    }
    IF (counter > num)
    {
        done ← false
    }
    DISPLAY(counter)
    RETURN (done)
}
```

(A) Boolean

(B) String

(C) Number

(D) Expression

GO ON TO THE NEXT PAGE.

14 ☐ Mark for Review

A company focused on space exploration has provided a set of criteria to determine whether an applicant is eligible for the next Mars mission. The person must be between the ages of 25 and 35, inclusive, and must be able to lift 50 pounds. The algorithm has a variable called `age` which represents the applicant's age and a variable called `capable` which stores the amount of weight an applicant can lift. Which of the following Boolean expressions will correctly evaluate whether an applicant is allowed to go on the next Mars mission?

(A) `age ≥ 25 OR (age ≤ 35 AND capable ≥ 50)`

(B) `age ≥ 25 OR age ≤ 35 AND capable ≥ 50`

(C) `(age ≥ 25 AND age ≤ 35) AND capable ≥ 50`

(D) `age > 25 OR age < 35 OR capable ≥ 50`

15 ☐ Mark for Review

For which of the following situations below would it be best to use a heuristic in order to find a solution that runs in a reasonable amount of time?

  I. How many moves it will take for a computer to beat a human player
 II. Finding the route to multiple desired destinations
III. Calculating student GPA

(A) II only

(B) I and II only

(C) III only

(D) I, II, and III

GO ON TO THE NEXT PAGE.

16   Mark for Review

Comparing the two algorithms below, which statement best compares time and identifies the algorithm that runs faster, given that calling the procedure `countX()` takes approximately 1 minute to run each time it is called?

```
Algorithm A

x ← 0
y ← 0
REPEAT n TIMES {
      x = countX();
}
REPEAT n TIMES {
      y = countX();
}
```

```
Algorithm B

x ← 0
y ← 0
REPEAT n TIMES {

      REPEAT n TIMES {
          countX();
      }
}
```

(A) Both algorithms take the same amount of time.

(B) Algorithm B is faster as it takes 2 * *n* minutes to run, while Algorithm A takes 4 * *n* minutes to run.

(C) Algorithm A is faster as it takes 4 * *n* minutes to run, while Algorithm B takes 8 * *n* minutes to run.

(D) Algorithm A is faster as it takes 2 * *n* minutes to run, while Algorithm B takes 1 * n^2 minutes to run.

GO ON TO THE NEXT PAGE.

17 ☐ Mark for Review

Given the following network configurations, which shows fault tolerance due to redundancy between terminals A and C?

I.   Network A

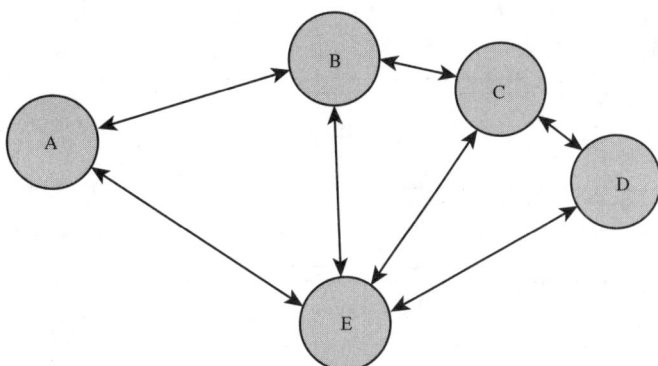

II.   Network B

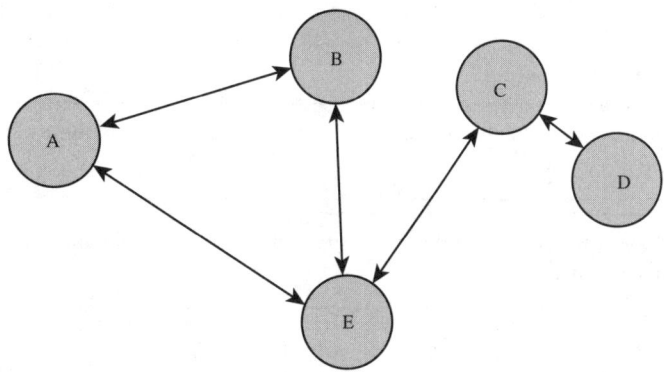

III.   Network C

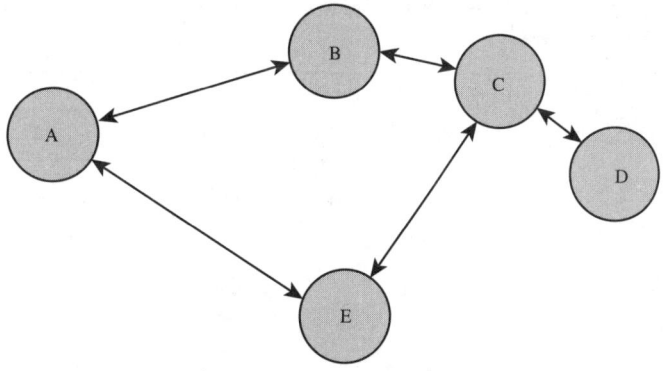

Ⓐ I, II, and III

Ⓑ I only

Ⓒ I and III only

Ⓓ I and II only

GO ON TO THE NEXT PAGE.

18 ▢ Mark for Review

Which of the following situations shows the use of Creative Commons?

(A) Sally needs images of dogs for her presentation at school, she does a Web search for pictures of dogs and, even though they are copyrighted, she doesn't have to credit the photographer.

(B) Preston is working on creating a new song to raise money by putting together sounds others have created; he uses audio clips that he found that had an attribution license.

(C) Mrs. Alexander photocopies pages out of her book to share with students in her class who haven't purchased the book.

(D) Steven quotes and cites an author who he interviewed for his book report.

19 ▢ Mark for Review

Which of the following is NOT an example of phishing?

(A) A user installs new software that they downloaded and then notices their computer is running slower and unexpected pop-up windows appear while browsing the Internet.

(B) The user receives a link to a spoofed version of a popular website, designed to look like the real one, that asks them to confirm or update their account credentials.

(C) Using an email address of the CEO of the company, the email asks the user to install a new app on their computer.

(D) An email alerts users that there is an issue with their order and to confirm their payment information by opening the attachment and responding via email.

GO ON TO THE NEXT PAGE.

20 ⬚ Mark for Review

Given the following code, which expression is equivalent to the output displayed after this code segment is run?

```
x ← 8
y ← 5

REPEAT UNTIL (x < y)
{
      y ← y - 2
      x ← x - 5
}
DISPLAY (x*y)
```

(A) 4 + 3 * -2 / 7

(B) 4 + 3 * -2 / 1

(C) 2 - 14 * -6 / 1

(D) -2 + 14 * -2 / 4

21 ⬚ Mark for Review

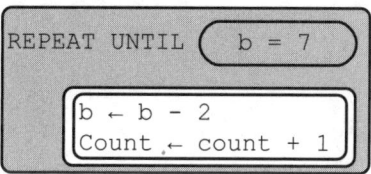

Currently the programmer wants this loop to take a value of b and decrease it until the value of b is 7 and count how many times it takes to change the value of b to 7. Unfortunately, it only works part of the time. What code could be changed to ensure that it works regardless of the value of b initially?

(A) Change condition for b to be equal to or greater than 7

(B) Change so that it sets b to 7 in loop

(C) Change so loop will repeat *n* times

(D) Change so that b is decreased by 1 each time

GO ON TO THE NEXT PAGE.

22   ◻ Mark for Review

Steve has created two variables that hold integer values named num1 and num2. He needs to switch the values held in these variables so that the data in num1 is now contained in num2 and the data in num2 will now be contained in num1. Which of the following codes below will switch the data correctly?

Ⓐ
```
num2 ← num1
num ← num2
num1 ← num2
```

Ⓑ
```
temp ← num2
num1 ← num2
num2 ← temp
```

Ⓒ
```
temp ← num1
num1 ← num2
num2 ← temp
```

Ⓓ
```
num1 ← num2
num2 ← num1
```

GO ON TO THE NEXT PAGE.

23 ☐ Mark for Review

A programmer wants to write code that will evaluate each number from 1 to 30 and determine whether it is an odd number. Odd numbers will be added to the list `oddNum` and displayed. Evaluate the two code segments below to determine whether they will output the correct list.

Code Segment #1

```
oddNum ← []
number ← 0
REPEAT 30 TIMES
{
    IF(number MOD 2 = 1)
    {
    oddNum[number] ← number
    }
    number ← number + 1
}
DISPLAY(oddNum)
```

Code Segment #2

```
oddNum ← []
number ← 0
REPEAT 30 TIMES
{
    IF(number MOD 2 = 0)
    {
        APPEND(oddNum, number + 1)
    }
    number ← number + 1
}
DISPLAY(oddNum)
```

(A) Both code segments will correctly add all odd numbers from 1 to 30 to the list.

(B) Only code segment #1 will correctly add all odd numbers from 1 to 30 to the list.

(C) Only code segment #2 will correctly add all odd numbers from 1 to 30 to the list.

(D) Neither code segment will correctly add all odd numbers from 1 to 30 to the list.

GO ON TO THE NEXT PAGE.

24 ☐ Mark for Review

The following code segment should allow a person to know how much the wind is blowing: If wind is less than 2 miles per hour, it should output "no wind at all"; if between 2 and 5 mph, it should output "a light breeze"; if greater than 15 mph but less than 30, it should say "getting gusty"; and if greater than 30 mph, it should say "make sure to hold on." The following conditional statement does not function properly for all cases.

```
IF   ( wind > 30 )
   DISPLAY (make sure to hold on)

IF ( wind > 15 OR wind < 30 )
   DISPLAY (getting gusty)

IF ( wind > 2 OR wind < 5 )
   DISPLAY (a light breeze)

IF   ( wind < 2 )
   DISPLAY (no wind at all)
```

Which of the following corrections would allow the code to work for all cases?

Ⓐ Make IF statements nested

Ⓑ Reverse the order of the IF statements

Ⓒ Change the OR to AND in both complex IF statements

Ⓓ Make all comparisons for Boolean conditions greater than or less than and equal to

GO ON TO THE NEXT PAGE.

25 ◻ Mark for Review

The `createNew` procedure takes 2 string parameters and concatenates the first 2 letters of the first string parameter in reverse order with the last 2 letters of the second string parameter and returns a string. The precondition of the procedure is that all strings will have a length greater than 3. Which of the following inputs will correctly create a variable name word containing "acid"?

Ⓐ `word ← createNew(acute, rapid)`

Ⓑ `word ← createNew(castle, avoid)`

Ⓒ `word ← createNew(car, paid)`

Ⓓ `word ← createNew(caper, disk)`

26 ◻ Mark for Review

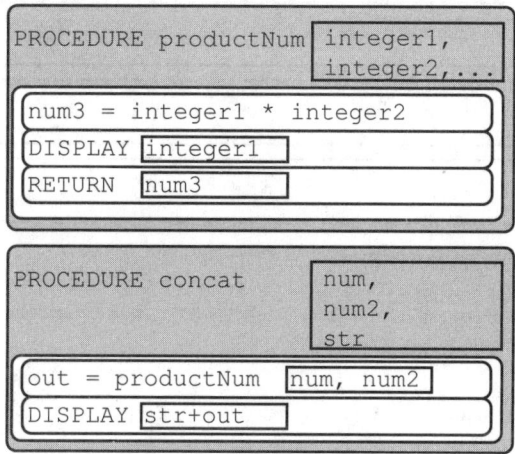

What is displayed as a result of the procedure call `concat(3,5, " answer ")`?

Ⓐ `3 answer 5`

Ⓑ `15 answer 15`

Ⓒ `5 answer 3`

Ⓓ `3 answer 15`

GO ON TO THE NEXT PAGE.

27 🔖 Mark for Review

Procedure `doSomething` takes in 2 parameters, a list and integer, and follows the following algorithm.

1. Let `min` be equal to 1 and `max` be the length of the list
2. If `max < min,` then stop: target is not present in array. `Return -1.`
3. Compute `guess` as the average of `max` and `min`, rounded down (so that it is an integer).
4. If `array[guess]` equals target, then stop. `Return guess.`
5. If the guess was too low, that is, `array[guess] < target,` then set `min = guess + 1.`
6. Otherwise, the guess was too high. Set `max = guess - 1.`
7. Go back to step 2, repeat until procedure returns `-1` or `guess`.

Which of the following are true statements about the procedure?

I. It implements a binary search.
II. It implements a sorted list from greatest to least.
III. It only works as intended when the list is sorted.

Ⓐ I only

Ⓑ II only

Ⓒ I and III only

Ⓓ II and III only

GO ON TO THE NEXT PAGE.

28 ☐ Mark for Review

A flowchart is a way to visually represent an algorithm. The flowchart below is used to display a message under certain Boolean conditions. The flowchart uses the integer variable `max`.

Block	Explanation
Oval	The start of the algorithm
Parallelogram	An input or output step
Diamond	A conditional or decision step, where execution proceeds to the side labeled "True" if the condition is true and to the side labeled "False"otherwise
Rectangle	The result of the algorithm

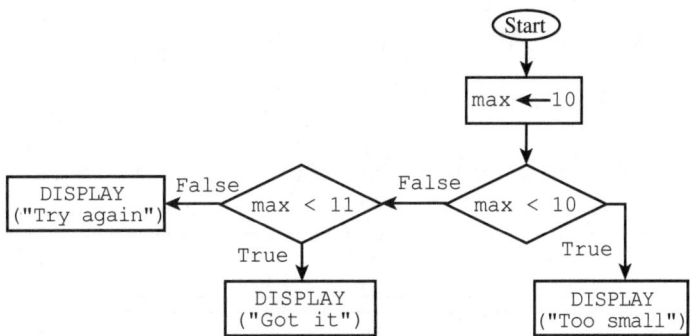

What is displayed as a result of executing the algorithm in the flowchart?

(A) Got it

(B) Too small

(C) Try again

(D) Not enough information is provided to determine the output.

GO ON TO THE NEXT PAGE.

29 ☐ Mark for Review

```
IF(closed)
{
        DISPLAY("Check back")
}
ELSE
{
        IF(code < 10)
        {
           DISPLAY("Open in next hour")
        }
        ELSE
        {
           DISPLAY("Open now")
        }
}
```

If the variable `closed` has the value false and `code` has the value of 10, what is displayed as a result of running the code segment above?

(A) Check back

(B) Open in next hour

(C) Check back Open in next hour

(D) Open now

GO ON TO THE NEXT PAGE.

30 ☐ Mark for Review

The division of motor vehicles uses the following system to determine whether a driver needs to take a driving test, which is stored in a Boolean variable called `test`. The program for the system contains two variables: `age`, which holds a numeric value for the applicant's age, and `class`, which is a Boolean variable that states whether they have taken a class. Fifteen-year-old drivers need to have taken a course but do not require a driving test. Those drivers 16 years and older must take a course but are still required to take a driving test. Which of the following code segments correctly sets the value of `test`?

Ⓐ
```
test ← false
  IF (class)
  {
          test ← true
  }
  IF(age = 15)
  {
          test ← false
  }
```

Ⓒ
```
test ← false
  IF(age ≠ 16)
  {
          test ← false
  }
  IF (class)
  {
          test ← true
  }
```

Ⓑ
```
test ← false
  IF (class)
  {
          test ← true
  }
  IF(age ≥ 16)
  {
          test ← false
  }
```

Ⓓ
```
test ← true
  IF(age < 16)
  {
          test ← false
  }
  IF (class)
  {
          test ← true
  }
```

GO ON TO THE NEXT PAGE.

31 ☐ Mark for Review

Which of the following code segments will allow the robot to get to the grey square from its current position?

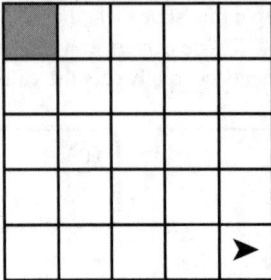

```
PROCEDURE TARGET(steps)
over ← steps/2
        REPEAT over TIMES
        {
            ROTATE LEFT()
            REPEAT steps TIMES
            {
                    FORWARD()
            }
        }
```

(A) TARGET(2)

(B) TARGET(4)

(C) TARGET(1)

(D) TARGET(5)

GO ON TO THE NEXT PAGE.

32 ☐ Mark for Review

```
list ← [5, 3, 12, 8, 9, 10]
a ← 1
b ← LENGTH(list)

REPEAT UNTIL (b < a)
{
    temp ← list[a]
    list[a] ← list[b]
    list[b] ← temp
    a++
    b--
}
```

Which of the following describes what is contained in the variable list after the code above runs?

(A) 5, 3, 12, 8, 9, 10

(B) 10, 9, 8, 12, 3, 5

(C) 10, 9, 8, 5, 3, 12

(D) 10, 9, 8, 12, 5, 3

33 ☐ Mark for Review

The police contacted Claire because they believed her identity had been stolen. New credit card accounts were opened with her personal information and certain existing accounts had been accessed by someone other than her. The police determined that software on her computer was recording all inputs to the computer and transmitting that data to another user. This best describes what type of cyberthreat?

(A) Malware

(B) Phishing

(C) Virus

(D) Keylogger

GO ON TO THE NEXT PAGE.

34 ☐ Mark for Review

Which of the following is true about the movement of data over the Internet?

(A) If a packet is not received or is "dropped," all packets, not just the dropped packet, need to be resent.

(B) Packets of data must be delivered in the same order they were sent otherwise the data will be corrupted.

(C) Packets may choose longer paths as they process the information and address data.

(D) A packet is divided into three parts; the header, payload, and trailer, either containing data or address information so that the packet can be put together at the desired destination.

35 ☐ Mark for Review

What is the benefit of having fault-tolerant Internet routing?

(A) Fault tolerance increases downtime, which may cause substantial data loss.

(B) Fault tolerance allows the reduction of redundancy, allowing for best cost efficiency of the system.

(C) Fault tolerance allows packets to follow the same paths, which allows for more traceability of data.

(D) Fault tolerance increases the complexity of the Internet and has worked so well that so far, no one has managed to break the entire Internet.

36 ☐ Mark for Review

Which of the following demonstrates the largest privacy concern?

(A) Katherine's bank sends her an email asking her to call her local branch about a potential security breach.

(B) A website uses cookies to track what users do when they visit it.

(C) When Anna searches using Google, the company is able to share data from its search engine across a wide variety of services, including third-party companies.

(D) Steve logs on to the personal Wi-Fi at his home.

GO ON TO THE NEXT PAGE.

37 ☐ Mark for Review

Which of the following would NOT be an unethical use of computer technology?

(A) Looking up code for to an assignment that you are struggling with as you prepare for the Create Task

(B) Weird Al Yankovic using the instrumental composition of the song "Smells Like Teen Spirit" as a base for his own lyrics, which poke fun at the band Nirvana

(C) Downloading the newest Star Wars movie since you aren't able to go see it in the theater

(D) A student putting images in his presentation from the Internet without checking the sources to determine copyright

38 ☐ Mark for Review

Which of the following cannot be represented by a single binary digit?

(A) Result in MOD

(B) Grade in school

(C) Black and white pixels in an image

(D) Position of a light switch

39 ☐ Mark for Review

Which of the following best describes lossless compression?

(A) A sound file is compressed and now has reduced size of data but has reduced sound quality.

(B) A sound file is compressed and emailed, and when it reaches final recipient it is restored to its original details, quality, and size.

(C) An image file has been compressed by averaging each color of pixel.

(D) A sound file is compressed by removing all redundant sounds in the file.

GO ON TO THE NEXT PAGE.

40 ☐ Mark for Review

In Florida, sharks are tagged to provide information on the health of the different species and also migration patterns. Tags that researchers place on sharks collect the following information.

- Location of shark
- Speed of shark
- Internal temperature of shark
- Depth of shark movements

Additionally, when the shark is tagged, data is collected on its species and gender.

What cannot be determined by this data alone?

(A) Whether sharks travel in groups

(B) Average body temperature of great white sharks

(C) How fast sharks can swim while in 30' deep water

(D) How location of shark causes a change in body temperature and speed

41 ☐ Mark for Review

The bookstore assigns a binary number to each reading level in the children's book section. Reading level 0 are picture books and those in the young adult section are assigned 1011101, which is equal to what decimal number?

(A) 93

(B) 101

(C) 109

(D) 189

GO ON TO THE NEXT PAGE.

42 ☐ Mark for Review

Which best describes the terms Internet and World Wide Web?

Ⓐ Both are the same and are interchangeable terms.

Ⓑ The World Wide Web is what the Internet was called before it expanded to be worldwide.

Ⓒ The Internet is a link of computers and servers, while the World Wide Web is a protocol which specifies how people can use the Internet.

Ⓓ World Wide Web is a system of linked pages, programs, and files and it uses the Internet.

43 ☐ Mark for Review

During a storm, Bob's computer is having difficulty loading websites, and when they do load, they seem to take a much longer time than normal. Which best describes what could be occurring?

Ⓐ The storm is causing issues and the network is fault-tolerant, which is causing a slow connection.

Ⓑ Because of lower available bandwidth, Bob's computer is having issues loading the websites.

Ⓒ Redundancy is causing Bob's computer to be slow when loading Web pages.

Ⓓ Packets may have not arrived at the correct router, which is causing Bob's computer to be unable to load the Web page.

44 ☐ Mark for Review

Johnny sends his friend a message about a party he went to at which there was illegal activity. He then realizes that this wasn't smart and deletes it. The following week, his school principal calls him into the office to discuss the party. Which best describes how this occurred?

Ⓐ Johnny's friend had to tell the principal because since Johnny deleted the message, it is not possible for the data to be available.

Ⓑ The principal is able to see messages that Johnny sent as it is public information.

Ⓒ The principal is talking to all students in the high school about the party and doesn't know if Johnny was there or not.

Ⓓ It is possible Johnny's message was reshared or used for an unintended purpose even if he deleted it because once information is placed online, it is very difficult to completely delete.

GO ON TO THE NEXT PAGE.

45 ◻ Mark for Review

Which of the following statements is most true about program documentation?

Ⓐ Program documentation is not required as it is mostly a tool for unskilled programmers and those just learning who do not know how to make descriptive variable names.

Ⓑ Program documentation only needs to be done when the program is complete; otherwise it is redundant.

Ⓒ Programming documentation should be done throughout program development so that what code segments do and how they were developed is documented.

Ⓓ Documentation is only required if you use code from other sources.

46 ◻ Mark for Review

When making a program, a student encounters code that, although it has no syntax issues and runs, still does not work correctly. What type of error is most likely occurring?

Ⓐ Syntax error

Ⓑ Run-time error

Ⓒ A user error

Ⓓ A logic error

GO ON TO THE NEXT PAGE.

47 ⬚ Mark for Review

What explanation best fits the data about Monthly Revenue over different periods of time in the graphs shown below?

Monthly Revenue

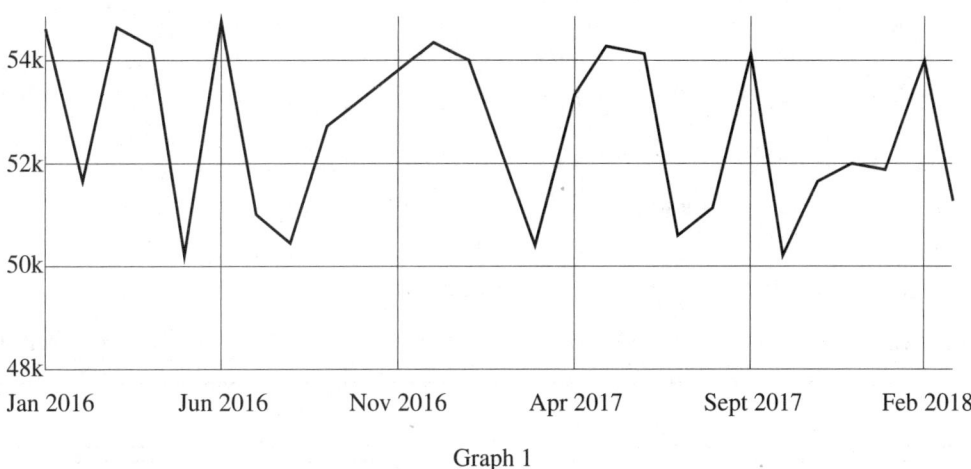

Graph 1

Monthly Revenue

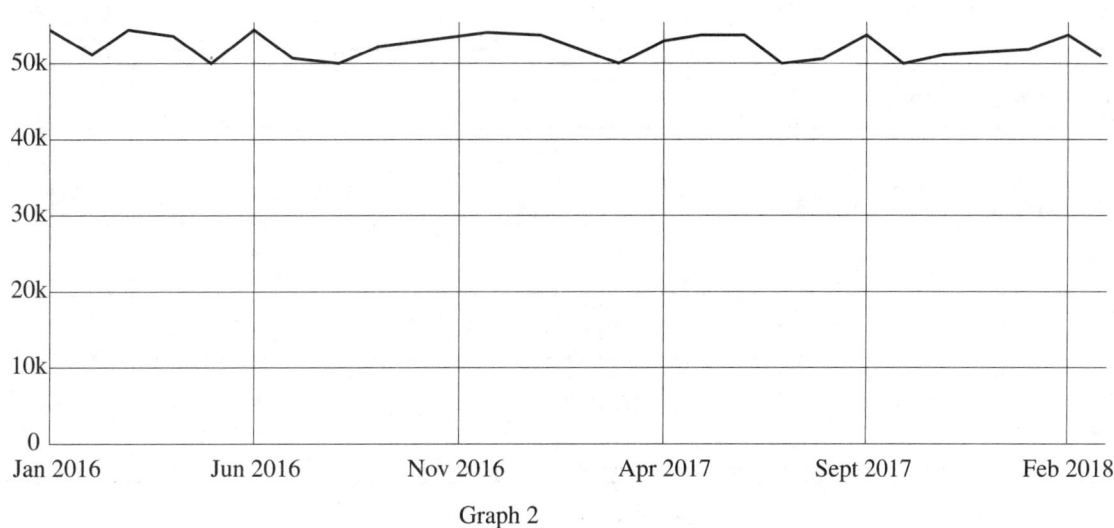

Graph 2

Ⓐ Monthly revenue for these years was almost identical as shown by Graph 2. Graph 1 must show outlier data.

Ⓑ Although the data looks fairly stable, when the axis is adjusted to better fit the data range, the visualization in Graph 1 shows there was variation across these years.

Ⓒ The two graphs must be two different data sets as they show different information and trends.

Ⓓ In order to best understand what is occurring with monthly revenue over these years, more data must be analyzed.

GO ON TO THE NEXT PAGE.

48 ☐ Mark for Review

A chef is unable to use the ovens in the kitchen when their temperature is at or below 120°C. The following code segment is intended to print a message indicating whether or not the chef is able to use the ovens based on the temperature. Assume that the variable `degrees` has been properly declared and initialized with the outside temperature.

```
IF (degrees ≥ 120)
{
    DISPLAY("Ovens can be used")
}
ELSE
{
    DISPLAY("Ovens cannot be operated")
}
```

Which of the following initializations for degrees, if any, will demonstrate that the code segment may not work as intended?

(A) `degrees = 120`

(B) `degrees = 119`

(C) `degrees = 130`

(D) All initializations will work for this code.

49 ☐ Mark for Review

What is the purpose of UDP protocol?

(A) UDP is more reliable than TCP, but both are used to transfer data on the Internet.

(B) UDP is a transfer protocol used by the Internet that speeds up transmissions by not formally establishing a connection before data is transferred.

(C) UDP has replaced TCP/IP as the main transfer protocol.

(D) UDP is a transport protocol but is not used by the Internet.

GO ON TO THE NEXT PAGE.

50 ☐ Mark for Review

A student creates an image file and then changes the metadata on the file. Which of the following is true?

(A) Changing the metadata may impact the colors or other appearance factors of the image.

(B) Although the metadata has been removed, the file will still contain information about when the image was created.

(C) Changing metadata will not affect the main data of the image.

(D) When metadata is deleted, it will not impact the image file size.

51 ☐ Mark for Review

Which of the following is not an effective tool for extracting information from a large data set?

(A) Search tools

(B) Data filtering systems

(C) Visualization of data through graphs and charts

(D) Compressing data

GO ON TO THE NEXT PAGE.

52 ☐ Mark for Review

Which of the following lines in the code segment show a data abstraction?

```
Line 1:   DISPLAY("Welcome to the Random Number Picker")
Line 2:   DISPLAY("Do you want to get a random number")
Line 3:   user ← INPUT()
Line 4:   numbers ← [5,12,7,3,0,9]
Line 5:   REPEAT UNTIL(user == "no")
Line 6:   {
Line 7:       choice ← RANDOM(1,LENGTH(numbers)-1)
Line 8:       DISPLAY(numbers[choice])
Line 9:       DISPLAY("Do you want to get a random number")
Line 10:      user ← INPUT()
Line 11:  }
```

(A) Line 5

(B) Line 3

(C) Line 4

(D) Line 7

53 ☐ Mark for Review

A new grading system is being used at High Valley High School. The grade average will be calculated traditionally, but the lowest and highest grades will be eliminated. The following procedures have been created:

1. NumberGrades() calculates how many grades are inputted by the user.
2. MaxGrade() finds the maximum grade inputted.
3. MinGrade() finds the minimum grade inputted.
4. SumGrades() finds the sum of all grades inputted.

Which of the following sequences will correctly calculate the grade average according to the new system?

(A) First MaxGrade() and MinGrade() are subtracted from SumGrades() and then divided by NumberGrades()

(B) SumGrades() divided by NumberGrades() minus 2

(C) SumGrades() divided by NumGrades() minus MaxGrade() minus MinGrade()

(D) First MaxGrade() and MinGrade() are subtracted from SumGrades() and then divided by NumberGrades() minus 2

GO ON TO THE NEXT PAGE.

54 ☐ Mark for Review

Consider the following code segment.

```
oldValues = [true, false, true, true]
Values2 = []
for EACH item IN oldValues
{
      IF (item)
      {
            APPEND(Values2, item)
      }
}
```

What, if anything, will be the contents of `Values2` as a result of executing the code segment?

(A) [true, false, true, true]

(B) [true, true, true]

(C) []

(D) [false]

55 ☐ Mark for Review

A medical device R&D team has a new drug delivery system to test and plans to use a simulation. Which of the following is NOT an advantage of using simulation?

(A) A simulation will allow researchers to help find unexpected behavior of the drug delivery system.

(B) Running a simulation will lessen the cost of developing the new drug delivery system.

(C) A simulation of a drug delivery system can allow researchers to examine possible long-term effects of the system itself.

(D) A simulation will allow a greater population to understand all possible effects of the new drug delivery system without having complete knowledge of the system.

GO ON TO THE NEXT PAGE.

56 ☐ Mark for Review

Computing innovations can be used in ways their original inventors did not intend or imagine. Which of the following is an unintended consequence of 3D printing?

(A) Production of small tools and parts for robotics has become easily accessible and has no health, monetary, or proprietary downsides.

(B) Toy makers may lose millions and have had to deal with increased piracy issues.

(C) Model making for architects and designers is becoming an increasingly specialized field.

(D) 3D printing is less of a health risk than most manufacturing processes, which has led to a healthier workforce.

57 ☐ Mark for Review

How does the computer system verify that a website is secure?

(A) The server hosting the website will present a digital certificate and your browser determines whether it is trusted.

(B) The trust model allows you to trust any website which claims it is secure without verification.

(C) Secure websites automatically encrypt all data using symmetric encryption.

(D) Computer systems use standard protocols to determine ownership by examining the IP address of the website.

GO ON TO THE NEXT PAGE.

Questions 58 through 62 refer to the following.

A company is developing an upgrade to its VR system. The current system uses a full room of equipment to create an experience so that a person is able to look around the artificial world, move around in it, and interact with virtual features or items. The new upgraded system will use a headset for a similar experience. Both systems incorporate sensory and force feedback that collect data on position, movement, and response, using haptic technology to ensure an immersive experience. The old system was a stationary system and used a single static IP at the company's location. A user would enter their height and gender in order to start a simulation each time they used the system. Data was collected on simulations and haptic sensor data.

The new headset has a built-in screen processor and battery, as well as several viewfinders that provide stable spatial orientation and position recognition relative to the coordinates of peripheral devices. A single processor is self-contained in the headset, in comparison to the older model which used to render better, higher quality images. The new system is able to be used with any stable Internet connection and will enable users to create an account. The account setup will require an email address, name, height, and gender to access the VR system. The new system will log data on length of play, scores, and simulations used and log haptic data. The company is hoping that by creating a system that can be used in any environment where the Internet is available, more users will be able to use their system.

---

58 ☐ Mark for Review

Which of the following is the MOST plausible data privacy concern of the upgraded system?

(A) The company could analyze which simulations are most popular and use this information to create new simulations of that type.

(B) Medical professionals could analyze the data to determine the effects of use of the system on response time of users.

(C) The storage of the upgraded system data will be much larger and could possibly require the company to utilize cloud storage.

(D) The new system will contain your information including email address, simulations used, and time spent in simulations. Since there is no disclosure by the company of how this data will be used, it may be possible for the company to sell your information to third-party vendors for targeted advertising.

---

59 ☐ Mark for Review

Which of the following is a potential effect of the VR application, rather than a purpose of the application?

(A) The immersive nature of virtual and augmented reality can induce stress or anxiety after wearing a full occlusion headset for more than a few minutes.

(B) Medical colleges are able train doctors and nurses in complex medical procedures easier.

(C) Students are able to interactively experience historical events while remaining in the classroom.

(D) A scientist is able to manipulate atoms and molecules without the use of an electron microscope, using VR simulation instead to analyze reactions.

GO ON TO THE NEXT PAGE.

60 ☐ Mark for Review

Which of the following statements is most likely to be true about the trade-offs of using the new VR system?

(A) Processing time and graphic quality may be decreased on the new stand-alone headset system.

(B) More people will be able to experience VR, but the company will have more control over personal data and the applications being used on their systems.

(C) Due to the less efficient processor in the stand-alone system, the stand-alone system will be less expensive but also run fewer detailed simulations.

(D) Although graphic quality may decrease, the processing time and types of simulations will increase on the new stand-alone headset.

61 ☐ Mark for Review

Which of the following data is necessary for the new VR system to process in order to enable a user to run it?

(A) IP address, email address, name, height, and gender

(B) Email address, height, gender, and name

(C) None: it can be run the same as the old system

(D) Email address, name, and age

62 ☐ Mark for Review

Which of the following data is not provided directly from the user but is necessary for the upgraded system to operate as described?

(A) Height of user

(B) Head movement and position data

(C) Age of user

(D) Choice of simulation

GO ON TO THE NEXT PAGE.

63 ☐ Mark for Review

What are the advantages of procedural abstraction?

Select two answers.

☐ An advantage of using procedural abstractions is that coding time is reduced.

☐ Procedural abstraction reduces debugging time since, when the same code is used in multiple places, changes to the code or fixing errors in the code only need to occur in a single spot.

☐ Procedural abstraction eliminates the need for global variables, which will cause the program to be much less complex.

☐ Procedural abstraction allows the solving of complex issues by focusing on the intricacies and not hiding any details.

64 ☐ Mark for Review

Which of the following are examples of distributed computing?

Select two answers.

☐ A one-player game where puzzles are complex

☐ Verizon cellular communication system

☐ Program which calculates GPA of an individual student

☐ Air traffic control systems

65 ☐ Mark for Review

Which of the following statements are always true about data compression of a larger file?

Select two answers.

☐ When data compression is completed, fewer bits means less information.

☐ When data compression is completed, quality is not always impacted, but you cannot revert to the original file.

☐ Data compression is dependent on two factors: the amount of redundancy and the type of compression used.

☐ Data compression reduces the number of bits of data but does not always impact the amount of information stored.

GO ON TO THE NEXT PAGE.

66 ☐ Mark for Review

Which of the following are challenges that are found with processing data, regardless of data size?

Select <u>two</u> answers.

☐ Data processing may require parallel systems since data may not be able to be processed with a single computer.

☐ Data may contain invalid or incomplete data.

☐ Data may need to be processed in order to make it uniform without changing the meaning of the data.

☐ Data processing may affect the amount of information that is able to be extracted from it.

67 ☐ Mark for Review

Which of the following are examples of analog data?

Select <u>two</u> answers.

☐ Position of a runner on a cross-country course

☐ Values on an abacus

☐ Blood pressure reading on blood pressure cuff

☐ Characters in an alphabet

GO ON TO THE NEXT PAGE.

68 ☐ Mark for Review

Which of the following describes asymmetric encryption?

Select <u>two</u> answers.

☐ Alice sends an encrypted message to Bob and tells him the key she used to encrypt the message so he can read it.

☐ Alice sends Bob an encrypted message which she used a private key to encrypt and then Bob uses a public key that Alice published online to decrypt the message.

☐ Alice stores her tax information on her computer and uses a password to protect it. Without the password, Alice will be unable to open the documents.

☐ A server at Bob's work generates both a public and private key so that different users can access the data.

69 ☐ Mark for Review

Ron and Brenda are designing a computer program together. They have produced a beta version for testing and want users to test the functionality of the program. What are some advantages of this collaboration?

Select <u>two</u> answers.

☐ Users are able to test the limitations of the program and report bugs, which will help both Ron and Brenda.

☐ Users are able to add code to the program and increase functionality that Ron and Brenda did not originally include in it.

☐ Having a diverse group of testers will allow for varied responses, enabling Ron and Brenda to anticipate the needs of varied users.

☐ Using collaboration for developing the program may increase bias because of the wide variety of possible users.

GO ON TO THE NEXT PAGE.

70 ▢ Mark for Review

If this code executes, what value could be displayed?

Select two answers.

```
x ← 2
b ← RANDOM(1, 5)
REPEAT UNTIL (b < 1)
{
      IF(b MOD 2 = 1)
      {
            x ← x * 2
      }
      ELSE
      {
            x ← x + 2
      }
      b ← b - 1
}
DISPLAY(x)
```

▢ 1

▢ 4

▢ 28

▢ 160

STOP

END OF EXAM

Practice Test 2:
Answers and
Explanations

PRACTICE TEST 2 ANSWER KEY

1.	A	36.	C
2.	D	37.	B
3.	C	38.	B
4.	B	39.	B
5.	A	40.	A
6.	B	41.	A
7.	A	42.	D
8.	C	43.	B
9.	A	44.	D
10.	D	45.	C
11.	D	46.	D
12.	A	47.	B
13.	A	48.	A
14.	C	49.	B
15.	B	50.	C
16.	D	51.	D
17.	C	52.	C
18.	B	53.	D
19.	A	54.	B
20.	B	55.	D
21.	D	56.	B
22.	C	57.	A
23.	C	58.	D
24.	C	59.	A
25.	B	60.	C
26.	D	61.	B
27.	C	62.	B
28.	A	63.	A, B
29.	D	64.	B, D
30.	A	65.	C, D
31.	B	66.	B, C
32.	B	67.	A, C
33.	D	68.	B, D
34.	D	69.	A, C
35.	D	70.	B, C

PRACTICE TEST 2 ANSWERS AND EXPLANATIONS

1. **A** Metadata summarizes basic information about data. The metadata is descriptive information about the image file. Most cameras store location, time, and file data, but metadata does not include descriptive information. The answer is (A).

2. **D** Binary is a base 2 system. In general, N bits (binary digits) are required to represent 2^N unique values. Using the same logic, 2^9, where 9 represents the number of bits, means that 512 unique values are able to be represented. The answer is (D).

3. **C** Multifactor authentication is a type of access control where at least 2 types of evidence are met by the user. The types of evidence are knowledge, possession, and inherence. Knowledge requires a user to answer a question about information they know. Possession requires a check-in with an alternative device, and inherence is normally completed via biometric authentication. Choice (A) gives two requests for evidence, but they are both of the knowledge type. Choices (B) and (D) only require one request for evidence. Choice (C) requires both a knowledge type of evidence shown by the password request and then a possession type of evidence required from the text message code. The answer is (C).

4. **B** A simple explanation of the digital divide is that people's access to computing and the Internet differs based on socioeconomic or geographic characteristics. Therefore, these satellites will help some groups access technology and content that they previously could not access. Therefore, the answer is (B).

5. **A** In the initial robot picture, the robot is facing towards the right of the page since the point of the arrow always displays which direction the robot is pointed. Following the code for (A), the robot will be in the space below its initial position but facing upward after repeating this code three times. After moving forward, it will be facing upward, and after repeating the loop two times, the robot will be two squares to the right of the gray square but facing down. Finally, the last three statements move the robot to the ending gray square, pointing to the left. The answer is (A).

6. **B** The MOD function analyzes whether there is remainder. If the remainder of the number of students when divided by 3 is zero, then the students can evenly distribute into groups of 3. In a MOD statement, the first number is the dividend, and the second number is the divisor. Therefore, (B) states if `numStudent` is divided by 3, then there will be equal groups of three students each. The answer is (B).

7. **A** Crowdsourcing is simply the idea that many online users are combining their work or efforts to help fund projects, generate ideas, or create services. Google uses crowdsourcing to allow students to have input into the brand and therefore effectively engage people with their company. The answer is (A).

8. **C** Personally Identifiable Information is any data that can be used to identify a specific individual. Social Security numbers, mailing or email addresses, and phone numbers have most commonly been considered PII, but technology has expanded the scope of PII considerably. It can include an

IP address, login IDs, social media posts, or digital images. Geolocation, biometrics, and behavioral data can also be classified as PII. Choice (C) is the correct answer because it shows the use of PII in order to create a new identity and commit crimes.

9. **A**   Lossy compression algorithms are techniques that reduce file size by discarding the less important information. Since pixel values are averaged, the original pixel value cannot be restored; therefore, this is lossy compression. The answer is (A).

10. **D**   The table shows processing times for 8 bits, 80 bits, and 800 bits. 1000 bytes is 8000 bits since each byte is 8 bits. Therefore, examining the pattern between the columns, you can see that increasing the number of bits by a multiple of 10 adds an additional second for creating a copy of an audio file; the processing time for 8000 bits would be 4 seconds. The processing time for backing up an audio file is 32 seconds, searching an audio file is 500 seconds, and deleting an audio file is 6.75 seconds. The answer is (D).

11. **D**   Computing bias is defined as errors in a computing system that create unfair and incorrect outcomes. In this example, Oprah Winfrey is incorrectly identified as a male. Computing bias is often seen in facial recognition systems since facial recognition algorithms vary in their performance across different face types. They have a tendency to perform worse on darker skin tones and the female population. The answer is (D).

12. **A**   Execution time is optimized when the workload of the two processors is as close to equal as possible, so that one processor does not finish too early and has to wait for the other processor to finish. In order to accomplish this, Y and Z would need to run sequentially, which would take 105 seconds, close to the 110 seconds that task X takes. The answer is (A).

13. **A**   The variable which is returned contains either the value `true` or `false`, which is best described as a Boolean variable. The answer is (A).

14. **C**   The first part of the Boolean expression determines if their age is between 25 and 35, inclusively, and the second part determines whether they are able to lift 50 lbs. The answer is (C).

15. **B**   A heuristic solution is an algorithm that finds an approximate solution. Calculating student GPA requires a very exact solution. I and II both require brute force to try every possible solution; however, the computer can approximate the result to determine a possible solution. The answer is (B).

16. **D**   Each time Algorithm A runs the first or second loop it takes 1 minute. The number of times it runs is dependent on n. Each time Algorithm B runs it takes 1 minute, but since it is a nested loop, it multiplied by n^2. The answer is (D).

17. **C**   In Network A, there are many paths, including A-B-C, A-E-B-C, and A-E-C, which make it fault-tolerant due to redundancy. Also, in Network C, there are 2 different paths, A-B-C and A-E-C. But in Network B, in order to access C from A, you must go through node E. Therefore, only Networks A and C are fault tolerant, which means that the answer is (C).

18.   **B**   Creative Commons licensing allows copyright owners to specify the ways in which their works can be used or distributed. Creative Commons licenses do not replace copyright law. Therefore, (A) would still be a violation of copyright. Also, (D) shows proper credit being given according to the copyright laws. Choice (C) is a violation of copyright. Choice (B) is the answer because Preston uses materials that have a Creative Commons license, which allows their use as long as attribution is given.

19.   **A**   A phishing attack is an attempt to trick individuals into providing personal information, often by getting them to fill out a form on a malicious website. All of the answer choices show examples of phishing except for (A), which is an example of a virus. Choice (A) is the correct answer.

20.   **B**   The loop runs two times first when x is 8 and y is 5. Since x is not less than y, y becomes 5 – 2 = 3 and x becomes 8 – 5 = 3. Since x is still not less than y, it runs again: y becomes 3 – 2 = 1 and x becomes 3 – 5 = –2. The loop does not run again since –2 is less than 1. So the code displays –2 times 1, which is –2. Looking at the answers, due to order of operations, the expressions should be multiplied first, then divided, and then added or subtracted. For (B), if you do this you get 4 + –6 / 1 and then 4 + –6, which equals –2. Choice (A) does not equal –2; instead it equals 3.14. Choice (C) equals 86 and (D) equals –9. Choice (B) is correct.

21.   **D**   Currently, if b is an even number and you decrease by 2 in the loop each time, it will never equal to 7. If you, instead, decrease by 1 each time, then when b is an even or odd number, it will work as intended. The correct choice is (D).

22.   **C**   In order for the data to not be overwritten, it needs to be stored in a temporary value. Choice (C) stores num1 in a temporary variable, then num2 value is put in num1 and, after that, num2 is assigned the value of num1, which was stored as a temporary variable. Choice (C) is the correct answer.

23.   **C**   Code Segment #1 correctly evaluates whether the number is odd, but it does not correctly add it to the list, since oddNum is a blank list and therefore cannot be indexed at each number. Code Segment #2 correctly evaluates whether the number is odd and then appends it to the list. Since only Code Segment #2 works, (C) is the correct answer.

24.   **C**   When the wind speed is greater than 30 then the current code will output "make sure to hold on", "getting gusty", and "a light breeze". The OR statements provide that, if either part of the conditional statement is true, it will display the output. It should require both parts of the statement to be true; for example, the wind needs to be greater than 15 AND less than 30 for "getting gusty" to be correct. The correct answer is therefore (C).

25.   **B**   In order to make the word "acid", you need the first 2 letters of the first parameter to be "ca" since the procedure extracts these letters and reverses their order. For the second parameter, you need the string to end with the letters "id". These two parameters are then concatenated, linked together. Choices (C) and (B) both appear to work, but the question states that there is a precondition for the procedure that requires the string parameters to have a length greater than 3; the parameter "car" is not, so therefore the answer is (B).

26. **D** The procedure `productNum` takes in two integers, displays the first parameter number and then returns the product of the two numbers. The procedure `concat` adds the string parameter to the output from the `productNum` procedure and displays the output. The answer is (D).

27. **C** The procedure `doSomething` implements a binary search, which works by repeatedly dividing in half the portion of the list that could contain the item until you've narrowed down the possible locations to just one, and if the item is not found, it returns −1. Therefore, statement I is correct. Eliminate (B) and (D), which do not include statement I. A binary search, though, requires the list to be sorted, so statement III is also true. Eliminate (A), which does not include statement III. The correct answer is (C).

28. **A** After `max` is set to 10, which is not less than 10, the flowchart evaluates whether `max` is less than 11, which is true. So it displays "`got it`". The answer is (A).

29. **D** For this conditional statement, if the variable `closed` is true, then it will display "`Check back`", otherwise it will go to the ELSE statement. Then, if `code` is less than 10, it will display "`Open in next hour`", otherwise it will display "`Open Now`". Since `closed` is false and the code has a value of 10, this will display "`Open Now`"; the answer is (D).

30. **A** Choice (A) sets `test` to `false`, and if they have taken a class, then it is set to `true`. It only sets to to `false` if `age` is 15. The correct answer is (A).

31. **B** Each time the procedure runs, the robot rotates to the left and then moves forward however many times indicated by the argument. In order to move to this spot, the robot would need to turn left and move forward four spots; if it does this twice, which is equal to steps divided by 2, then the robot will reach the destination. The answer is (B).

32. **B** The code creates a list and two variables, which initializes a with the value of 1 and b to the length of the list. The loop repeats until b is less than a. It then swaps the items at the end of the list with those at the beginning. Once the loop is complete, all items of the list will be reversed. The answer is (B).

33. **D** Keylogger is a program that records user input, allowing a third party to gain fraudulent access to passwords and other confidential information. The answer is (D).

34. **D** Data is broken into a number of packets that are sent independently over whatever route is most efficient and reassembled at the destination. Each packet contains address information that identifies the sending computer and intended recipient. Using these addresses, network switches and routers determine the most efficient way to transfer the packet to its destination. Because it is possible for packets to follow very different routes, the receiving end needs to know the order in which the packets are to be assembled and to request any be re-sent if they are received corrupted or incomplete. Due to this, the answer is (D).

35. **D** A fault-tolerant system is one that can experience failure (or multiple failures) in its components but still continue operating properly. Although there have been some catastrophic failures around the world, due to the fault tolerance of the Internet, not one of these has managed to disable the entire Internet system. The answer is (D).

36. **C** Computer privacy issues deal with storing, reusing, and sharing data with third parties, and sharing information about oneself on the Internet. For (A), replying to such an email may be risky, but calling a local branch does not carry the same risks. For (B), although it seems it would be a possible privacy issue, cookies traditionally cannot be used to obtain personal information from your computer. For (D), though public Wi-Fi can be an easy access point for cybercriminals to eavesdrop and gain private information, private Wi-Fi in your home is more secure. Google has been frequently in the news for their privacy issues and sharing of data. Even the CEO has stated that if you don't want someone knowing what you are doing then you probably shouldn't be doing it. The answer is (C).

37. **B** Weird Al Yankovic is covered by fair use since it is a parody. All others contain ethical issues, including plagiarism and piracy. The answer is (B).

38. **B** A binary digit can be used to express anything with two possible values. Choice (A) can be expressed as a binary digit if the divisor is 2, since the result of an integer MOD 2 is either 1 or 0. Choice (C) can be expressed as a binary digit since there are only two possible colors. Choice (D) can be expressed as a binary digit as well since the light switch can be either in position "on" or "off." The only choice that cannot be expressed as a binary digit is a grade in school, which is either 0 to 100 or A, B, C, D, or F. The answer is (B).

39. **B** Lossless compression restores and rebuilds data to its original form after decompression, while lossy compression eliminates the data which is not noticeable and cannot be restored to its original form. Therefore, (B) is the correct answer.

40. **A** The individual tag on a shark does not contain data about the location of sharks nearby, and while it is possible to correlate this data with other shark tags, whether sharks travel in groups cannot be determined by this data alone. The answer is (A).

41. **A** Binary numbers are 8 bits where each bit is either a 0 or a 1. To convert to a decimal number, add the power of 2 represented by each bit, if the bit in that place is 1. Here there is a 1 in 2^0 column, 2^2 column, 2^3 column, 2^4 column, and 2^6 column. Adding these values together $(1 + 4 + 8 + 16 + 64)$ yields 93. The correct answer is (A).

42. **D** As the correct answer, (D) states the World Wide Web is simply a system of linked pages, programs, and files, while the Internet is a computer network consisting of interconnected networks. The World Wide Web does use the Internet.

43. **B** Bandwidth of a computer network is the maximum amount of data that can be sent in a fixed amount of time. During a storm, people are more likely to be home using Internet-connected devices, limiting the amount of broadband available per customer. Thus, Web pages will either not load or load slowly. The correct answer is (B).

44. **D**   Materials posted online are very difficult to delete and can be used in ways not intended by the original creator. For example, tweets can be retweeted, or screenshots can be taken of snaps or text messages. The correct answer is (D).

45. **C**   Program documentation is a written description of the function of code segments, events, procedures, or programs and how they were developed. Documentation should be completed throughout development and is a helpful tool whether working individually or especially when working collaboratively. Choice (C) is the correct answer.

46. **D**   A logic error is a mistake in the program that causes it to act incorrectly, while a syntax error occurs when the programming rules are not followed. A run-time error occurs when a mistake occurs in the program when it operates. The correct answer is (D).

47. **B**   The data is identical in these two graphs. The first graph has a y-axis that goes from 48,000 to 56,000, while the second graph shows a y-axis range from 0 to 60k. When the x-axis is adjusted, the trends are able to be better visualized. Choice (B) is the correct answer.

48. **A**   When degrees is 120, the expression `degrees ≥ 120` evaluates to true, so "`Ovens can be used`" is printed. This shows that the code does not work as intended because it was supposed to display "`Ovens cannot be operated`" when the temperature is at or below 120°C. The answer is (A).

49. **B**   HTTP, UDP, TCP and IP are all open protocols used by the Internet. UDP is a standardized method for transferring data between two computers in a network. Compared to other protocols, UDP accomplishes this process in a simple fashion: it sends packets (units of data) directly to a target computer without establishing a connection first. The correct answer is (B).

50. **C**   Metadata is defined as data about data. It may contain information such as date of creation, file size, camera used, etc. Deleting this data will not impact the overall primary data. Choice (C) is correct.

51. **D**   Data compression can reduce the number of bits used to store data, but it does not help extract information for analysis. The correct answer is (D).

52. **C**   Data abstraction is assigning a collection of data a single name as a reference to help manage complexity of code. Here the data abstraction, `numbers`, is created using a list. The answer is (C).

53. **D**   In order to calculate the grade average in the new system, the maximum grade and the minimum grade are subtracted. Since two grades are removed, the total number of grades will be what is returned from the procedure `NumberGrades()` minus two. The answer is (D).

54. **B**   When the IF statement is true and when the item in the list contains the value `true`, then `true` will be added to the `newVals` list. Since there are three true values in the initial list, `oldValues`, then the new list, `Values2`, will contain three true values. The answer is (B).

55. **D** To create a simulation, a thorough understanding is needed of the system and an awareness of all the factors involved with it. Without this understanding, it is difficult to interpret the results. Additionally, it is not possible to test all possible effects. The answer is (D).

56. **B** Computing innovations, such as the 3D printer, often have both beneficial and harmful effects, which are often unintended. Since 3D printing models and CAD software are so readily available and easy to learn, the toy market is struggling with copyright and piracy issues. The correct answer is (B).

57. **A** Certificate based authentication, which is the basis of the trust model, allows users to securely access a server by exchanging a digital certificate. Since the certificate is signed, it is only possible to connect to the real server and is therefore secure. The correct answer is (A).

58. **D** Both (A) and (B) do not connect the user's identity to the data. Choice (C) provides only a storage concern. Data privacy concerns often revolve around whether and how data is shared with third parties. Choice (D) states that user data may be shared with other companies and used for targeting advertising without the user's consent or knowledge. The answer is (D).

59. **A** The purpose of the VR innovation is the why: Why does it exist? What problem does it address? What is the goal/objective? An effect is something that can occur from using the VR application. Choices (B), (C), and (D) all discuss potential purposes of the VR application, but (A) is a possible negative effect of VR.

60. **C** A trade-off is a decision that involves diminishing or losing one quality or property of a system in return for gains in other aspects. In the new VR system, the system went from requiring a whole room setup to now being a stand-alone headset, but due to this trade-off, the new system uses a less powerful processor and cannot render images and graphics of the same quality. Choice (C) is the correct answer.

61. **B** The new system requires email address and name in addition to the previously required height and gender. The answer is (B).

62. **B** The user must provide height and choose which simulation to use, but sensors analyze head movement and position data in order for the VR environment to function. Choice (B) is correct.

63. **A, B** If you only have to write a code segment one time and code statements that call it, you save the time of coding the same routine multiple times; this reduces programming and debugging time. The correct answers are (A) and (B).

64. **B, D** Distributed computing is defined as a computational model in which multiple devices are used to run a single program. Air traffic control systems rely heavily on information about the location of hundreds or thousands of airplanes and sensors at each airfield working together. Cellular networks require multiple cell phone towers and coverage areas to communicate and work together to allow users to travel without losing service. The correct answers are (B) and (D).

65. **C, D** Data compression is the process of reducing the amount of data or bits needed for storage or transfer of particular information. Lossless data compression reduces the number of bits but stores all the same information so the original files can be restored. The amount of data compression that can be achieved is dependent on whether lossy or lossless compression is done and the amount of redundant data. The answers are (C) and (D).

66. **B, C** Data processing has four main challenges that are not dependent on the size of the data set. These include the need to clean data, the need to combine data sources, elimination of incomplete data, and invalid data. The answers are (B) and (C).

67. **A, C** Analog data has values that change smoothly over time. Digital data represents discrete measurements. Both (A) and (C) are examples of analog data and are the correct answers.

68. **B, D** Asymmetric encryption requires two different keys that are linked to encrypt and decrypt the data. Choices (B) and (D) are the answers since they describe the use of two different keys for encryption.

69. **A, C** Having a variety of users will increase perspective, and allowing more users to test the code will allow a greater chance of all errors being located. Users are not able to add code and collaboration decreases bias. The answers are (A) and (C).

70. **B, C** When b is given the lowest value of 1, then the loop only iterates one time, since b modulus 1 equals 1, it takes x which has a value of 2 and multiplies it by 2 yielding 4. This value is displayed by the program. When b is given the maximum value of 5, then the loop iterates five times. The first iteration b is 5 and x is 2, and since b modulus 2 is 1, then x becomes 4. The second iteration b is 4 and x is 4, and since b modulus 2 is not 1, then x becomes 6. The third iteration b is 3 and x is 6, and since b modulus 2 is 1, then x becomes 12. The fourth iteration b is 2 and x is 12, and since b modulus 2 is not 1, then x becomes 14. The fifth iteration b is 1 and x is 14, and since b modulus 2 is 1, then x becomes 28. The answers are (B) and (C).

HOW TO SCORE PRACTICE TEST 2

Section I: Multiple Choice

———————————— × 1.5000 = ————————————
Number Correct   Weighted
(out of 70)   Section I Score
                                  (Do not round)

Section II: Create Performance Task

(This is completed and submitted outside of test time. Do your best to
score your Create Performance Task using the guidelines in Chapter 2.)

Task Score: ———————— × 7.5000 =   ————————
             (out of 6)   (Task Score
                                 Do not round)

AP Score Conversion Chart Computer Science Principles	
Composite Score Range	AP Score
112–150	5
98–111	4
80–97	3
55–79	2
0–54	1

Composite Score

———————————— + ———————————— = ————————————
Weighted   Weighted   Composite Score
Section I Score   Section II Score   (Round to nearest
                                            whole number)

Practice Test 3

AP® Computer Science Principles Exam

SECTION I: Multiple-Choice Questions

DO NOT BEGIN THE EXAM UNTIL YOU ARE TOLD TO DO SO.

At a Glance

Total Time
2 hours
Number of Questions
70
Percent of Total Score
70%

DISCLAIMER: The official AP Computer Science Principles will be administered digitally. Instructions for the digital exam may differ from this practice test.

Instructions

Section I has 70 multiple-choice questions and lasts 2 hours.

Each question is followed by four suggested answers.

For questions 1–62, select the single best answer choice for each question.

For questions 63–70, **two** of the suggested answers are correct. **For each of these questions, you must select both correct choices to earn credit.** No partial credit will be earned if only one correct choice is selected. Select the two that are best in each case.

Reference information for programming questions is available in this application and can be accessed throughout Section I.

GO ON TO THE NEXT PAGE.

Quick Reference

Instruction	Explanation
Assignment, Display, and Input	
Text: a ← expression Block: `a ◄— expression`	Evaluates expression and then assigns a copy of the result to the variable a.
Text: DISPLAY(expression) Block: `DISPLAY expression`	Displays the value of expression, followed by a space.
Text: INPUT() Block: INPUT	Accepts a value from the user and returns the input value.
Arithmetic Operators and Numeric Procedures	
Text and Block: a + b a - b a * b a / b	The arithmetic operators +, -, *, and / are used to perform arithmetic on a and b. For example, 17 / 5 evaluates to 3.4. The order of operations used in mathematics applies when evaluating expressions.
Text and Block: a MOD b	Evaluates to the remainder when a is divided by b. Assume that a is an integer greater than or equal to 0 and b is an integer greater than 0. For example, 17 MOD 5 evaluates to 2. The MOD operator has the same precedence as the * and / operators.
Text: RANDOM(a, b) Block: RANDOM `a, b`	Generates and returns a random integer from a to b, including a and b. Each result is equally likely to occur. For example, RANDOM(1, 3) could return 1, 2, or 3.

Instruction	Explanation
Relational and Boolean Operators	
Text and Block: a = b a ≠ b a > b a < b a ≥ b a ≤ b	The relational operators =, ≠, >, <, ≤, and ≥ are used to test the relationship between two variables, expressions, or values. A comparison using relational operators evaluates to a Boolean value. For example, a = b evaluates to true if a and b are equal; otherwise it evaluates to false.
Text: NOT condition Block: NOT (condition)	Evaluates to true if condition is false; otherwise evaluates to false.
Text: condition1 AND condition2 Block: (condition1) AND (condition2)	Evaluates to true if both condition1 and condition2 are true; otherwise evaluates to false.
Text: condition1 OR condition2 Block: (condition1) OR (condition2)	Evaluates to true if condition1 is true or if condition2 is true or if both condition1 and condition2 are true; otherwise evaluates to false.
Selection	

Text:
 	
IF(condition)
 	
{
 	
\<block of statements>
 	
}
 	
Block:
 	
IF (condition)
 	
(block of statements)
	The code in block of statements is executed if the Boolean expression condition evaluates to true; no action is taken if condition evaluates to false.

Instruction	Explanation
Selection—Continued	

Text:
 	
`IF(condition)`
 	
`{`
 	
`<first block of statements>`
 	
`}`
 	
`ELSE`
 	
`{`
 	
`<second block of statements>`
 	
`}`
 	
Block:
 	
IF (`condition`)
    `first block of statements`
ELSE
    `second block of statements`
	The code in `first block of statements` is executed if the Boolean expression `condition` evaluates to `true`; otherwise the code in `second block of statements` is executed.

Iteration	

Text:
 	
`REPEAT n TIMES`
 	
`{`
 	
`<block of statements>`
 	
`}`
 	
Block:
 	
REPEAT n TIMES
    `block of statements`
	The code in `block of statements` is executed n times.

Text:
 	
`REPEAT UNTIL(condition)`
 	
`{`
 	
`<block of statements>`
 	
`}`
 	
Block:
 	
REPEAT UNTIL (`condition`)
    `block of statements`
	The code in `block of statements` is repeated until the Boolean expression `condition` evaluates to `true`.

Instruction	Explanation
List Operations	
For all list operations, if a list index is less than 1 or greater than the length of the list, an error message is produced and the program terminates.	

Text:
 	
`aList ← [value1, value2, value3, ...]`
 	
Block:
 	
`aList ◄— value1, value2, value3`
	Creates a new list that contains the values `value1`, `value2`, `value3`, and ... at indices `1`, `2`, `3`, and ... respectively and assigns it to `aList`.

Text:
 	
`aList ← []`
 	
Block:
 	
`aList ◄— []`
	Creates an empty list and assigns it to `aList`.

Text:
 	
`aList ← bList`
 	
Block:
 	
`aList ◄— bList`
	Assigns a copy of the list `bList` to the list `aList`.
	
	For example, if `bList` contains `[20, 40, 60]`, then `aList` will also contain `[20, 40, 60]` after the assignment.

Text:
 	
`aList[i]`
 	
Block:
 	
`aList i`
	Accesses the element of `aList` at index `i`. The first element of `aList` is at index `1` and is accessed using the notation `aList[1]`.

Text:
 	
`x ← aList[i]`
 	
Block:
 	
`x ◄— aList i`
	Assigns the value of `aList[i]` to the variable `x`.

Text:
 	
`aList[i] ← x`
 	
Block:
 	
`aList i ◄— x`
	Assigns the value of `x` to `aList[i]`.

Text:
 	
`aList[i] ← aList[j]`
 	
Block:
 	
`aList i ◄— aList j`
	Assigns the value of `aList[j]` to `aList[i]`.

Text:
 	
`INSERT(aList, i, value)`
 	
Block:
 	
`INSERT aList, i, value`
	Any values in `aList` at indices greater than or equal to `i` are shifted one position to the right. The length of the list is increased by 1, and `value` is placed at index `i` in `aList`.

Instruction	Explanation
List Operations—Continued	
Text: APPEND(aList, value) Block: APPEND aList, value	The length of aList is increased by 1, and value is placed at the end of aList.
Text: REMOVE(aList, i) Block: REMOVE aList, i	Removes the item at index i in aList and shifts to the left any values at indices greater than i. The length of aList is decreased by 1.
Text: LENGTH(aList) Block: LENGTH aList	Evaluates to the number of elements in aList.

Text:
 	
FOR EACH item IN aList
 	
{
 	
\<block of statements>
 	
}
 	
Block:
 	
FOR EACH item IN aList
   block of statements
	The variable item is assigned the value of each element of aList sequentially, in order, from the first element to the last element. The code in block of statements is executed once for each assignment of item.

Procedures and Procedure Calls	

Text:
 	
PROCEDURE procName(parameter1,
               parameter2, ...)
 	
{
 	
\<block of statements>
 	
}
 	
Block:
 	
PROCEDURE procName parameter1,
               parameter2, ...
   block of statements
	Defines procName as a procedure that takes zero or more arguments. The procedure contains block of statements.
	
	The procedure procName can be called using the following notation, where arg1 is assigned to parameter1, arg2 is assigned to parameter2, etc.:
	procName(arg1, arg2, ...)

Instruction	Explanation
Procedures and Procedure Calls—Continued	

Text:
 	
`PROCEDURE procName(parameter1,`
`            parameter2, ...)`
 	
`{`
 	
`<block of statements>`
 	
`RETURN(expression)`
 	
`}`
 	
Block:
 	
`PROCEDURE procName parameter1,`
`                   parameter2, ...`
`   block of statements`
`   RETURN expression`
	Defines `procName` as a procedure that takes zero or more arguments. The procedure contains `block of statements` and returns the value of `expression`. The `RETURN` statement may appear at any point inside the procedure and causes an immediate return from the procedure back to the calling statement.
	
	The value returned by the procedure `procName` can be assigned to the variable `result` using the following notation:
	`result ← procName(arg1, arg2, ...)`

Text:
 	
`RETURN(expression)`
 	
Block:
`RETURN expression`
	Returns the flow of control to the point where the procedure was called and returns the value of `expression`.

Robot	
If the robot attempts to move to a square that is not open or is beyond the edge of the grid, the robot will stay in its current location and the program will terminate.	

Text:
 	
`MOVE_FORWARD()`
 	
Block:
`MOVE_FORWARD`
	The robot moves one square forward in the direction it is facing.

Text:
 	
`ROTATE_LEFT()`
 	
Block:
`ROTATE_LEFT`
	The robot rotates in place 90 degrees counterclockwise (i.e., makes an in-place left turn).

Text:
 	
`ROTATE_RIGHT()`
 	
Block:
`ROTATE_RIGHT`
	The robot rotates in place 90 degrees clockwise (i.e., makes an in-place right turn).

Text:
 	
`CAN_MOVE(direction)`
 	
Block:
`CAN_MOVE direction`
	Evaluates to `true` if there is an open square one square in the direction relative to where the robot is facing; otherwise evaluates to `false`. The value of `direction` can be `left`, `right`, `forward`, or `backward`.

This page intentionally left blank.

GO ON TO THE NEXT PAGE.

AP COMPUTER SCIENCE PRINCIPLES
SECTION I
Time—2 hours

Number of Questions—70

Percent of total exam grade—70%

Directions: Choose one best answer for each question. Some questions at the end of the test will have more than one correct answer; for these, you will be instructed to choose two answer choices.

---

1 ☐ Mark for Review

What would be the next three binary numbers after 1000 1101?

(A) 1000 1111, 1001 0000, 1001 0001

(B) 1000 1101, 1001 0011, 1001 0100

(C) 1000 1110, 1000 1111, 1001 1111

(D) 1000 1110, 1000 1111, 1001 0000

---

2 ☐ Mark for Review

What are large amounts of structured or unstructured data that can be potentially mined, examined, and used by organizations known as?

(A) Data collection

(B) Data set

(C) Usable data

(D) Big data

GO ON TO THE NEXT PAGE.

3 🔖 Mark for Review

Which of the following can be represented as a Boolean variable?

(A) Temperature of water coming out of a tap

(B) State of a traffic light

(C) State of a light bulb

(D) Number of lights on a light string

4 🔖 Mark for Review

What would the code below output?

```
count ← 0
 n ← 1
REPEAT UNTIL (n ≥ 10) {
    n ← 1
    count ← count + n
    n ← n + 1
}
DISPLAY (count)
```

(A) 1

(B) 9

(C) 45

(D) There would be no output as the program is in an infinite loop.

5 🔖 Mark for Review

Which of the following is always true of metadata?

(A) Metadata references other data.

(B) Metadata is collected at run-time.

(C) Metadata is transmitted with raw data.

(D) Metadata is stripped during compression.

GO ON TO THE NEXT PAGE.

6 ☐ Mark for Review

Which of the following is NOT a Boolean expression?

(A) `IF (role = supervisor AND shift > 1)`

(B) `REPEAT UNTIL (speed = SoundSpeed)`

(C) `IF (NOT (pet = CAT))`

(D) `x ← x + 15`

7 ☐ Mark for Review

How does the Internet ensure reliably transmitted data?

(A) Ensuring data never gets lost

(B) Sending data in order along the same route

(C) Using TCP

(D) Creating redundancy

8 ☐ Mark for Review

A movie streaming service makes individualized recommendations on movies for users to watch based on their viewing history and user movie rating. How does the streaming service most likely make its recommendations?

(A) It recommends the most watched movies.

(B) It recommends random movies.

(C) It uses data mining techniques to determine patterns in the movies and ratings that are similar.

(D) It recommends movies from the user's viewing history.

GO ON TO THE NEXT PAGE.

9 ☐ Mark for Review

Brew-haha Coffee Shop's register displays the change due to a customer as $0.999999 instead of $1.00. How is this possible?

(A) The register has a faulty program.

(B) Decimal numbers are stored imprecisely, hence this is a rounding error.

(C) The number displayed is on hexadecimal not decimal.

(D) The cashier made an error while entering prices.

10 ☐ Mark for Review

What is the act of chaining or placing two (or more) things side-by-side so they are treated as one object called?

(A) Indexing

(B) Truncating

(C) Concatenation

(D) Extraction

11 ☐ Mark for Review

Consider the code segment below.

```
REPEAT UNTIL ( x > 10 )

    x ← x * 3

Display x
```

If the first time the code is run, x = 1, what would display at the end?

(A) 1

(B) 9

(C) 27

(D) 3^{10}

GO ON TO THE NEXT PAGE.

12 ⬚ Mark for Review

A journalist demonstrates computer automation to a group of visiting high school students. As part of his demonstration, he uploads a random news story and changes all the "p" characters to "q." To restore the file back to its original form, he converts all the "q" characters to "p." Did the journalist restore the file to its original form?

(A) Yes, the file was restored to its original form as the second action undid what was done by the first action.

(B) Yes, but he may have to verify that formatting was not changed.

(C) No, he will have to restore the original file from the company's backup drive.

(D) No, he has corrupted the file, and the story will have to be rewritten.

13 ⬚ Mark for Review

A Social Services bureau uses a kiosk where clients sign in. They enter their name (user input), address (user input), and service (drop-down list). The kiosk provides a unique number and adds the client to a queue. In an effort to improve services, the bureau installs an algorithm that predicts client wait times. Which of the following inputs is likely to cause computing bias?

(A) Number of people in queue

(B) Type of service requested

(C) Number of service windows operating

(D) Zip code

14 ⬚ Mark for Review

Eight-bit storage (as used for RGB colors) can store $2^8 = 256$ levels for each color. If an integer is stored in eight-bit memory, what is its maximum value?

(A) 8

(B) 255

(C) 256

(D) 32,767

GO ON TO THE NEXT PAGE.

15 ☐ Mark for Review

The British Library created a well-designed website to allow anyone from around the world to become a "digital member." These members have access to all the library's digital collections, including archives and recordings, and can email their librarians. However, the library found that there are no members from certain countries. What is the most likely reason for this?

(A) Computing bias

(B) Scalability

(C) Digital divide

(D) Creative Commons

16 ☐ Mark for Review

Why are "citizen scientists" used on projects?

(A) They can record local data to be included in global databases.

(B) They are paid minimum wage.

(C) They have specialized knowledge in that field.

(D) They are retired scientists engaged in their area of expertise.

17 ☐ Mark for Review

What is the purpose of the Digital Millennium Copyright Act (DMCA) as it relates to the Creative Commons for digital content?

(A) To provide protection for intellectual property in digital format that has copyright status.

(B) To enable music and movie downloads to be more widely shared.

(C) To protect individuals using copyright content for personal or non-profit use.

(D) To provide software for legally sharing digital content.

GO ON TO THE NEXT PAGE.

18 ⬚ Mark for Review

Which of the following would be LEAST likely to help bridge the digital divide gap within a small city?

(A) Mandate that the local school system not assign homework that needs internet access.

(B) Raise taxes to provide free citywide internet access.

(C) Loan each high school student a computer for the duration of the school year.

(D) Provide low-cost or no-cost training services to city residents on how to use the World Wide Web.

19 ⬚ Mark for Review

Fast Fastfood Inc. values its quick service and collects the following daily data on its employees that interact with its customers: Attendance (0 for showing up when scheduled to show up, +1 for showing up when covering somebody else's shift, –1 for missing or rescheduling one's shift at the last minute), total tip amount collected by shift, total number of orders by shift, service time (time between when the customer places an order and the time the customer is served), tenure (number of months an employee has been working for *Fast* Fastfood Inc.). The company wants to promote some of its workers to managers using the following criteria: the worker needs to have been employed for a minimum of three years, should have a fast service time, and should have helped cover a shift at least ten times. A program will be written to select top candidates who will then be interviewed for the open manager positions. Which of the following programs would be most suitable as an initial screen?

(A) Do not include employees with tenure less than 36 months, do not include employees if sum of attendance is less than 10, rank average order amount (looking for highest value).

(B) Do not include employees with tenure less than 36 months, do not include employees if sum of attendance is less than 10, rank average shift tip (looking for highest value).

(C) Do not include employees with tenure less than 36 months, do not include employees if sum of attendance is less than 10, rank average order amount divided by service time (looking for highest value).

(D) Do not include employees with tenure less than 36 months, do not include employees if sum of attendance is less than 10, rank average order amount divided by service time (looking for lowest value).

GO ON TO THE NEXT PAGE.

20 ☐ Mark for Review

Which of the following is NOT an example of computing innovation?

Ⓐ A program that interacts with customers to schedule and book vacation travel and activities.

Ⓑ A program that interacts with patients to book doctor appointments and order refills.

Ⓒ A program that plays pre-recorded info on a museum exhibit.

Ⓓ A program that shows highway driving conditions from user inputs of origin, destination, and start time.

21 ☐ Mark for Review

Refer to the logic diagram below.

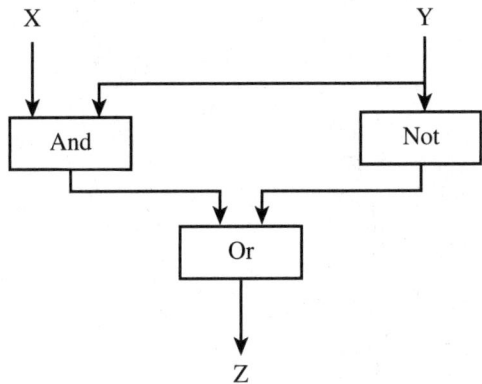

Under what conditions is Z false?

Ⓐ X is true and Y is true.

Ⓑ X is true and Y is false.

Ⓒ X is false and Y is true.

Ⓓ X is false and Y is false.

GO ON TO THE NEXT PAGE.

22 ☐ Mark for Review

Which of the following situations would NOT be acceptable under one of the Creative Commons licenses?

(A) Latisha writes computer code. Someone else publishes the unedited computer code on a blog site and credits Latisha.

(B) James makes an informative video and puts it online. Someone else adds another segment to the end of the video and publishes it online.

(C) Jing takes a picture of a deer at a sanctuary. Someone else puts that picture on a throw blanket and sells it online.

(D) Pia records a trumpet solo. Someone else adds a beat to the solo and publishes it on their website with Pia's name.

23 ☐ Mark for Review

Consider the following code segment `eval` that takes `n` as its input (`tVal1` is a variable internal to the procedure `eval`):

```
PROCEDURE eval (n)
{
    tVal1 ← false
    IF (n > 5) ·
    {
        IF (n > 10)
            tVal1 ← true
    }
    ELSE
    {
        IF (n < -5)
            tVal1 ← true
    }
    RETURN (tVal1)
}
```

Which of the following statements assigns the same value to the variable `tEquiv` as the return value of the code above?

(A) `tEquiv ← (n > -5) AND (n < 10)`

(B) `tEquiv ← (n > -5) OR (n < 10)`

(C) `tEquiv ← (n < -5) AND (n > 10)`

(D) `tEquiv ← (n < -5) OR (n > 10)`

GO ON TO THE NEXT PAGE.

24 ☐ Mark for Review

A medical team using private health records has made a discovery that could help healthcare providers better serve their communities. However, the results are only pertinent if location and demographic data (age, gender, and race) are also provided. If the medical team wishes to publish its findings in a medical journal it needs to:

  I.   Disguise patient name and personal information.
 II.   Omit demographic data.
III.   It cannot publish its findings as that would make the information public.

(A) I only

(B) II only

(C) III only

(D) I and II only

25 ☐ Mark for Review

Consider the following programming code:

```
a ← User Input
b ← 2 * a
c ← 40
b ← b + c
e ← b/2
e ← e - a
Display e
```

Which of the following best describes the result of running the program code?

(A) The user input is displayed.

(B) The number 40 is displayed.

(C) The number 20 is displayed.

(D) Depends on the user input.

GO ON TO THE NEXT PAGE.

26 ☐ Mark for Review

Heuristic approaches would be most appropriate under which of the following conditions?

Ⓐ When a problem cannot be solved in a reasonable time and an approximate solution is acceptable

Ⓑ When a problem cannot be solved in a reasonable time and an exact solution is required

Ⓒ When a problem can be solved in a reasonable time and an approximate solution is acceptable

Ⓓ When a problem can be solved in a reasonable time and an exact solution is required

27 ☐ Mark for Review

For a particular controller, variables declared as `int` are allocated 16-bit memory, which allows for 2^{16} (or 65,536) possible combinations. What is the greatest integer that can be stored in 16-bit memory?

Ⓐ 32,767

Ⓑ 32,768

Ⓒ 65,535

Ⓓ 65,536

28 ☐ Mark for Review

Which one of the following is LEAST likely to cause legal or ethical concerns?

Ⓐ A presidential photographer writes a program to change one picture she has taken with another every four hours on her Web page.

Ⓑ A musician uses a peer-to-peer network to exchange digital content that was used on his album, but to which he does not own the copyright.

Ⓒ An engineer uses authenticated access to download the latest upgrades to the sensors her company manufactures on her personal computer.

Ⓓ A high school student accesses geolocation and browsing history of those who visit his website.

GO ON TO THE NEXT PAGE.

29 ☐ Mark for Review

Consider the code segments below, which are designed to display the number of parking spots available in a parking garage. "Entry" and "Exit" are Boolean variables. "Entry" becomes true when a car enters the parking garage, and "Exit" becomes true when a car exits the parking garage. When the parking garage becomes full, no more cars can enter the garage, and at the beginning of the day there are no cars in the parking garage.

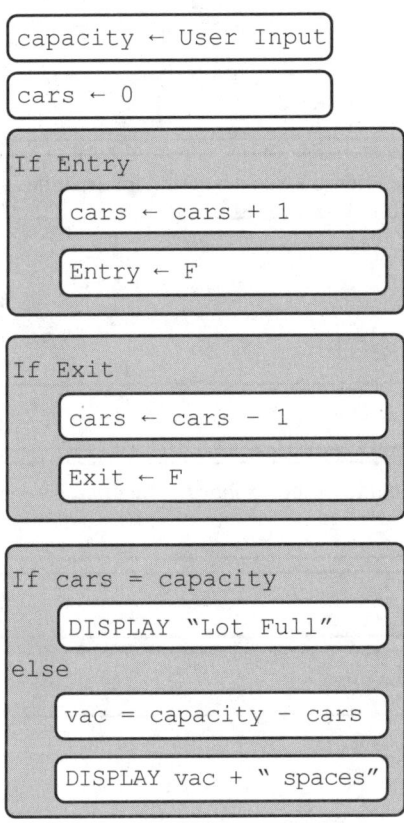

Assume that the program never resets the value of `capacity`, and only resets the value of `cars` just before the parking garage opens in the morning. If its capacity is 160 cars, and it currently has 108 cars, what will the program display after two cars leave and one car enters the parking garage?

Ⓐ It depends on prior activity.

Ⓑ The program will display 51 spaces.

Ⓒ The program will display 52 spaces.

Ⓓ The program will display 53 spaces.

GO ON TO THE NEXT PAGE.

30 ☐ Mark for Review

What is the relationship between the World Wide Web and the Internet?

(A) The Internet connects servers to devices, and the World Wide Web uses the Internet to transmit and receive HTML to those devices.

(B) The Internet creates web pages, while the World Wide Web sends those pages to and from devices.

(C) The Internet can log off and log on, while the World Wide Web is always on and connected.

(D) The World Wide Web was created first for data sharing, while the Internet came after to assist in sharing information.

31 ☐ Mark for Review

Which of the following is NOT likely to yield Personally Identifiable Information (PII)?

(A) A picture of a car clearly showing its license plate.

(B) A map of a residential community showing the house number, owner's name, and registered political affiliation (note: this data is publicly available).

(C) A picture of a coworker showing only his new jacket.

(D) A video clip of a football game with a date and location tag showing some of the fans.

32 ☐ Mark for Review

Which type of programming error will prevent the compiler from compiling the code?

(A) Syntax error

(B) Run-time error

(C) Logic error

(D) Overflow error

GO ON TO THE NEXT PAGE.

33 ⬚ Mark for Review

The algorithm used by a bot is shown in the flowchart below:

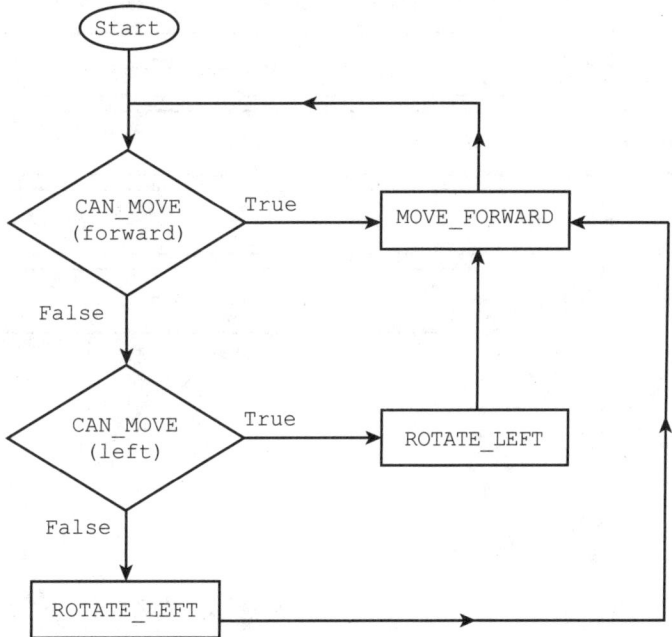

The bot starts at the beginning of a maze facing "forward" as shown below:

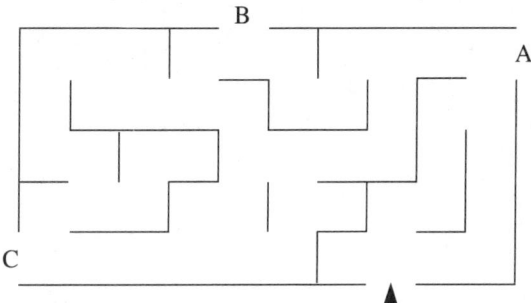

Where will the bot exit the maze?

Ⓐ At A

Ⓑ At B

Ⓒ At C

Ⓓ The bot will never exit the maze.

GO ON TO THE NEXT PAGE.

34 ☐ Mark for Review

A musician records a piece of music and saves it on her computer. She notices that the saved version is of lower quality than the original piece. Which one of the following could be a possible explanation of the decrease in quality?

(A) The musical piece was saved using fewer bits per second than the original piece.

(B) The musical piece was saved using more bits per second than the original piece.

(C) The piece was saved using lossless compression techniques.

(D) Some information is lost every time a file is saved from one location to another.

GO ON TO THE NEXT PAGE.

35 ☐ Mark for Review

Which of the following reverses the characters of a string? (For example, `reverse` (`"desserts"`) returns the string "stressed".) Assume the input string is a valid (non-null) string.

```
I.  PROCEDURE reverse (str) {
        outStr ← " "                  // initialize outStr as Empty String
        n ← LENGTH (str)
        i ← 1
        REPEAT n TIMES {
            outStr ← INSERT (outStr, 1, str[i])
            i ← i + 1
        }
        RETURN (outStr)
    }


II. PROCEDURE reverse (str) {
        outStr ← " "                  // initialize outStr as Empty String
        n ← LENGTH (str)
        i ← n
        REPEAT n TIMES {
            outStr ← APPEND (outStr, str[i])
            i ← i - 1
        }
        RETURN (outStr)
    }
```

(A) I only

(B) II only

(C) I and II

(D) Neither

GO ON TO THE NEXT PAGE.

36 ▢ Mark for Review

A program requires the execution of three independent steps. The time for each step is provided below:

Process	Time
Step A	50 msec
Step B	40 msec
Step C	80 msec

If the computer has two identical processors that can run in parallel, what is the minimum time required to execute the program?

Ⓐ 40 msec

Ⓑ 80 msec

Ⓒ 90 msec

Ⓓ 170 msec

GO ON TO THE NEXT PAGE.

37 ☐ Mark for Review

A store usually sells an item for $12 to non-members and $10 to members. It is currently offering a special 20% discount to only those members who have a discount coupon. Consider the two sets of code designed to correctly price the item.

Program A

```
cost ← 12
```

```
If member
    cost ← 10
```

```
If discount
    cost ← cost * 0.8
```

Program B

```
cost ← 10
```

```
If discount
    cost ← cost * 0.8
```

```
If non-member
    cost ← 12
```

Which of the following is true of Program A and Program B?

(A) Both programs correctly calculate the item price.

(B) Program A correctly calculates the item price, but Program B does not.

(C) Program B correctly calculates the item price, but Program A does not.

(D) Neither program correctly calculates the item price.

GO ON TO THE NEXT PAGE.

38 ☐ Mark for Review

Which one of the following is MOST likely a violation of the DMCA (Digital Millennium Copyright Act), which is intended to provide copyright protections for digital media, including Creative Commons licenses?

Ⓐ A political cartoonist downloads a color Disney picture, changes it to black and white, replaces the heads of the original characters with caricatures of politicians, touches up the background so it suits the current political landscape, and publishes it on her employer's subscription-based website.

Ⓑ A programmer copies a piece of code from a MATLAB blog (where programmers post code to help each other), incorporates it into his larger code, and sells it for commercial purposes.

Ⓒ A researcher downloads demographic data and includes it in her paper that is published in a subscription-based academic journal.

Ⓓ An independent seller copies an image from the product manufacturer's website and posts it to show what they're selling.

39 ☐ Mark for Review

Programmers usually add comments to their programs to help other users understand the code's characteristics (like function, valid input, and output). Another function comments serve is to document revisions, maintain version control, and assert authorship. They are also used as trackers as the compiled code would have commented information in human readable form. Which of the following are also uses of comments in programs?

Ⓐ Comment out alternate code

Ⓑ Debug the program

Ⓒ Note which portions need fixing or have been tested

Ⓓ All the above

GO ON TO THE NEXT PAGE.

40 ☐ Mark for Review

Which of the following are NOT common protocols used on the Internet or the World Wide Web?

(A) TCP

(B) HTTP

(C) UDP

(D) IETF

41 ☐ Mark for Review

The code below is intended to sort the elements in the list `aList` in ascending order. The procedure `swap` exchanges elements at indexes `i` and `j` in `aList`:

```
len ←LENGTH(aList)
i←1
j←2
REPEAT UNTIL (j>len)
{
    IF (aList[j]<aList[i])
    {
        swap(aList,i,j)
    }
    j←j+1
}
```

Will the code sort `aList` as intended?

(A) No, `i` should start at 0, and `j` should start at 1.

(B) No, only the smallest element of `aList` will be in the first position of the list

(C) No, only the largest element of `aList` will be in the first position of the list

(D) Yes, the code will sort `aList` in ascending order

GO ON TO THE NEXT PAGE.

42 Mark for Review

Consider the method below, `biggest`, which is intended to return the greatest of three integers (a, b, and c). It does not always work as intended.

```
PROCEDURE biggest (a, b, c)
 {
    IF ((a > b) AND (a > c))
    {
        RETURN (a)
    }
    ELSE
    {
        IF ((b > a) AND (b > c))
        {
            RETURN (b)
        }
        ELSE
        {
            RETURN (c)
        }
    }
}
```

Which of the following describes the error in the method?

(A) `biggest` may not work correctly when a and b have the same value.

(B) `biggest` may not work correctly when a and c have the same value.

(C) `biggest` may not work correctly when b and c have the same value.

(D) `biggest` may not work correctly when c is the biggest value.

GO ON TO THE NEXT PAGE.

43 ☐ Mark for Review

Which of the following is NOT an example of crowdsourcing?

(A) A notice by a lake that asks visitors to text a visible salinity readout to a posted number.

(B) A company sends out a survey to all of its customers soliciting new product ideas.

(C) A company's top executives meet offsite to outline the company's strategic direction.

(D) An activist sets up a website to solicit donations that will be used to fight climate change.

44 ☐ Mark for Review

While at a library, a person logs into the public Wi-Fi network labeled "Library" with their private device. The person then uses their device to make a deposit into their bank account. That deposit never reaches the user's bank account, but is instead rerouted to another account. It turns out that the public Wi-Fi network was not from the library, but instead, a cybercriminal installed an access point on the library's Wi-Fi without the library's permission and used that access point to reroute the money into the cybercriminal's account.

What type of attack would this be considered?

(A) Malware

(B) Keylogging

(C) Phishing

(D) Rogue Access Point

GO ON TO THE NEXT PAGE.

A company is networked to its offices as shown in the figure below. Any node connected to another node represents two offices that can communicate with each other. HQ is the headquarters and processes more information than any other office. Offices C and H have the more current hardware, and hence the fastest processing times and the lowest maintenance times (downtimes). Offices D and E have aging hardware, the slowest processing times, and the longest maintenance times. Due to their hardware, they also have the most unscheduled maintenance time.

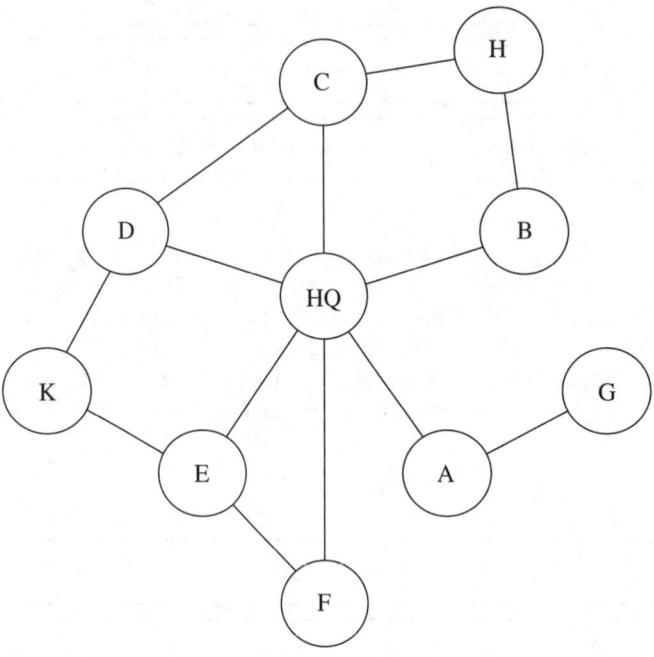

If a message is generated from HQ, which office is expected to be the last to get it, and which office is the least fault tolerant?

Ⓐ   Office G is the last to get the message from HQ because it has the fewest number of connections. Office D and Office E are the least fault tolerant as they have the worst performing hardware.

Ⓑ   Office K is the last to get the message as it is connected to the slowest nodes. Office G is least fault tolerant as it is connected to only one node.

Ⓒ   Office E or D is the last to get the message as they have the least efficient hardware. Office G is least fault tolerant as it is connected to only one node.

Ⓓ   Office G is the last to get the message from HQ because it has the fewest number of connections. Office K is least fault tolerant as it is connected to offices that have the least efficient hardware.

GO ON TO THE NEXT PAGE.

46 ☐ Mark for Review

A computer keeps time through its CMOS clock, which essentially counts the number of "ticks." Computer A's CMOS is rated at 35kHz (number of ticks per sec) while Computer B uses a frequency doubler and has an effective CMOS rating of 70kHz. At noon the system clock for Computer A was reading 11:58 A.M. while that for Computer B was reading 12:03 P.M. Which of the following could explain the time discrepancies?

(A) Computer A's CMOS has an actual frequency of lower than 35kHz, while Computer B's CMOS has an actual frequency of higher than 70kHz.

(B) CMOS ratings tend to overestimate clock speeds and therefore Computer A's system clock is slower than it should be. Frequency doublers overclock the CMOS and as a result speed up the system clock. Thus, Computer B's system clock is faster than it should be.

(C) Computer A's CMOS has an actual frequency of higher than 35kHz, while Computer B's CMOS has an actual frequency of lower than 70kHz.

(D) CMOS chips rarely hit their rated frequency and generally have a self-correcting algorithm. Computer A and Computer B either have faulty or non-functioning self-correcting algorithms.

GO ON TO THE NEXT PAGE.

47 ☐ Mark for Review

An accounting manager gets the following email:

Sarah Templeton (URGENT)

Sarah,
 	
   I'm in meetings all day, but we need to complete a wire transfer as soon as possible for a payment Charlie wants to complete today.
 	
   Can you take care of it this morning? Let me know if you can and I'll send you the details.
 	
Thanks,
Teresa Holler
CEO Custom Build Inc.

Assume that Teresa, Sarah, and Charlie all work for Custom Build Inc. and that Teresa is the president. However, if Teresa did not send the above email, then it is an example of which type of phishing?

- (A) Deception phishing
- (B) Spear phishing
- (C) Whaling
- (D) Angler phishing

GO ON TO THE NEXT PAGE.

48 ☐ Mark for Review

Which of the following correctly depicts the behavior of the algorithm represented by the flowchart below (assume *a* and *b* are integers)?

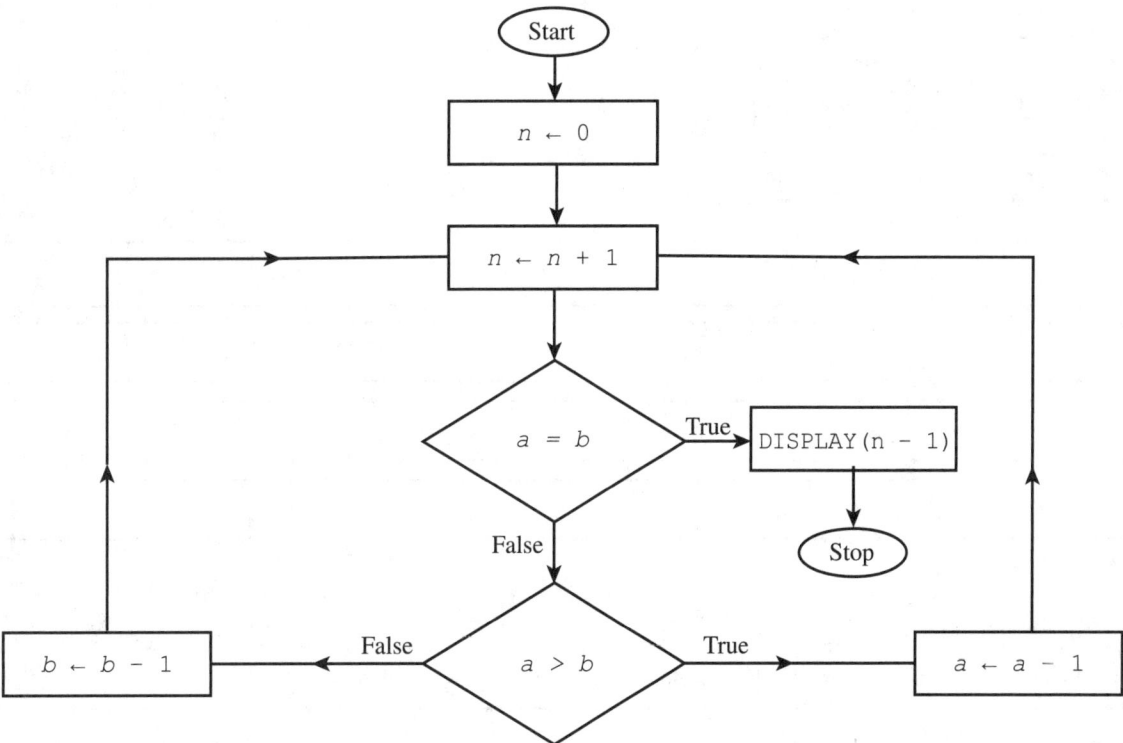

(A) It displays the sum of *a* and *b*.

(B) It displays the difference of *a* and *b*.

(C) It displays neither the sum nor the difference between *a* and *b*.

(D) It gets stuck in an infinite loop.

GO ON TO THE NEXT PAGE.

49 ▢ Mark for Review

What condition makes the program an infinite loop?

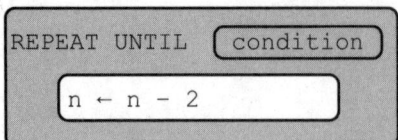

```
n ← 5

REPEAT UNTIL ( condition )
    n ← n – 2
```

Ⓐ n = 1

Ⓑ n ≠ 3

Ⓒ n ≤ -24

Ⓓ n = -12

50 ▢ Mark for Review

Which of the following is a characteristic of a low-level language (such as machine language)?

Ⓐ Simple to maintain

Ⓑ Needs an assembler to translate

Ⓒ Less memory efficient

Ⓓ Portable

GO ON TO THE NEXT PAGE.

51 ⬜ Mark for Review

A game is designed such that a treasure is buried in one cell of a 10 × 10 grid. When a user picks a cell to try to find the treasure, the program provides a hint which advises the user whether the treasure is buried north or south and east or west of the current cell. If a player uses binary search to locate the treasure, what is the maximum number of trials that the user needs to successfully locate the treasure?

(A) 4

(B) 8

(C) 10

(D) 25

52 ⬜ Mark for Review

Which of the following is NOT an advantage of parallel computing?

(A) Race condition

(B) Can use commodity components for hardware

(C) Ability to solve large or complex problems

(D) Can use computing resources over Wide Area Network (WAN)

53 ⬜ Mark for Review

Which one of the following is most likely to cause bias?

(A) A program that predicts future tax returns based on graduation rates, SAT scores, and demographic data.

(B) A program used to screen medical school applicants based on GPA and MCAT (standardized test) scores.

(C) A program that predicts election outcomes based on demographic and economic data.

(D) All the above.

GO ON TO THE NEXT PAGE.

54 ☐ Mark for Review

Speedup is the ratio of the time it takes to complete the task sequentially to the time it takes to complete the task in parallel. Which of the following is/are true about speedup?

I.   Speedup is always less than or equal to 1.
II. Speedup is always greater than or equal to 1.
III. Speedup cannot be a higher value than the number of processing cores.

Ⓐ I only

Ⓑ II only

Ⓒ III only

Ⓓ II and III only

55 ☐ Mark for Review

Popular antivirus software uses heuristic algorithms for detecting viruses and other malware. What is an advantage of using this algorithm?

Ⓐ It looks for behavioral patterns common to a class of viruses.

Ⓑ It can detect all viruses.

Ⓒ It implements the optimal solution for scanning and neutralizing malware threats.

Ⓓ It can detect future viruses without requiring the virus to be first detected elsewhere.

56 ☐ Mark for Review

Which of the following is NOT a characteristic of clustering?

Ⓐ It is an iterative process.

Ⓑ It utilizes a specific algorithm.

Ⓒ It is inherently qualitative.

Ⓓ It enables multi-objective formulation.

GO ON TO THE NEXT PAGE.

57 🔖 Mark for Review

A hardware manufacturing company monitors its bandwidth usage and has compiled the following data.

Top 5 Applications

Application	Usage
YouTube	1.2 MB
http	669.8 kB
Google	220.5 kB
Ebay	120.3 kB
Wikipedia	62.3 kB

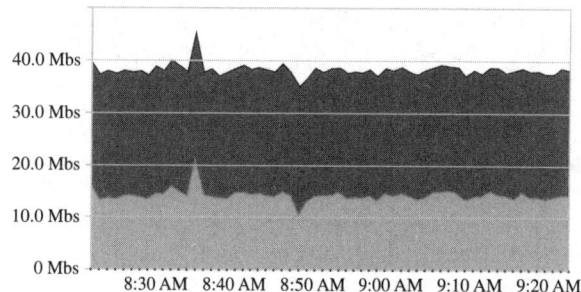

Typical Bandwidth Usage Per Hour

As overall bandwidth usage is close to the company's limits, what should it do?

I.   Limit access to certain websites.
II. Limit VoIP network usage to strictly business needs.
III. Add additional bandwidth.

- (A) III only
- (B) I and II only
- (C) I, II, and III
- (D) Not enough information to decide.

GO ON TO THE NEXT PAGE.

Questions 58 through 62 refer to the following.

A school is trying to figure out a more efficient way to sign in students every day. Because of a recent health crisis, every student's temperature must be verified to be in a normal range, and every student must be asked a series of questions about his or her recent health history. The school only has a small population of students coming in at this time, but soon all students will again be attending in-person full time. During the time the smaller population is coming in, the school has hired extra security members at each door to take each student's temperature and ask them all health screening questions. When the entire student population returns, the school is planning to switch to an automated system and will therefore not need security staff members at each door.

This new system requires every student to have a student ID that can be scanned. The school also purchased a walk-through temperature scanner that will take each student's temperature. This data is linked to each student's ID number, which is linked to all of the student's information in a database (name, class schedule, medical history, etc.). Before each student shows up to school each day, they must have answered a series of questions about their current health using devices such as a cell phone, laptop, etc. To do this, they must log in to a system that is linked to all their school information. Here is a flowchart of the system and the use of each block in the flowchart.

Block	Explanation
Oval	The start of the algorithm
Parallelogram	An input or output step
Diamond	A conditional or decision step, where execution proceeds to the side labeled "True" if the condition is true and to the side labeled "False" otherwise
Rectangle	The result of the algorithm

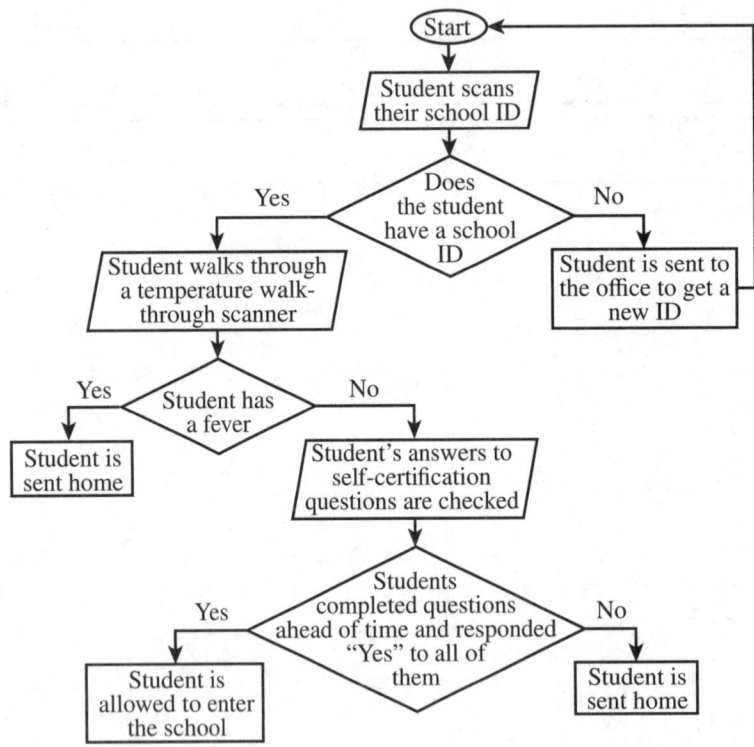

GO ON TO THE NEXT PAGE.

58 ☐ Mark for Review

Which of the following has a potential harmful effect on society, culture, or economy when using the new system?

Ⓐ The entire process of students entering the building will be sped up, resulting in less lost time.

Ⓑ The need to hire more security personnel is eliminated, saving money, but resulting in job loss.

Ⓒ Having an automated attendance system will help track the spread of the health crisis within their school and community.

Ⓓ There will be less contact with the security staff since students' temperatures will be taken by a machine.

59 ☐ Mark for Review

Which of the following actions would do the LEAST to address any problems that may occur due to a possible digital divide in this school's population?

Ⓐ Provide every student with a device and Internet connectivity so they are all able to answer the self-certification questions ahead of time.

Ⓑ Allow students to answer the self-certification questions on school devices when they get to school, instead of ahead of time.

Ⓒ Make sure that every student has an ID before they come to school, and if they do not have an ID, send them to the office to get one for free.

Ⓓ Ensure that every student has knowledge of how to use a device and how to use the self-certification system before starting to use the new system.

60 ☐ Mark for Review

Which of the following is a potential data privacy concern with this new system?

Ⓐ The student's class schedule can be used in case the student needs to be removed during a certain class period because of a medical issue.

Ⓑ If a student falls ill, the school can use their attendance and class schedule to contact other students about them being in contact with an ill student.

Ⓒ When a student falls ill at school, the staff members can use their medical information to quickly assist with any major issues that can occur.

Ⓓ Access to student information, including medical information, would be given to all staff, security, and district personnel.

GO ON TO THE NEXT PAGE.

61 ☐ Mark for Review

When students log in to the school's self-certification system, they also have access to their attendance, personal information, school schedule, and medical history. Which of the following is the LEAST effective measure taken to ensure that this information stays private?

(A) After each login, if the user does not do anything on the self-certification website for 30 minutes, it automatically logs out.

(B) Use multifactor authentication to ensure that there are multiple authentications needed to be completed before logging in to the self-certification website.

(C) Require the users to create strong passwords that are easy to remember, but difficult to guess. This would include requiring the passwords have a certain length and use characters other than just letters.

(D) Make sure the self-certification website uses public key encryption and certificates.

62 ☐ Mark for Review

When the entire student and staff population returned and the school started using their new system, several students still got sick. Which of the following data would be MOST effective when trying to find a correlation between which students got sick and if they got other students sick, with the hopes of proving a causal relationship between sick students getting other students sick due to proximity?

(A) Comparing all the students who got sick to their medical history

(B) Checking for overlap in each sick student's class schedules

(C) Checking the time each student answers their self-certification questions in the morning

(D) Comparing the students' temperatures each day with their medical history

GO ON TO THE NEXT PAGE.

63 🔖 Mark for Review

Which of the following can be stored in a bit?

Select <u>two</u> answers.

- [ ] The result of a number MOD 2

- [ ] A Boolean variable

- [ ] A variable which is a single digit positive integer

- [ ] An electronic device that is in "on," "off," or "sleep" mode

64 🔖 Mark for Review

NASA routinely makes publicly available data collected on stars, exoplanets, and the universe. The data is freely available for all to use and analyze in the hopes that other scientists will provide novel insights into the structure or origins of space. What is this an example of?

Select <u>two</u> answers.

- [ ] Citizen science

- [ ] Crowd sourcing

- [ ] Open data

- [ ] Crowd funding

65 🔖 Mark for Review

Which of the following is an appropriate variable name for an `int` variable?

Select <u>two</u> answers.

- [ ] `v1`

- [ ] `spots`

- [ ] `intSpot`

- [ ] `numberOfAvailableSpots`

GO ON TO THE NEXT PAGE.

66 ☐ Mark for Review

Montreal-Trudeau International Airport is installing new kiosks to enhance the user experience and increase the efficiency of those going through immigration. Considering that there will be international travelers going through this airport, what should the user interface provide?

Select <u>two</u> answers.

☐ Text in the most common languages worldwide: English, French, Spanish, Mandarin, Hindi, and Arabic.

☐ Interface with a translation website.

☐ Provide a link to an online dictionary so travelers can quickly look up words they don't know.

☐ Use images and animation to represent program functionality.

67 ☐ Mark for Review

Which of the following are the main reasons organizations analyze big data?

Select <u>two</u> answers.

☐ To verify findings and insights from smaller datasets

☐ To gain hidden insight

☐ To enable more holistic decision-making

☐ To leverage economies of scale

68 ☐ Mark for Review

Which of the following can tolerate lossy compression for transmission?

Select <u>two</u> answers.

☐ Medical images

☐ Executable programs

☐ Text documents

☐ Military voice communication

GO ON TO THE NEXT PAGE.

69 ☐ Mark for Review

Which of the following are weaknesses of 2FA (two-factor authentication)?

Select <u>two</u> answers.

☐ Luring the user to a phishing site

☐ Using a passcode and personal PIN

☐ Sniff session cookies

☐ Authenticating the user via two separate devices

70 ☐ Mark for Review

Which of the following is a function that can be done by the World Wide Web, but not by the Internet?

Select <u>two</u> answers.

☐ Transfer data among computers

☐ Enable computers to communicate

☐ Interlink sites

☐ Interpret Web pages

STOP

END OF EXAM

Practice Test 3:
Answers and
Explanations

PRACTICE TEST 3 ANSWER KEY

1.	D	36.	C
2.	D	37.	C
3.	C	38.	D
4.	D	39.	D
5.	A	40.	D
6.	D	41.	B
7.	C	42.	A
8.	C	43.	C
9.	B	44.	D
10.	C	45.	B
11.	C	46.	A
12.	C	47.	C
13.	D	48.	B
14.	B	49.	D
15.	C	50.	B
16.	A	51.	A
17.	A	52.	A
18.	A	53.	B
19.	C	54.	D
20.	C	55.	D
21.	C	56.	B
22.	C	57.	D
23.	D	58.	B
24.	A	59.	C
25.	C	60.	D
26.	A	61.	A
27.	A	62.	B
28.	A	63.	A, B
29.	D	64.	B, C
30.	A	65.	B, C
31.	C	66.	B, D
32.	A	67.	B, C
33.	D	68.	A, D
34.	A	69.	A, C
35.	C	70.	C, D

PRACTICE TEST 3 ANSWERS AND EXPLANATIONS

1. **D** To get the first number, add 1 to 1000 1101. Start at the far right digit and add 1 + 1 to get 10, causing the far right digit to become 0 and for the 1 to be carried to the digit to the left of it. Once you do, add 1 + 0 to get 1, leaving you with 1000 1110. To get the second number add 1 again to the far right to get 0 + 1 = 1, leaving you with 1000 1111. Finally to get the third number, add 1 to the far right to get 1 + 1 = 10, causing the far right digit to become 0 and for the 1 to be carried to the digit to the left of it. Once you do that, you'll add 1 + 1 again to make the second digit from the right 0, and carrying the 1 to the third digital from the right. Repeat two more times until you get to the fifth digit from the right. Add 1 + 0 to get 1, leaving you with 1001 0000.

First number	Second number	Third number
1000 1101	1000 1110	1000 1111
+ 1	+ 1	+ 1
1000 1110	1000 1111	1001 0000

The answer is (D).

2. **D** Choice (A) is the process of data collection, so eliminate it. Choice (B) is a collection of related sets of information composed of separate elements and usually of the same data structure or data type. As it does not incorporate both structured and unstructured data, eliminate it. Choice (C) is data that has been adapted to the end-user's need (that is, formatted to be useful to user needs). As the description does not include unstructured data, eliminate it. Choice (D) usually refers to large data sets. Even though size is not mentioned, the disparate variety of data types and structure are characteristic of big data. This is the closest (and credited) answer. The answer is (D).

3. **C** Boolean variables can only take two values, and so can only represent things that exist in one of two states. Choice (A) can take on a range of values and should be represented as a double. Choice (B) needs three states (red, green, and amber), and so cannot be represented as a Boolean variable. Choice (C) is the credited answer, as the state of a light bulb is either on or off: two states, which can be represented as a Boolean. Choice (D) can take on a range of values and would most appropriately be represented as an integer. The answer is (C).

4. **D** As the variable n is reset to 1 each time the loop executes, n will always be less than 10, and hence will never be able to exit the loop. Choice (A) is the value of n at the beginning of the loop. As the program never exits the loop that value will never display. Choice (B) is the greatest value n can be and still execute the loop. However, as it is reset each time the loop runs, it will never be able to get as large as 9. Choice (C) is all the integers from 1 to 9 added up. Normally one would expect this to be the output, except for the fact that the program is stuck in an infinite loop. Choice (D) correctly identifies that n is reset and the program will never get to the DISPLAY statement. The answer is (D).

5. **A** Metadata provides information about other data, but not the content of the data—for instance, the column labels (like first name, last name, address, city, state) but none of the actual values. Choice (A) is the credited answer. Metadata always refers to raw data. Choice (B) is not true as metadata tends to be set up before run time (at which point raw data is collected). Choice (C) is not always true as there is no need to transmit metadata if it is structured data and the receiving party knows the structural format. Choice (D) is not true as metadata would be needed if unstructured data is compressed. The answer is (A).

6. **D** Boolean expressions are either true or false. Choice (A) is either true or false, eliminate it. Choice (B) is trickier, but the expression inside the parenthesis is either true or false, making it a Boolean expression, so eliminate it. Work through each set of parentheses to see that (C) is a Boolean expression that can be eliminated. Choice (D) is an assignment, it adds 15 to x, and is not a Boolean expression. The answer is (D).

7. **C** When streaming data over the Internet, the data is divided into individually transmitted packets. These may be sent via different routes and may arrive at the destination out of order. Transmission Control Protocol (TCP) continuously sends packets until it receives acknowledgment that the packets have reached the destination. You can eliminate (A) because data can get lost during transmission. You can eliminate (B) because while most sequential data to the same receiver does travel along the same route, the Internet is designed to divert data along different paths if needed (to be more fault tolerant). Choice (C) is the credited answer as TCP governs data flow over the Internet. It keeps track of which packets are received successfully, resends lost, missing, or damaged data, and specifies the order for reassembling data. Choice (D) can be eliminated because while redundancy is only one part of reliability, and even with all the redundancy built in the Internet, data packets still get lost. The answer is (C).

8. **C** To individualize suggestions, the streaming service would most likely make recommendations based on user profile and movie characteristics. This would involve some level of data mining and comparison to similar patterns and movies. Choices (A) and (B) are not individualized for the user, and so they can be eliminated. You can also eliminate (D), which would only recommend films that users have already seen. Choice (C) provides individualized recommendations based on user preferences and prior history. The answer is (C).

9. **B** Non-terminating decimals are rounded when stored in a computer's memory. This may cause a rounding (or floating point) error. Choice (C) is false, and neither (A) nor (D) describes the observed error. The answer is (B).

10. **C** Choice (A) is structuring data to facilitate fast lookup (usually used in databases). Choice (B) is shortening something, generally a decimal, to fewer digits. Choice (C) is the credited answer. Choice (D) is retrieving a piece of data, usually from a larger set. The answer is (C).

11. **C**   The loop will continue until x > 10. This means that when x > 10 the program will exit the loop. During the first iteration through the loop, x = 1, and at the end of the loop, x = 3. After the next iteration, x = 9. As 9 < 10, the loop will execute one more time, making x = 27. Choice (A) is false as the loop executes at least once. Choice (B) is false as since x < 10, the loop will execute again. Choice (C) is the credited answer as this is the smallest number (greater than 10) that x can be so as to exit the loop. Choice (D) is false as x is not a counter and 3 is not multiplied by itself. The answer is (C).

12. **C**   Usually performing an action and then performing its reverse does not alter the original file. However, in this case, all the "q" that were originally "q" would also change to "p" with the second action. Choices (A) and (B) are false as the file may not be restored to its original form. Choice (C) is the credited answer as it restores the original file before the journalist made his changes. Choice (D) is false as a corrupted file has become inoperable or unusable due to a defect or bug in the software used to create and manipulate the file. In this case, the change was willfully made by the journalist, and hence the file was not corrupted. The answer is (C).

13. **D**   Bias, in its broadest sense, means "slant." For instance, a grocery shopper can be biased based on their preference for one type of fruit over another. In computing, bias is defined by a system that systematically and unfairly discriminates against certain individuals or groups. It is reasonable to use the number of people in the queue, type of services requested (and hence complexity of the service demanded), and the number of windows open. However, using the zip code would imply that people living in certain zip codes need more (or less) customer support than those living in other zip codes. This may lead to favoring one group of people over another. The answer is (D).

14. **B**   The integer could have 256 distinct values. However, as storage starts with zero, the max integer would be 256 − 1 = 255. Choice (A) is just the power that 2 is raised to and can be eliminated. Choice (B) is $2^8 - 1$, which is the highest number that can be stored in eight-bit memory (including zero) and is the credited answer. Choice (C) is 2^8, which does not account for storing zero. Choice (D) is the highest integer, which is usually stored as `int` variable, traditionally using sixteen-bit memory. The answer is (B).

15. **C**   Censorship, remote locations, computing know-how, and socioeconomic factors are the major barriers to the World Wide Web. This is what creates the digital divide, (C). Computing bias (A) is when automated decisions lead to systematic bias. There is no evidence that the process of becoming a digital member is different for people from different countries, and hence this choice can be eliminated. Scalability refers to how easily a program can be sized up or down to accommodate shifts in demand. Its impact would be felt by all users, not those in specific countries. Eliminate (B). The Creative Commons, (D), are a set of standards that allow the creators of digital content to safely share their content under a legal framework. The question is about uneven access, not the legal issues of making content digitally available, so eliminate (D). The answer is (C).

16. **A**   Choice (A) is the credited answer as citizen scientists can record local data to be incorporated into global databases. Choice (B) is incorrect as most of them are unpaid volunteers. Choice (C) is incorrect as most of them don't have (or need) any specialized training. Choice (D) is false. The answer is (A).

17. **A**   The Digital Millennium Copyright Act (DMCA) is a copyright law that criminalizes production and dissemination of technology, devices, or services intended to circumvent measures that control access to copyrighted works regardless of actual copyright infringement. Choice (A) is the credited answer. Choices (B) and (D) are the opposite of DMCA. Choice (C) is false. The answer is (A).

18. **A**   Bridging the digital divide entails offering opportunities to access digital information to those subpopulations who would otherwise be unable to access it. Choice (A), the credited response, only makes it possible for all students to do their homework *without* digital resources; those who have access may still have an advantage. Choice (B) takes steps to provide equal (and free) internet access to all residents. While it does not guarantee that those who do not currently have access will get it, it does remove the geographical obstacle (and to a lesser degree a financial obstacle) for removing a barrier to internet access. Choice (C) provides all students with an opportunity to access digital resources, and hence moves toward bridging the digital divide gap. Choice (D) provides training for those who may not know how to use digital resources and hence does move toward bridging the digital divide gap. The answer is (A).

19. **C**   Tenure and attendance are threshold criteria that candidates need to meet. Achieving more than the required threshold does not confer additional consideration. As *Fast* Fastfood Inc. values service time, service time per dollar should be ranked with low values as desirable. This would account for large orders that take more time to fulfill. Choice (A) does not consider service time and can be eliminated. Choice (B) does not consider service time and can be eliminated. Choice (C) considers order amount divided by service time. As service time should be as short as possible, this variable should be as large as possible. This is the credited answer. Choice (D) considers order amount divided by service time. As service time should be as short as possible, this variable should be as large as possible. The ranking is reversed, so eliminate (D). The answer is (C).

20. **C**   Computing innovation requires inputs, a processing of inputs, and an output. Usually, the output changes based on the input. Choice (A) is a computing innovation as different clients would be choosing different destinations and vacation activities. Choice (B) is a computing innovation as different patients would be booking appointments with different doctors and requesting different refills. Choice (C) is not a computing innovation as the information for the museum exhibit would be the same each time. Hence it is the credited answer. Choice (D) is a computing innovation as different origins and destinations, as well as changing weather conditions, would provide different outputs for different users. The answer is (C).

21. **C** For Z to be false, both inputs to the "Or" junction need to be false. This means that not Y has to be false, making Y true. Eliminate (B) and (D). For the output from "And" to be false, either X or Y has to be false. Since Y is true already, it means that X has to be false. Hence the answer is (C). You can also make a truth table to check out the other choices:

X	Y	X and Y	Not Y	Z	
T	T	T	F	T	Choice A
T	F	F	T	T	Choice B
F	T	F	F	F	Choice C
F	F	F	T	T	Choice D

The answer is (C).

22. **C** A Creative Commons (CC) license grants users the ability to use copyrighted work under certain conditions. The intent is to help creators freely distribute and share their work with a wider audience within the framework of copyright law. Choices (A), (B), and (D) might be covered under BY-NC-ND, NC, and BY-NC, respectively, but (C), which does not credit the author and is used for commercial purposes, would not be covered by CC. The answer is (C).

23. **D** It may be easier to see the code as a flowchart:

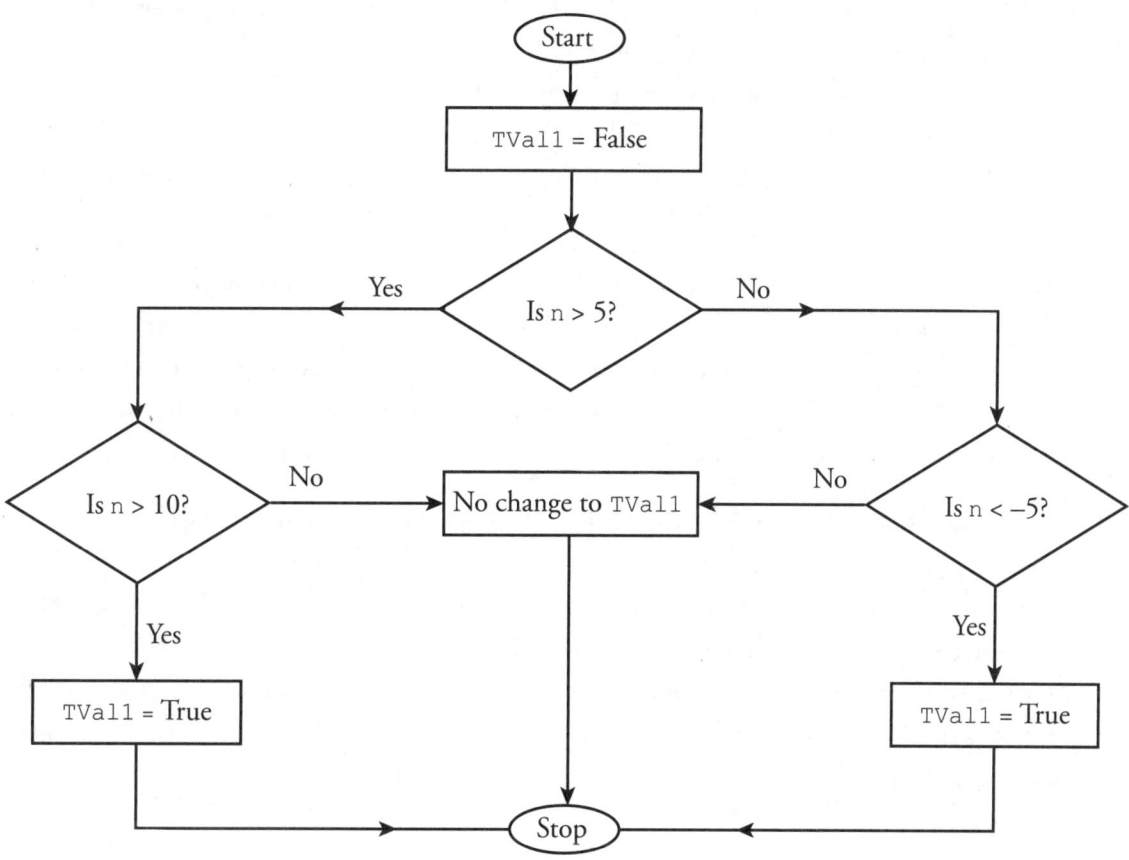

`tVal1` is true when n > 10 or when n < –5. The answer choice needs to be "or" not "and," so eliminate (A) and (C). Of the remaining choices, (D) matches the output range. Choice (A) makes `tEquiv` true when n is between –5 and 10. This is not the program output. Choice (B) makes `tEquiv` true for all values of n. The first condition is that n > –5 or n < 10. No matter what the value of n, it will satisfy one of these conditions, and hence will be true for all values of n. Choice (C) will always make `tEquiv` false as n cannot be less than –5 and greater than 10 at the same time. Choice (D) makes `tEquiv` true when n < –5 or n > 10, which matches the program output. The answer is (D).

24. **A** Data published needs to be such that participants cannot be identified by readers not privy to the private (and possibly confidential) data used by the study. Ideally, all personal information should be omitted, or at least disguised such that specific results can't be traced back to the study participants. At a minimum, patient names and personal information that would identify the patient should be omitted, as in (A). You can eliminate (B) and (D) because the data is only meaningful with demographic data included. In this case, the team should try to lump similar demographic findings together to make it more difficult for others outside the research team to identify individual study participants. Choice (C) would maintain the most privacy, but those concerns must be balanced with public health concerns. If there are significant public health advantages, then the research team may need to publish its findings.

25. **C** No matter what the user input is, the program will always display a value that is half of c. In this case, it is 20 (half of 40). Choice (A) is false as the user input is subtracted in Step 6. Choice (B) is false because in Step 5 e is divided by two (hence halving c). Choice (C) is the credited answer. In Step 4 c is added to b, then in Step 5 half of b is designated as e (effectively the sum of a and half of c). Choice (D) is false as the program consistently displays 20, regardless of input. The answer is (C).

26. **A** The objective of heuristic algorithms (heuristics) is to produce a solution in a reasonable time frame that approximates the actual solution. Choice (A) fits the definition of heuristics and is the credited answer. Choice (B) requires an exact solution and would not be appropriate for heuristic approaches. Choices (C) and (D) have problems that can be solved in a reasonable time and hence would not be good candidates for heuristic approaches. The answer is (A).

27. **A** When storing integers, one bit is allocated for the integer's sign (negative or positive). This means that the integer can only use 15 bits for its value. 2^{15} is 32,768. However, as integers start from zero (not one), the maximum integer that can be stored is 32,768 – 1 = 32,767. Choice (A) is the credited answer (see explanation above). Choice (B) is incorrect as it does not consider that integers start from zero. Choice (C) is incorrect as it does not consider that one bit is reserved for the integer's sign. Choice (D) is incorrect as it neither considers that one bit is reserved for the integer's sign nor that the integers begin from zero, not one. The answer is (A).

28. **A** This question is really asking about the potential for copyright violations or infringing on privacy considerations. Choice (A) is the credited answer as the photographer is using her pictures and loading them to her Web page. She presumably owns the rights to her pictures, and loading them to her Web page is not an ethical or legal violation. With (B), the musician may be exchanging copyrighted content and may not know if he is using it correctly, especially if there is no copyright designation. (Something creative without copyright designation is by default protected by law.) For (C), the sensor upgrades are the company's intellectual property, and the engineer may be improperly storing them if they are on her personal computer. With (D), extracting personal information of visitors to a Web page—especially if it can be used to identify an individual (as it could be with geolocation data)—is unethical. The answer is (A).

29. **D** The program seems to be functioning as intended, and the variable cars is the number of cars in the parking garage. With 108 cars, the current number of open spots is 160 – 108 = 52. If two cars leave and one car enters, then it will have one more open spot, or 53 spaces. Choice (A) is false as the program does function as intended. Choice (B) is false as the number of spaces has *increased* from 52. Choice (C) is false as it is the number of spots before the cars left and entered the garage. Choice (D) is the credited answer as there was a net increase in parking spots. The answer is (D).

30. **A** Choice (B) is incorrect because the World Wide Web uses HTML to create pages, and the HTML is transmitted over the Internet. Eliminate (C) because the Internet is never off; there are protocols set up to prevent this. Choice (D) can also be eliminated because the Internet came first as a way to share information; the World Wide Web was then created to have a shared language to transmit information. The answer is (A).

31. **C** The general test for PII is that if the information can be used to identify an individual, then it is PII. Choice (A) provides information that could be used to identify the car's owner and hence is PII. Choice (B) clearly links names to addresses and political affiliation. While the information is publicly available (hence legal), compiling that information does reveal PII. Choice (C) is the credited answer as it does not show or identify the coworker. The focus of this picture is just the jacket. Choice (D) shows the fans (who can be identified) and the location tag, which makes it PII. This could be a video clip that someone took while at the game and uploaded to a personal Facebook page (hence legal), but it is still PII because some of the fans at the game can be identified (potentially without their permission). The answer is (C).

32. **A** Choice (A) is an error where the rules of a programming language are not followed. Hence the compiler cannot "understand" the programmer's intent and will error out. Choice (B) is a mistake that happens during execution. For instance, the code may want to divide a by b. However, if the user did not define b, or set it equal to zero, then the program will error out during its execution. Choice (C) is a mistake between what a program should display and what it does display. There may be no error flags for this type of mistake, and it is usually caused by referencing the element or not accounting for all possible behaviors that the program could encounter. Choice (D) happens when the program attempts to handle a value that is outside the defined range of values. The answer is (A).

33.   **D**   The bot will exit only if a wall makes it turn left or right into an exit or if it is headed directly toward that exit. This isn't the case for Exits A and B, so (A) and (B) can be eliminated. If you map out the path the bot will take (remember that it has a bias for turning left with respect to the direction it is facing), you will see whether it reaches Exit C.

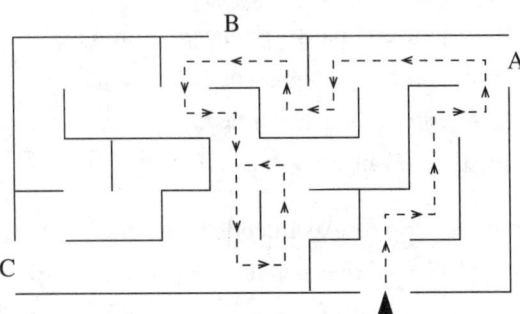

Because the bot gets stuck in a loop, it never reaches Exit C, so eliminate (C). The answer is (D).

34.   **A**   Choice (A) is the credited answer. If a sound file is saved using fewer bits per second, then there would be information loss (or averaging) that would produce a file of lower sound quality. Choice (B) could potentially render a higher resolution file (and would require more storage than would the original), but would not decrease in quality, so eliminate (B). Choice (C) would not result in a lower quality file as lossless techniques are designed to maintain the same quality as that of the original file, so eliminate (C). Choice (D) is not true and can be eliminated. The answer is (A).

35.   **C**   Program I starts picking characters from the beginning of the input string and adds them to the beginning. This means that it puts the second character before the first character when adding characters to `outStr`. Hence it reverses the string. Program II starts at the end of the input string and adds subsequent letters behind the first ones added to `outStr`. This effectively reverses the original string. Choice (A) incorrectly selects only Program I, but not Program II. Choice (B) incorrectly selects Program II but not Program I. Choice (C) is the credited answer as it correctly selects both programs. Choice (D) incorrectly selects neither program. The answer is (C).

36.   **C**   As each step is independent, they can be run simultaneously. With three steps and two processors, the most efficient utilization would be to have one processor execute the two fast steps, and the other processor execute the slowest step. The minimum time would be the higher of either the sum of the times of the two fast steps, or the time of the slowest step. In this case, the minimum time would be the sum of the two fastest steps, which is 90 msec. Choice (A) is the time for the fastest step and can be eliminated. Choice (B) is the time for the slowest step, but as this is faster than the sum of the two fast steps, eliminate it. Choice (C) is the sum of the two fast steps, which, in this case, is longer than the slowest step and therefore the credited answer. Choice (D) is the sum of all the steps and would be the time if a single processor were executing the program, so eliminate it. The answer is (C).

37. **C** Program A will correctly calculate the price for members (with or without a coupon). However, it gives the discount to non-members with a coupon, hence it does not correctly price the item. Program B correctly calculates the price of the item. Choice (A) is false as Program A does not correctly calculate the item price. Choice (B) reverses the two programs and can be eliminated. Choice (C) is the credited answer as it correctly identifies that Program A does not correctly calculate the item price, while Program B does. Choice (D) is false as Program B correctly calculates the item price. The answer is (C).

38. **D** Copyright laws are intended to protect the rights of creators of original works. However, there are areas of copyright law that permit use of the work. These include fair use (you can make a copy of work you own for your personal use), educational use (an academic institution can make multiple copies of a work it owns for instructional purposes), and works in the public domain, which can be used without restriction. Non-commercial works are typically more likely to be considered fair use than those from which users monetarily benefit. In (A), because the cartoonist has made substantial changes to the original picture, it is likely to be considered a new work. For (B), pieces of code that are posted in programming blogs are generally meant for programmers to use in their projects (both commercial and non-commercial). If they are open source, they can be used with no restriction. With (C), data cannot be copyrighted as it is not considered an original work (the *interpretation* of that data can, however, be protected by copyright law). Because only the data was used, this is not a violation of DMCA. When it comes to (D), images and other digital content on commercial websites are protected intellectual property. Copying and using any of that, especially for commercial purposes, is a violation of DMCA. In this case, the violation is more blatant if the seller did not seek permission. Putting up a copyright notice on a Web page is not required, as by default created content is protected. The answer is (D).

39. **D** For programmers who work in teams, comments can be very useful for keeping everyone on the same page and, as in (A), providing alternative (usually less efficient) code in the event the program needs to be debugged or optimized later, which is also addressed by (B): programmers may want to keep tabs on how far a program can properly execute or to test whether an error is in the code or the problem itself (which may not have a solution). Because both (A) and (B) are valid uses, (D) must be the correct answer, and indeed, (C) is also true, as with complex code, it is helpful to keep track of which parts already work as intended and which are still being worked on. The answer is (D).

40. **D** TCP is an acronym for Transmission Control Protocol and works with the IP (Internet Protocol) to send packets, making it a common protocol of the Internet. UDP is an acronym for User Datagram Protocol, and is also an IP that is an alternative to the TCP. HTTP stands for Hypertext Transfer Protocol and is a protocol established by the World Wide Web to view web pages. IETF, the Internet Engineering Task Force, promotes open standards for the Internet, but is not a protocol. Note, IETF is the only acronym that does not end in "P" for protocol. The answer is (D).

41. **B**   Choice (B) is correct because after the code executes, the smallest element will be in the first position (index 1) of the list. Since the value of i does not increment, the elements in the second through last positions (indexes 2,3,...*length*) will not have gone through the sorting process. Choice (A) is not correct because the index of the first element in a list is 1, not 0. Choice (C) is not correct because the code swaps elements if the element at index j is *less than* the element at index i. Choice (D) is not correct because the elements in the second through last positions (indexes 2,3,...*length*) will not have gone through the sorting process. The answer is (B).

42. **A**   The method works if a, b, and c are distinct. If all the inputs are distinct, the first condition tests if a is the greatest, and the second tests if b is the greatest. If neither is true, then c must be the greatest (and that is what the method returns). The issue arises when two of the inputs are the same. In this case, the method only needs to return the greatest, or it may default to returning c. Choice (A) is the credited answer. If a and b are the same value, and c is less than a or b, then it will not go through the first if statement or the second if statement. Hence it will return c, which is not the greatest value. Choice (B) works if b is the greatest and distinct from a and c, then the second if condition will flag it as the greatest value. If b is not the greatest, then the method will return c, which is the greatest value. Choice (C) works if a is the greatest value, then the first condition will return a. If a is not the greatest value, then the last ELSE will return c which is the greatest value. Choice (D) works and will return c – if it is the greatest value – regardless of the relative values of a and b. The answer is (A).

43. **C**   Crowdsourcing is obtaining input or information from a large number of people usually (but not always) via the Internet. The idea is to reach out to a much larger or more diverse group. Choice (A), which asks visitors to report data, is citizen science (where the public participates voluntarily in the scientific endeavor) and is part of crowdsourcing. Choice (B) is asking customers to provide input on product development and therefore is an example of crowdsourcing. Choice (C) involves a very small group and involves an activity that is part of that group's function. This is not an example of crowdsourcing, and it is therefore the credited answer. Choice (D) is reaching out to others to fund a common cause and hence is part of crowdsourcing. The answer is (C).

44. **D**   Malware is software that damages or takes over a system, so (A) can be eliminated. Choice (B) is not correct, since keylogging involves recording the keystrokes made by the user. Phishing is tricking a user into giving up their personal information, so eliminate (C). A rogue access point is a wireless access point that will give a cybercriminal unauthorized access to a network. The answer is (D).

45. **B**   The office that would be among the last to receive a message from HQ would be one that is not directly connected to HQ (like G, H, or K), so eliminate (C). You can further eliminate (A) and (D) because the office connected only to the least efficient nodes, in this case, K, would most likely get the message last. To double-check the remaining answer, (B), look at office G. Fault tolerance means that if a node (office) is unable to communicate, the other nodes can still function, as the communication will get rerouted through other nodes. Because G has the fewest number of connections—messages must go through A to reach it, whereas H can get a message from B or C—it is the least fault tolerant. The answer is (B).

46. **A**   A computer's internal clock will be fast if its clock frequency is higher than its rated (assumed) frequency. Choice (A) is the credited answer. If Computer A's CMOS frequency is lower than its rated frequency, then its system clock will be behind the actual time. Similarly, if Computer B's CMOS frequency is higher than its rated frequency, then its clock will be ahead of the actual time. Choice (B) is not true as CMOS ratings are generally not overrated. A frequency doubler does overclock, but usually frequency multipliers are implemented with correcting routines that account for the multiplier. Choice (C) states that Computer A's CMOS has the higher frequency, which would cause it to gain time (not lose time). Similarly, the answer choice is backward for Computer B's CMOS. Choice (D) correctly offers a solution, but the question is asking why there is a discrepancy in times, so eliminate this choice. The answer is (A).

47. **C**   The email is highly targeted and seems to be coming from a top corporate executive. This rules out (A), deception phishing, which would be a more generic email, such as a claim that the victim's account has been hacked with a link to reset the password. Choice (B) is a targeted attack based on knowledge of the specifics about the victim, like their name, place of employment, and job title. Keep it for now but look at the other options to see if anything is even more accurate. Choice (C), whaling, is when the criminal sends an email impersonating a top executive in order to get an employee to do something (usually transfer funds). This exactly matches this scenario, and is the credited answer. Choice (D), angler phishing, is when criminals use social media posts to persuade victims to divulge sensitive information or download malware, but because this has come through email, this can be eliminated. The answer is (C).

48. **B**   The algorithm decrements the larger integer until both integers are equal. The counter *(n)* keeps track of how many times the larger integer is decremented, but it is offset by one. Hence it displays $n - 1$ (and not *n*) to get the correct difference, which is described by the credited answer, (B). Choices (A) and (C) are false as the algorithm correctly displays the difference. Choice (D) is false as the algorithm does exit the loop (as long as *a* and *b* are integers, which is given). The answer is (B).

49. **D**   The program starts at n = 5 and decrements by 2. Hence n will never reach a value greater than its initial value, and will never attain an even value. Choice (A) is incorrect as n = 1 on the second iteration. Choice (B) will terminate the program without it going through the loop as n ≠ 3 from its initial value. Choice (C) will terminate the program as soon as n = –25. Choice (D) is the credited answer as n will always be odd. The answer is (D).

50. **B**   Examples of high-level languages include Java, Python, and C++. Two of the most common low-level languages are machine language and assembly language. Low-level languages are machine-friendly languages, tough for humans to understand (which matches (B)), complex to debug and maintain (which rules out (A)), machine specific (which rules out (D)), and generally not used except in specialized circumstances where high execution speeds and very low computational overhead are a requirement (which rules out (C)). The answer is (B).

51.　**A**　In a 2 × 2 binary search, the area is reduced by a quarter after each hint. Divide the total area (100) by 4 and keep dividing until the result is less than one. In other words, you are looking for the minimum n such that $100/4^n < 1$. In this case $n = 4$, so the answer is (A).

52.　**A**　Parallel computing offers several advantages, the biggest of which is computing speed, as the processing is distributed over several centers. A disadvantage is that it takes more time up front to break down computing tasks so they can be solved simultaneously across several processing units. Solve this question by eliminating the answer choices that represent advantages of parallel computing. With (B), because the computational load is distributed, less expensive (commodity) hardware can be used instead of that which is specialized for supercomputers. With (C), parallel computing is most effective for large, complex problems. And for (D), certain tasks can leverage underutilized computational capacity to run other resources over WAN. That leaves (A), which is when a variable has to be processed *before* being picked up for additional processing or as an input. In a parallel system, there is the possibility of the variable being picked up *before* it is modified, which is no good. The answer is (A).

53.　**B**　The question is very specific in that it asks what will cause bias. Predictions like (A) and (C) are unlikely to cause bias—that is, the prediction may have bias, but the program is not acting on it. Choice (B), however, executes a certain function and is likely to cause bias based on data that may underrepresent certain demographics. The answer is (B).

54.　**D**　Consider the following two scenarios each using two processing cores and three independent tasks:

Example:

Process	Time
Step A	50 msec
Step B	40 msec
Step C	80 msec

Time to execute the program in parallel is 50 + 40 = 90 msec.

Time to execute the program in sequence is 50 + 40 + 80 = 170 msec.

Speedup = 170 / 90 = 1.89

For (I), speedup is the sequential time divided by the parallel time. As the sequential time will always be greater than the parallel time, the ratio will always be one or greater. Eliminate this choice. Choice (II) is true (see explanation for Choice I). Choice (III) is true for the most efficient combination of process times. In this case, there is no ideal time for any processor, and the computational time for parallel processing is the reciprocal of the number of cores. In other words, if the processing time is 1000 msec and the computer has four cores, then the time for the entire task is 1000 / 4 = 250 msec. This would have a speedup of 1000 / 250 = 4 (which is the number of cores). Choice (III) is correct. The answer is (D).

55. **D** The objective of heuristic algorithms (heuristics) is to produce a solution in a reasonable time frame that is good enough for solving the problem at hand. Choice (A) is how most algorithms function, but it is not an *advantage* of deploying heuristics. Choice (B) is false. In fact, heuristics don't work against highly randomized self-modifying (polymorphic) viruses. Choice (C) is false. Heuristics find a solution, and there is no guarantee (or even attempt) to verify that it is the most optimal solution. Choice (D) is the credited answer. By looking for certain behaviors, heuristics can detect future viruses before they are detected and identified in prior applications. The answer is (D).

56. **B** Cluster analysis (clustering) is the task of grouping a set of objects in such a way that objects in the same group (cluster) are more similar (in some sense) to each other than to those in other clusters. This technique has found great success in pattern recognition, image analysis, and machine learning. Choice (A) is a feature of clustering as it is often used for knowledge discovery, which involves trial and failure. It is often necessary to modify data pre-processing and model parameters until the result achieves the desired properties. Choice (B) is the credited answer as it is not a characteristic of clustering. Clustering algorithms include grouping data with small distances between cluster members, identifying dense areas of data space, or sampling intervals or particular statistical distributions. Hence, cluster analysis itself is not one specific algorithm, but the general task to be solved. Choice (C) is a characteristic of clustering as the objective is to determine which clusters data belong (or do not belong) in. Choice (D) is a characteristic of clustering as one of its objectives is knowledge discovery. This process is both iterative and interactive as it involves multi-objective optimization. This means that it is often necessary to modify data pre-processing and model parameters until the result achieves the desired properties. The answer is (B).

57. **D** Many companies do restrict access to certain websites, as suggested by (I), and a deeper dive into what employees are using the remaining sites for may be in order here. VoIP (voice over Internet protocol) referred to by (II), can take up a lot of bandwidth, but nothing indicates that employees are using it for personal reasons. And finally, while adding bandwidth would help to avoid hitting the limits, as suggested by (III), the first step would be to investigate those top five applications—marketing may be uploading critical videos to YouTube; employees may be doing research relevant to their jobs. The answer is (D).

58. **B** Choices (A), (C), and (D) are all beneficial effects since they are saving time, tracking the health crisis, and having less contact with other people. Although the school has the beneficial effect of saving money by hiring less personnel, there is the harmful effect on society by jobs being lost. The answer is (B).

59. **C** Choice (A) would enable all students to have access to the self-certification system from home, removing the digital divide dealing with access. Choice (B) would eliminate any issues that students might have if they do not have access to the Internet at home to complete the self-certification system. Choice (D) eliminates the issues that students might have who have not had access to computers or devices during their lifetime and will need assistance with tasks such as completing a self-certification system. Choice (C) will not do anything for the digital divide since IDs are a physical item. The answer is (C).

60. **D** Choices (A), (B), and (C) are all ways that the school can assist with medical issues since there is access to student medical history. Choice (D) is a concern. When there are too many people with access to private information, the chances of that information being stolen increases because of phishing attacks, etc. The answer is (D).

61. **A** Choice (B) would make it extremely difficult for someone to access someone else's login since they would have to know most of that person's personal information or various other pieces of information. Whenever a password becomes longer and uses more than just letters, the odds of cracking that password becomes significantly more difficult, so (C) can be eliminated. The use of public key encryption makes unauthorized access difficult, and certificates validate ownership and security with the keys, eliminating (D). While (A) does help security, the length of 30 minutes is long enough for someone to access a student's account if they forget to logout. The answer is (A).

62. **B** When looking for a causal relationship, you want to see if one data set will affect another and if the two are connected because of the data correlation. In this situation, you are trying to find if one student being infected will cause other students to become infected because of their proximity to already infected people. The medical history will most likely not affect other students, so (A) and (D) can be eliminated. What time a student self-certifies cannot be used to determine if that student infected other students, so (C) can be eliminated. When comparing infected students to other infected students, it can be determined whether they were around other students to make them infected, so the data can be useful in determining whether a causal relationship exists. The answer is (B).

63. **A, B** A bit is either 0 or 1 and can therefore only store two options. Choice (A) has only two options, hence it can be stored in a bit. Choice (B) can only be either true or false and can be stored in a bit. There are nine possible choices (zero is not positive) for (C), so eliminate it, as it cannot be stored in a bit. Choice (D) describes three possible states, so eliminate it, as it cannot be stored in a bit. The answers are (A) and (B).

64. **B, C** Choice (A) uses volunteers to *collect* data, not analyze it, so eliminate (A). Choice (B) is obtaining information or data from a large group of people. Choice (C) refers to data that is accessible for anyone to use, redistribute, or republish without major restrictions (like copyrights). Choice (D) leverages the internet to encourage many small investors to invest in a common cause, which is irrelevant to this scenario. The answers are (B) and (C).

65. **B, C** To make a program readable, variable names should appropriately describe the variables they represent. However, if the variable name is too long, then it increases the possibility that the programmer may make typographic errors when writing (or modifying) the code, especially if the variable is used in several different places. Choice (A) is a nondescript variable name and does not convey any hint of what the variable could stand for, so eliminate it. Choice (B) describes what the variable could be. Choice (C) describes not only the variable, but also the datatype. (Some programming standards actually require this.) Choice (D) is too long, making it a poor choice for a variable name. The answers are (B) and (C).

66. **B, D** Choice (A) address most of the common languages, but leaves out travelers who may not be as fluent in those six languages. As there are ways of enhancing traveler experience without excluding those who are not fluent in these languages, eliminate (A). Choice (B) allows the interface to be translated into any of the languages in the database. Usually, these translation algorithms have most spoken languages in their database, and certainly the most widely spoken languages. This option would ensure that virtually all travelers are working in a language they are fluent in. Choice (C) is a cumbersome option that would not enhance one's experience, especially if the user needs to keep referring to the dictionary, so eliminate (C). Choice (D) moves away from written language and towards pictures and animation. This option is the best option when accommodating different languages. The answers are (B) and (D).

67. **B, C** Big data analytics is more resource-intensive not only because there is more data, but because the work requires analyzing structured and unstructured data. Within structured data, there may be different data structures that add another layer of complexity. One primary reason businesses invest in big data analytics is that it helps them uncover insights that they would not be able to uncover with traditional (small data) analysis, which is (B). The other major reason is it helps them with overall optimization, as focusing on individual components doesn't always do this; this would be (C). Choice (A) is the opposite—larger datasets are desired, not smaller ones. Choice (D) is not a main reason to leverage big data. In fact, it is leveraged by small (even startup) businesses. The answers are (B) and (C).

68. **A, D** Lossy data transmission and storage is used when the restored data needs only to approximate the original. Generally, image, movie, or voice files are tolerant of lossy compression. Lossless algorithms are used when approximations cannot be tolerated and restored data needs to be exactly like the original. Executable programs, text documents, and source code typically require lossless compression. Images, (A), can tolerate lossy compression. Executable code, (B), would not function as intended if even a small piece is approximated, so eliminate it. Text documents, (C), if approximated, may render a different letter and potentially a different meaning (imagine receiving a text like "you need to shake a tower" instead of "you need to take a shower"). You can also eliminate (C). Military voice communication, (D), has traditionally been lossy compression as speed is typically the most critical element. Voice communications, in general, are tolerant of lossy compression. The answers are (A) and (D).

69. **A, C** 2FA is a legitimate method of secondary security that in many cases has the potential to prevent cyber attacks, but it's not as foolproof as many believe. This is especially true for phishing attacks that manipulate users into handing over sensitive information but reinforce a false sense of security. Users may receive a phishing message requesting them to log into their account. Since users generally trust their real accounts, they may log in and enter their credentials and 2FA information, completely unaware that it is a phishing site, thereby rendering 2FA useless, (A). In addition, 2FA data can be recorded in session cookies. Once users add their 2FA code to a website, a hacker has the ability to sniff session cookies using a developer tool. With these session cookies, a hacker can

simply paste the session cookie into a browser and log into the victim's account, (C). You can eliminate (B) because this is describing how 2FA works. You can also eliminate (D) because this is what 2FA is working toward to make things harder for hackers. The answers are (A) and (C).

70. **C, D** The Internet and the World Wide Web are often used interchangeably. While they are related, they serve different functions: The World Wide Web is a collection of interlinked websites that can be viewed through a Web browser. The Internet enables computers to communicate with each other and hence enables services like email exchanges and file transfer. Choice (A) is an Internet function as it facilitates data transfer (and hence communication) among computers. Choice (B) is an Internet function as it allows computers to communicate with each other. Choice (C) is a Web function as it links websites together. Choice (D) is a Web function as it works directly with Web pages on websites. The answers are (C) and (D).

HOW TO SCORE PRACTICE TEST 3

Section I: Multiple Choice

_____ × 1.5000 = _____
Number Correct   Weighted
(out of 70)   Section I Score
                                   (Do not round)

Section II: Create Performance Task

(This is completed and submitted outside of test time. Do your best to score your Create Performance Task using the guidelines in Chapter 2.)

Task Score: _____ × 7.5000 = _____
            (out of 6)   (Task Score
                                   Do not round)

AP Score Conversion Chart Computer Science Principles	
Composite Score Range	AP Score
112–150	5
98–111	4
80–97	3
55–79	2
0–54	1

Composite Score

_____ + _____ = _____
Weighted   Weighted   Composite Score
Section I Score   Section II Score   (Round to nearest
                                      whole number)

Glossary

GLOSSARY

A

Abstraction: A way of hiding information

Algorithm: A clear, step-by-step, detailed, computable set of instructions that returns a result in a finite amount of time

Algorithm Efficiency: How an algorithm performs with regard to both time and space

Application Program Interface (API):   Specifications for using a library's procedures and understanding how they behave

Artificial Intelligence: The development of computing systems capable of performing tasks that would otherwise rely on human intelligence

Assignment: The storing of a value to a variable

B

Bandwidth: The maximum amount of data that can be sent over a particular computer network in a fixed amount of time

Base Conversion: Taking a number written in one base (e.g., decimal) and rewriting it in another (e.g., binary)

Bias: The intentional or unintentional skewing of data to favor a particular result

Binary: Numbers represented with base 2 digits

Binary Search: A method of seeking an item in an ordered list through an iterated process of comparing the target to the middle item in the list

Boolean Expression: An expression that evaluates to true or false

C

Citizen Science: Crowdsourcing in scientific research

Cleaning Data: Making data uniform without changing its meaning

Computing Innovations: A new method, product, or idea that requires a computer

Creative Commons: A not-for-profit organization that has various forms of licenses that can be used to protect original work from being plagiarized

Crowdsourcing: The practice of obtaining input or information from a large number of people via the Internet

Cybersecurity: The protection of a system against unauthorized or criminal use of a system

D

Data: Anything stored, transmitted, or processed by computing systems in numerical form

Data Abstraction: Filtering out specific details to focus on the information needed to process the data

Data Compression: A reduction in the size (number of bits) of data transmitted or stored

Data Types: A specified kind of information that is stored in a variable

Decimal: Numbers represented with base 10 digits

Decryption: The process of converting encrypted data into its original form

Digital Divide: The disparity between those who have access to technology and those who do not

Distributed Computing: A model in which multiple devices run a program

E

Encryption: The process in which data is encoded to another form

F

Fault Tolerance: The ability of a network to find a different path between sender and receiver

G

Graphs: A visual representation of data used to give quick information on trends

H

Heuristic: An algorithm that finds an approximate solution rather than an exact solution

Hexadecimal: Numbers represented with base 16 digits

Hypertext Transfer Protocol (HTTP):   A protocol used to interpret a Web page

I

Information: See Data

Information Security: See Cybersecurity

Integer Overflow: The attempt to store a number that is too big for the data type

Integer Roundoff: Impression caused by limits in size of data type

Intellectual Property: A product that is protected from unauthorized use by others

Internet Protocol: Any protocol governing the Internet or other network

Iteration: The process in which a part of an algorithm repeats until it meets a condition or for a fixed number of times, either of which is selected by the programmer or user

L

Libraries: A collection of precompiled procedures that can be used by other programs

List: A data type that holds a collection of values

Loops: Sections of code statements that need to be repeated more than once

Lossless Compression: A reduction of the number of bits stored or transmitted that guarantees complete restoration of the original data

Lossy Compression: A significant reduction in the number of bits stored or transmitted that only allows for an approximation of the original data

M

Machine Learning: The ability of a computing system to train on data fed into software systems

Metadata: Data about data such as author, date created, usage, file size, etc.

O

Open Source: Software development that allows programmers and developers to access the source code and to modify and improve the code as they see the need

P

Parallel Computing: Breaking a program into smaller sequential operations using multiple processors

Path: A sequence of directly connected computing devices between two computing devices on a computer network

Patterns: Recognizable forms in sets of data

Personally Identifiable Information (PII):   Information about a person that can uniquely identify them, such as educational, medical, financial, or employment information

Plagiarism: The copying of someone's work and passing it off as one's own

Precision: The number of significant figures or meaningful decimal places in measurement or calculation

Procedural Abstraction: The calling of a function with concern only for the end result rather than how the code functions

Procedures: A named group of programming code that performs a specific task

Protocol: An agreed upon set of rules that specify the behavior of a system

Pseudocode: A way of describing an algorithm that is not the specific code of any language

R

Random Number Generator: A program that picks a number at random from a range of values

Redundancy: Additional paths in a network to create fault tolerance

Route: See Path

Routing: The process of finding a path from sender to receiver

S

Scalability: The capacity for a system to change in size and scale to meet new demands

Selection: The use of a Boolean condition to evaluate which of two parts of an algorithm to use

Sequencing: The outlining of each step of an algorithm in a specific order to solve a problem

Sequential Computing: A process in which program instructions are processed one at a time

Simulation Models: Collections of computer software that respond to real-time input data to emulate a response that would resemble the real world

String: A collection of characters

T

Transmission Control Protocol (TCP/IP): An Internet protocol in which packets are repeatedly sent until receipt is confirmed

Trends: General direction in which something is developing or changing over time

U

Undecidable Problem: A problem that cannot be solved using an algorithm

V

Variable: An abstraction inside a program that can hold a value

W

World Wide Web: A system of linked pages, programs, and files

Exam Reference
Sheet

Quick Reference

Instruction	Explanation
Assignment, Display, and Input	
Text: a ← expression Block: \[a ⬅ expression \]	Evaluates expression and then assigns a copy of the result to the variable a.
Text: DISPLAY(expression) Block: (DISPLAY \[expression\])	Displays the value of expression, followed by a space.
Text: INPUT() Block: INPUT	Accepts a value from the user and returns the input value.
Arithmetic Operators and Numeric Procedures	
Text and Block: a + b a - b a * b a / b	The arithmetic operators +, -, *, and / are used to perform arithmetic on a and b. For example, 17 / 5 evaluates to 3.4. The order of operations used in mathematics applies when evaluating expressions.
Text and Block: a MOD b	Evaluates to the remainder when a is divided by b. Assume that a is an integer greater than or equal to 0 and b is an integer greater than 0. For example, 17 MOD 5 evaluates to 2. The MOD operator has the same precedence as the * and / operators.
Text: RANDOM(a, b) Block: RANDOM \[a, b\]	Generates and returns a random integer from a to b, including a and b. Each result is equally likely to occur. For example, RANDOM(1, 3) could return 1, 2, or 3.

Instruction	Explanation
Relational and Boolean Operators	

Text and Block:
 	
`a = b`
`a ≠ b`
`a > b`
`a < b`
`a ≥ b`
`a ≤ b`
	The relational operators =, ≠, >, <, ≤, and ≥ are used to test the relationship between two variables, expressions, or values. A comparison using relational operators evaluates to a Boolean value.
	
	For example, `a = b` evaluates to `true` if a and b are equal; otherwise it evaluates to `false`.

Text:
 	
`NOT condition`
 	
Block:
 	
`NOT (condition)`
	Evaluates to `true` if `condition` is `false`; otherwise evaluates to `false`.

Text:
 	
`condition1 AND condition2`
 	
Block:
 	
`(condition1) AND (condition2)`
	Evaluates to `true` if both `condition1` and `condition2` are `true`; otherwise evaluates to `false`.

Text:
 	
`condition1 OR condition2`
 	
Block:
 	
`(condition1) OR (condition2)`
	Evaluates to `true` if `condition1` is `true` or if `condition2` is `true` or if both `condition1` and `condition2` are `true`; otherwise evaluates to `false`.

Selection	

Text:
 	
`IF(condition)`
`{`
`<block of statements>`
`}`
 	
Block:
 	
`IF (condition)`
`  (block of statements)`
	The code in `block of statements` is executed if the Boolean expression `condition` evaluates to `true`; no action is taken if `condition` evaluates to `false`.

Instruction	Explanation
Selection—Continued	

Text:
 	
`IF(condition)`
`{`
`<first block of statements>`
`}`
`ELSE`
`{`
`<second block of statements>`
`}`
 	
Block:
	The code in `first block of statements` is executed if the Boolean expression `condition` evaluates to `true`; otherwise the code in `second block of statements` is executed.

Iteration	

Text:
 	
`REPEAT n TIMES`
`{`
`<block of statements>`
`}`
 	
Block:
	The code in `block of statements` is executed n times.

Text:
 	
`REPEAT UNTIL(condition)`
`{`
`<block of statements>`
`}`
 	
Block:
	The code in `block of statements` is repeated until the Boolean expression `condition` evaluates to `true`.

Instruction	Explanation
List Operations	
For all list operations, if a list index is less than 1 or greater than the length of the list, an error message is produced and the program terminates.	

Text:
 	
`aList ← [value1, value2, value3, ...]`
 	
Block:
 	
`aList ← [value1, value2, value3]`
	Creates a new list that contains the values `value1`, `value2`, `value3`, and ... at indices `1`, `2`, `3`, and ... respectively and assigns it to `aList`.

Text:
 	
`aList ← []`
 	
Block:
 	
`aList ←`
	Creates an empty list and assigns it to `aList`.

Text: `aList ← bList` Block: `aList ← bList`	Assigns a copy of the list `bList` to the list `aList`. For example, if `bList` contains `[20, 40, 60]`, then `aList` will also contain `[20, 40, 60]` after the assignment.

Text:
 	
`aList[i]`
 	
Block:
 	
`aList i`
	Accesses the element of `aList` at index `i`. The first element of `aList` is at index `1` and is accessed using the notation `aList[1]`.

Text:
 	
`x ← aList[i]`
 	
Block:
 	
`x ← aList i`
	Assigns the value of `aList[i]` to the variable `x`.

Text:
 	
`aList[i] ← x`
 	
Block:
 	
`aList i ← x`
	Assigns the value of `x` to `aList[i]`.

Text:
 	
`aList[i] ← aList[j]`
 	
Block:
 	
`aList i ← aList j`
	Assigns the value of `aList[j]` to `aList[i]`.

Text:
 	
`INSERT(aList, i, value)`
 	
Block:
 	
`INSERT aList, i, value`
	Any values in `aList` at indices greater than or equal to `i` are shifted one position to the right. The length of the list is increased by 1, and `value` is placed at index `i` in `aList`.

Instruction	Explanation
List Operations—Continued	

Text:
`APPEND(aList, value)`
 	
Block:
`APPEND aList, value`
	The length of `aList` is increased by 1, and `value` is placed at the end of `aList`.

Text:
`REMOVE(aList, i)`
 	
Block:
`REMOVE aList, i`
	Removes the item at index `i` in `aList` and shifts to the left any values at indices greater than `i`. The length of `aList` is decreased by 1.

Text:
`LENGTH(aList)`
 	
Block:
`LENGTH aList`
	Evaluates to the number of elements in `aList`.

Text:
`FOR EACH item IN aList`
`{`
`<block of statements>`
`}`
 	
Block:
`FOR EACH item IN aList`
`block of statements`
	The variable `item` is assigned the value of each element of `aList` sequentially, in order, from the first element to the last element. The code in `block of statements` is executed once for each assignment of `item`.

Procedures and Procedure Calls	

Text:
`PROCEDURE procName(parameter1,`
`                parameter2, ...)`
`{`
`<block of statements>`
`}`
 	
Block:
`PROCEDURE procName parameter1, parameter2, ...`
`block of statements`
	Defines `procName` as a procedure that takes zero or more arguments. The procedure contains `block of statements`.
	
	The procedure `procName` can be called using the following notation, where `arg1` is assigned to `parameter1`, `arg2` is assigned to `parameter2`, etc.:
	`procName(arg1, arg2, ...)`

Instruction	Explanation
Procedures and Procedure Calls—Continued	

Text:
 	
`PROCEDURE procName(parameter1,`
`                  parameter2, ...)`
 	
`{`
 	
`<block of statements>`
 	
`RETURN(expression)`
 	
`}`
 	
Block:
 	
`PROCEDURE procName` `parameter1,`
`                    parameter2, ...`
`block of statements`
`RETURN expression`
	Defines `procName` as a procedure that takes zero or more arguments. The procedure contains `block of statements` and returns the value of `expression`. The RETURN statement may appear at any point inside the procedure and causes an immediate return from the procedure back to the calling statement.
	
	The value returned by the procedure `procName` can be assigned to the variable `result` using the following notation:
	`result ← procName(arg1, arg2, ...)`

Text:
 	
`RETURN(expression)`
 	
Block:
 	
`RETURN expression`
	Returns the flow of control to the point where the procedure was called and returns the value of `expression`.

Robot	
If the robot attempts to move to a square that is not open or is beyond the edge of the grid, the robot will stay in its current location and the program will terminate.	

Text:
 	
`MOVE_FORWARD()`
 	
Block:
 	
`MOVE_FORWARD`
	The robot moves one square forward in the direction it is facing.

Text:
 	
`ROTATE_LEFT()`
 	
Block:
 	
`ROTATE_LEFT`
	The robot rotates in place 90 degrees counterclockwise (i.e., makes an in-place left turn).

Text:
 	
`ROTATE_RIGHT()`
 	
Block:
 	
`ROTATE_RIGHT`
	The robot rotates in place 90 degrees clockwise (i.e., makes an in-place right turn).

Text:
 	
`CAN_MOVE(direction)`
 	
Block:
 	
`CAN_MOVE direction`
	Evaluates to `true` if there is an open square one square in the direction relative to where the robot is facing; otherwise evaluates to `false`. The value of `direction` can be `left`, `right`, `forward`, or `backward`.

01 14

J

Completely darken bubbles with a No. 2 pencil. If you make a mistake, be sure to erase mark completely. Erase all stray marks.

1.

YOUR NAME: _____
(Print)   Last   First   M.I.

SIGNATURE: _____   DATE: __ / __ / __

HOME ADDRESS: _____
(Print)   Number and Street

_____
City   State   Zip Code

PHONE NO.: _____

IMPORTANT: Please fill in these boxes exactly as shown on the back cover of your test book.

2. TEST FORM

3. TEST CODE

4. REGISTRATION NUMBER

⓪	Ⓐ	Ⓙ	⓪	⓪	⓪	⓪	⓪	⓪	⓪
①	Ⓑ	Ⓚ	①	①	①	①	①	①	①
②	Ⓒ	Ⓛ	②	②	②	②	②	②	②
③	Ⓓ	Ⓜ	③	③	③	③	③	③	③
④	Ⓔ	Ⓝ	④	④	④	④	④	④	④
⑤	Ⓕ	Ⓞ	⑤	⑤	⑤	⑤	⑤	⑤	⑤
⑥	Ⓖ	Ⓟ	⑥	⑥	⑥	⑥	⑥	⑥	⑥
⑦	Ⓗ	Ⓠ	⑦	⑦	⑦	⑦	⑦	⑦	⑦
⑧	Ⓘ	Ⓡ	⑧	⑧	⑧	⑧	⑧	⑧	⑧
⑨			⑨	⑨	⑨	⑨	⑨	⑨	⑨

6. DATE OF BIRTH

Month	Day		Year	
◯ JAN				
◯ FEB	⓪	⓪	⓪	⓪
◯ MAR	①	①	①	①
◯ APR	②	②	②	②
◯ MAY	③	③	③	③
◯ JUN		④	④	④
◯ JUL		⑤	⑤	⑤
◯ AUG		⑥	⑥	⑥
◯ SEP		⑦	⑦	⑦
◯ OCT		⑧	⑧	⑧
◯ NOV		⑨	⑨	⑨
◯ DEC				

5. YOUR NAME

First 4 letters of last name				FIRST INIT	MID INIT
Ⓐ	Ⓐ	Ⓐ	Ⓐ	Ⓐ	Ⓐ
Ⓑ	Ⓑ	Ⓑ	Ⓑ	Ⓑ	Ⓑ
Ⓒ	Ⓒ	Ⓒ	Ⓒ	Ⓒ	Ⓒ
Ⓓ	Ⓓ	Ⓓ	Ⓓ	Ⓓ	Ⓓ
Ⓔ	Ⓔ	Ⓔ	Ⓔ	Ⓔ	Ⓔ
Ⓕ	Ⓕ	Ⓕ	Ⓕ	Ⓕ	Ⓕ
Ⓖ	Ⓖ	Ⓖ	Ⓖ	Ⓖ	Ⓖ
Ⓗ	Ⓗ	Ⓗ	Ⓗ	Ⓗ	Ⓗ
Ⓘ	Ⓘ	Ⓘ	Ⓘ	Ⓘ	Ⓘ
Ⓙ	Ⓙ	Ⓙ	Ⓙ	Ⓙ	Ⓙ
Ⓚ	Ⓚ	Ⓚ	Ⓚ	Ⓚ	Ⓚ
Ⓛ	Ⓛ	Ⓛ	Ⓛ	Ⓛ	Ⓛ
Ⓜ	Ⓜ	Ⓜ	Ⓜ	Ⓜ	Ⓜ
Ⓝ	Ⓝ	Ⓝ	Ⓝ	Ⓝ	Ⓝ
Ⓞ	Ⓞ	Ⓞ	Ⓞ	Ⓞ	Ⓞ
Ⓟ	Ⓟ	Ⓟ	Ⓟ	Ⓟ	Ⓟ
Ⓠ	Ⓠ	Ⓠ	Ⓠ	Ⓠ	Ⓠ
Ⓡ	Ⓡ	Ⓡ	Ⓡ	Ⓡ	Ⓡ
Ⓢ	Ⓢ	Ⓢ	Ⓢ	Ⓢ	Ⓢ
Ⓣ	Ⓣ	Ⓣ	Ⓣ	Ⓣ	Ⓣ
Ⓤ	Ⓤ	Ⓤ	Ⓤ	Ⓤ	Ⓤ
Ⓥ	Ⓥ	Ⓥ	Ⓥ	Ⓥ	Ⓥ
Ⓦ	Ⓦ	Ⓦ	Ⓦ	Ⓦ	Ⓦ
Ⓧ	Ⓧ	Ⓧ	Ⓧ	Ⓧ	Ⓧ
Ⓨ	Ⓨ	Ⓨ	Ⓨ	Ⓨ	Ⓨ
Ⓩ	Ⓩ	Ⓩ	Ⓩ	Ⓩ	Ⓩ

The **Princeton** Review®

1. Ⓐ Ⓑ Ⓒ Ⓓ
2. Ⓐ Ⓑ Ⓒ Ⓓ
3. Ⓐ Ⓑ Ⓒ Ⓓ
4. Ⓐ Ⓑ Ⓒ Ⓓ
5. Ⓐ Ⓑ Ⓒ Ⓓ
6. Ⓐ Ⓑ Ⓒ Ⓓ
7. Ⓐ Ⓑ Ⓒ Ⓓ
8. Ⓐ Ⓑ Ⓒ Ⓓ
9. Ⓐ Ⓑ Ⓒ Ⓓ
10. Ⓐ Ⓑ Ⓒ Ⓓ
11. Ⓐ Ⓑ Ⓒ Ⓓ
12. Ⓐ Ⓑ Ⓒ Ⓓ
13. Ⓐ Ⓑ Ⓒ Ⓓ
14. Ⓐ Ⓑ Ⓒ Ⓓ

15. Ⓐ Ⓑ Ⓒ Ⓓ
16. Ⓐ Ⓑ Ⓒ Ⓓ
17. Ⓐ Ⓑ Ⓒ Ⓓ
18. Ⓐ Ⓑ Ⓒ Ⓓ
19. Ⓐ Ⓑ Ⓒ Ⓓ
20. Ⓐ Ⓑ Ⓒ Ⓓ
21. Ⓐ Ⓑ Ⓒ Ⓓ
22. Ⓐ Ⓑ Ⓒ Ⓓ
23. Ⓐ Ⓑ Ⓒ Ⓓ
24. Ⓐ Ⓑ Ⓒ Ⓓ
25. Ⓐ Ⓑ Ⓒ Ⓓ
26. Ⓐ Ⓑ Ⓒ Ⓓ
27. Ⓐ Ⓑ Ⓒ Ⓓ
28. Ⓐ Ⓑ Ⓒ Ⓓ

29. Ⓐ Ⓑ Ⓒ Ⓓ
30. Ⓐ Ⓑ Ⓒ Ⓓ
31. Ⓐ Ⓑ Ⓒ Ⓓ
32. Ⓐ Ⓑ Ⓒ Ⓓ
33. Ⓐ Ⓑ Ⓒ Ⓓ
34. Ⓐ Ⓑ Ⓒ Ⓓ
35. Ⓐ Ⓑ Ⓒ Ⓓ
36. Ⓐ Ⓑ Ⓒ Ⓓ
37. Ⓐ Ⓑ Ⓒ Ⓓ
38. Ⓐ Ⓑ Ⓒ Ⓓ
39. Ⓐ Ⓑ Ⓒ Ⓓ
40. Ⓐ Ⓑ Ⓒ Ⓓ
41. Ⓐ Ⓑ Ⓒ Ⓓ
42. Ⓐ Ⓑ Ⓒ Ⓓ

43. Ⓐ Ⓑ Ⓒ Ⓓ
44. Ⓐ Ⓑ Ⓒ Ⓓ
45. Ⓐ Ⓑ Ⓒ Ⓓ
46. Ⓐ Ⓑ Ⓒ Ⓓ
47. Ⓐ Ⓑ Ⓒ Ⓓ
48. Ⓐ Ⓑ Ⓒ Ⓓ
49. Ⓐ Ⓑ Ⓒ Ⓓ
50. Ⓐ Ⓑ Ⓒ Ⓓ
51. Ⓐ Ⓑ Ⓒ Ⓓ
52. Ⓐ Ⓑ Ⓒ Ⓓ
53. Ⓐ Ⓑ Ⓒ Ⓓ
54. Ⓐ Ⓑ Ⓒ Ⓓ
55. Ⓐ Ⓑ Ⓒ Ⓓ
56. Ⓐ Ⓑ Ⓒ Ⓓ

57. Ⓐ Ⓑ Ⓒ Ⓓ
58. Ⓐ Ⓑ Ⓒ Ⓓ
59. Ⓐ Ⓑ Ⓒ Ⓓ
60. Ⓐ Ⓑ Ⓒ Ⓓ
61. Ⓐ Ⓑ Ⓒ Ⓓ
62. Ⓐ Ⓑ Ⓒ Ⓓ
63. Ⓐ Ⓑ Ⓒ Ⓓ
64. Ⓐ Ⓑ Ⓒ Ⓓ
65. Ⓐ Ⓑ Ⓒ Ⓓ
66. Ⓐ Ⓑ Ⓒ Ⓓ
67. Ⓐ Ⓑ Ⓒ Ⓓ
68. Ⓐ Ⓑ Ⓒ Ⓓ
69. Ⓐ Ⓑ Ⓒ Ⓓ
70. Ⓐ Ⓑ Ⓒ Ⓓ

Completely darken bubbles with a No. 2 pencil. If you make a mistake, be sure to erase mark completely. Erase all stray marks.

1.

YOUR NAME: _____
(Print)   Last   First   M.I.

SIGNATURE: _____ DATE: ___ / ___ / ___

HOME ADDRESS: _____
(Print)   Number and Street

_____
City   State   Zip Code

PHONE NO.: _____

IMPORTANT: Please fill in these boxes exactly as shown on the back cover of your test book.

2. TEST FORM

_____

3. TEST CODE

4. REGISTRATION NUMBER

⓪	Ⓐ	Ⓙ	⓪	⓪	⓪	⓪	⓪	⓪	⓪	⓪	⓪
①	Ⓑ	Ⓚ	①	①	①	①	①	①	①	①	①
②	Ⓒ	Ⓛ	②	②	②	②	②	②	②	②	②
③	Ⓓ	Ⓜ	③	③	③	③	③	③	③	③	③
④	Ⓔ	Ⓝ	④	④	④	④	④	④	④	④	④
⑤	Ⓕ	Ⓞ	⑤	⑤	⑤	⑤	⑤	⑤	⑤	⑤	⑤
⑥	Ⓖ	Ⓟ	⑥	⑥	⑥	⑥	⑥	⑥	⑥	⑥	⑥
⑦	Ⓗ	Ⓠ	⑦	⑦	⑦	⑦	⑦	⑦	⑦	⑦	⑦
⑧	Ⓘ	Ⓡ	⑧	⑧	⑧	⑧	⑧	⑧	⑧	⑧	⑧
⑨			⑨	⑨	⑨	⑨	⑨	⑨	⑨	⑨	⑨

6. DATE OF BIRTH

Month		Day		Year	
◯ JAN					
◯ FEB	⓪	⓪	⓪	⓪	
◯ MAR	①	①	①	①	
◯ APR	②	②	②	②	
◯ MAY	③	③	③	③	
◯ JUN		④	④	④	
◯ JUL		⑤	⑤	⑤	
◯ AUG		⑥	⑥	⑥	
◯ SEP		⑦	⑦	⑦	
◯ OCT		⑧	⑧	⑧	
◯ NOV		⑨	⑨	⑨	
◯ DEC					

5. YOUR NAME

First 4 letters of last name				FIRST INIT	MID INIT
Ⓐ	Ⓐ	Ⓐ	Ⓐ	Ⓐ	Ⓐ
Ⓑ	Ⓑ	Ⓑ	Ⓑ	Ⓑ	Ⓑ
Ⓒ	Ⓒ	Ⓒ	Ⓒ	Ⓒ	Ⓒ
Ⓓ	Ⓓ	Ⓓ	Ⓓ	Ⓓ	Ⓓ
Ⓔ	Ⓔ	Ⓔ	Ⓔ	Ⓔ	Ⓔ
Ⓕ	Ⓕ	Ⓕ	Ⓕ	Ⓕ	Ⓕ
Ⓖ	Ⓖ	Ⓖ	Ⓖ	Ⓖ	Ⓖ
Ⓗ	Ⓗ	Ⓗ	Ⓗ	Ⓗ	Ⓗ
Ⓘ	Ⓘ	Ⓘ	Ⓘ	Ⓘ	Ⓘ
Ⓙ	Ⓙ	Ⓙ	Ⓙ	Ⓙ	Ⓙ
Ⓚ	Ⓚ	Ⓚ	Ⓚ	Ⓚ	Ⓚ
Ⓛ	Ⓛ	Ⓛ	Ⓛ	Ⓛ	Ⓛ
Ⓜ	Ⓜ	Ⓜ	Ⓜ	Ⓜ	Ⓜ
Ⓝ	Ⓝ	Ⓝ	Ⓝ	Ⓝ	Ⓝ
Ⓞ	Ⓞ	Ⓞ	Ⓞ	Ⓞ	Ⓞ
Ⓟ	Ⓟ	Ⓟ	Ⓟ	Ⓟ	Ⓟ
Ⓠ	Ⓠ	Ⓠ	Ⓠ	Ⓠ	Ⓠ
Ⓡ	Ⓡ	Ⓡ	Ⓡ	Ⓡ	Ⓡ
Ⓢ	Ⓢ	Ⓢ	Ⓢ	Ⓢ	Ⓢ
Ⓣ	Ⓣ	Ⓣ	Ⓣ	Ⓣ	Ⓣ
Ⓤ	Ⓤ	Ⓤ	Ⓤ	Ⓤ	Ⓤ
Ⓥ	Ⓥ	Ⓥ	Ⓥ	Ⓥ	Ⓥ
Ⓦ	Ⓦ	Ⓦ	Ⓦ	Ⓦ	Ⓦ
Ⓧ	Ⓧ	Ⓧ	Ⓧ	Ⓧ	Ⓧ
Ⓨ	Ⓨ	Ⓨ	Ⓨ	Ⓨ	Ⓨ
Ⓩ	Ⓩ	Ⓩ	Ⓩ	Ⓩ	Ⓩ

The **Princeton** Review®

1. Ⓐ Ⓑ Ⓒ Ⓓ
2. Ⓐ Ⓑ Ⓒ Ⓓ
3. Ⓐ Ⓑ Ⓒ Ⓓ
4. Ⓐ Ⓑ Ⓒ Ⓓ
5. Ⓐ Ⓑ Ⓒ Ⓓ
6. Ⓐ Ⓑ Ⓒ Ⓓ
7. Ⓐ Ⓑ Ⓒ Ⓓ
8. Ⓐ Ⓑ Ⓒ Ⓓ
9. Ⓐ Ⓑ Ⓒ Ⓓ
10. Ⓐ Ⓑ Ⓒ Ⓓ
11. Ⓐ Ⓑ Ⓒ Ⓓ
12. Ⓐ Ⓑ Ⓒ Ⓓ
13. Ⓐ Ⓑ Ⓒ Ⓓ
14. Ⓐ Ⓑ Ⓒ Ⓓ

15. Ⓐ Ⓑ Ⓒ Ⓓ
16. Ⓐ Ⓑ Ⓒ Ⓓ
17. Ⓐ Ⓑ Ⓒ Ⓓ
18. Ⓐ Ⓑ Ⓒ Ⓓ
19. Ⓐ Ⓑ Ⓒ Ⓓ
20. Ⓐ Ⓑ Ⓒ Ⓓ
21. Ⓐ Ⓑ Ⓒ Ⓓ
22. Ⓐ Ⓑ Ⓒ Ⓓ
23. Ⓐ Ⓑ Ⓒ Ⓓ
24. Ⓐ Ⓑ Ⓒ Ⓓ
25. Ⓐ Ⓑ Ⓒ Ⓓ
26. Ⓐ Ⓑ Ⓒ Ⓓ
27. Ⓐ Ⓑ Ⓒ Ⓓ
28. Ⓐ Ⓑ Ⓒ Ⓓ

29. Ⓐ Ⓑ Ⓒ Ⓓ
30. Ⓐ Ⓑ Ⓒ Ⓓ
31. Ⓐ Ⓑ Ⓒ Ⓓ
32. Ⓐ Ⓑ Ⓒ Ⓓ
33. Ⓐ Ⓑ Ⓒ Ⓓ
34. Ⓐ Ⓑ Ⓒ Ⓓ
35. Ⓐ Ⓑ Ⓒ Ⓓ
36. Ⓐ Ⓑ Ⓒ Ⓓ
37. Ⓐ Ⓑ Ⓒ Ⓓ
38. Ⓐ Ⓑ Ⓒ Ⓓ
39. Ⓐ Ⓑ Ⓒ Ⓓ
40. Ⓐ Ⓑ Ⓒ Ⓓ
41. Ⓐ Ⓑ Ⓒ Ⓓ
42. Ⓐ Ⓑ Ⓒ Ⓓ

43. Ⓐ Ⓑ Ⓒ Ⓓ
44. Ⓐ Ⓑ Ⓒ Ⓓ
45. Ⓐ Ⓑ Ⓒ Ⓓ
46. Ⓐ Ⓑ Ⓒ Ⓓ
47. Ⓐ Ⓑ Ⓒ Ⓓ
48. Ⓐ Ⓑ Ⓒ Ⓓ
49. Ⓐ Ⓑ Ⓒ Ⓓ
50. Ⓐ Ⓑ Ⓒ Ⓓ
51. Ⓐ Ⓑ Ⓒ Ⓓ
52. Ⓐ Ⓑ Ⓒ Ⓓ
53. Ⓐ Ⓑ Ⓒ Ⓓ
54. Ⓐ Ⓑ Ⓒ Ⓓ
55. Ⓐ Ⓑ Ⓒ Ⓓ
56. Ⓐ Ⓑ Ⓒ Ⓓ

57. Ⓐ Ⓑ Ⓒ Ⓓ
58. Ⓐ Ⓑ Ⓒ Ⓓ
59. Ⓐ Ⓑ Ⓒ Ⓓ
60. Ⓐ Ⓑ Ⓒ Ⓓ
61. Ⓐ Ⓑ Ⓒ Ⓓ
62. Ⓐ Ⓑ Ⓒ Ⓓ
63. Ⓐ Ⓑ Ⓒ Ⓓ
64. Ⓐ Ⓑ Ⓒ Ⓓ
65. Ⓐ Ⓑ Ⓒ Ⓓ
66. Ⓐ Ⓑ Ⓒ Ⓓ
67. Ⓐ Ⓑ Ⓒ Ⓓ
68. Ⓐ Ⓑ Ⓒ Ⓓ
69. Ⓐ Ⓑ Ⓒ Ⓓ
70. Ⓐ Ⓑ Ⓒ Ⓓ

Completely darken bubbles with a No. 2 pencil. If you make a mistake, be sure to erase mark completely. Erase all stray marks.

1.

YOUR NAME: _____
(Print)   Last   First   M.I.

SIGNATURE: _____   DATE: ___ / ___ / ___

HOME ADDRESS: _____
(Print)   Number and Street

_____
City   State   Zip Code

PHONE NO.: _____

IMPORTANT: Please fill in these boxes exactly as shown on the back cover of your test book.

2. TEST FORM

3. TEST CODE

4. REGISTRATION NUMBER

5. YOUR NAME

First 4 letters of last name				FIRST INIT	MID INIT

6. DATE OF BIRTH

Month	Day	Year
JAN		
FEB	0 0	0 0
MAR	1 1	1 1
APR	2 2	2 2
MAY	3 3	3 3
JUN	4	4 4
JUL	5	5 5
AUG	6	6 6
SEP	7	7 7
OCT	8	8 8
NOV	9	9 9
DEC		

The **Princeton** Review®

1. Ⓐ Ⓑ Ⓒ Ⓓ
2. Ⓐ Ⓑ Ⓒ Ⓓ
3. Ⓐ Ⓑ Ⓒ Ⓓ
4. Ⓐ Ⓑ Ⓒ Ⓓ
5. Ⓐ Ⓑ Ⓒ Ⓓ
6. Ⓐ Ⓑ Ⓒ Ⓓ
7. Ⓐ Ⓑ Ⓒ Ⓓ
8. Ⓐ Ⓑ Ⓒ Ⓓ
9. Ⓐ Ⓑ Ⓒ Ⓓ
10. Ⓐ Ⓑ Ⓒ Ⓓ
11. Ⓐ Ⓑ Ⓒ Ⓓ
12. Ⓐ Ⓑ Ⓒ Ⓓ
13. Ⓐ Ⓑ Ⓒ Ⓓ
14. Ⓐ Ⓑ Ⓒ Ⓓ

15. Ⓐ Ⓑ Ⓒ Ⓓ
16. Ⓐ Ⓑ Ⓒ Ⓓ
17. Ⓐ Ⓑ Ⓒ Ⓓ
18. Ⓐ Ⓑ Ⓒ Ⓓ
19. Ⓐ Ⓑ Ⓒ Ⓓ
20. Ⓐ Ⓑ Ⓒ Ⓓ
21. Ⓐ Ⓑ Ⓒ Ⓓ
22. Ⓐ Ⓑ Ⓒ Ⓓ
23. Ⓐ Ⓑ Ⓒ Ⓓ
24. Ⓐ Ⓑ Ⓒ Ⓓ
25. Ⓐ Ⓑ Ⓒ Ⓓ
26. Ⓐ Ⓑ Ⓒ Ⓓ
27. Ⓐ Ⓑ Ⓒ Ⓓ
28. Ⓐ Ⓑ Ⓒ Ⓓ

29. Ⓐ Ⓑ Ⓒ Ⓓ
30. Ⓐ Ⓑ Ⓒ Ⓓ
31. Ⓐ Ⓑ Ⓒ Ⓓ
32. Ⓐ Ⓑ Ⓒ Ⓓ
33. Ⓐ Ⓑ Ⓒ Ⓓ
34. Ⓐ Ⓑ Ⓒ Ⓓ
35. Ⓐ Ⓑ Ⓒ Ⓓ
36. Ⓐ Ⓑ Ⓒ Ⓓ
37. Ⓐ Ⓑ Ⓒ Ⓓ
38. Ⓐ Ⓑ Ⓒ Ⓓ
39. Ⓐ Ⓑ Ⓒ Ⓓ
40. Ⓐ Ⓑ Ⓒ Ⓓ
41. Ⓐ Ⓑ Ⓒ Ⓓ
42. Ⓐ Ⓑ Ⓒ Ⓓ

43. Ⓐ Ⓑ Ⓒ Ⓓ
44. Ⓐ Ⓑ Ⓒ Ⓓ
45. Ⓐ Ⓑ Ⓒ Ⓓ
46. Ⓐ Ⓑ Ⓒ Ⓓ
47. Ⓐ Ⓑ Ⓒ Ⓓ
48. Ⓐ Ⓑ Ⓒ Ⓓ
49. Ⓐ Ⓑ Ⓒ Ⓓ
50. Ⓐ Ⓑ Ⓒ Ⓓ
51. Ⓐ Ⓑ Ⓒ Ⓓ
52. Ⓐ Ⓑ Ⓒ Ⓓ
53. Ⓐ Ⓑ Ⓒ Ⓓ
54. Ⓐ Ⓑ Ⓒ Ⓓ
55. Ⓐ Ⓑ Ⓒ Ⓓ
56. Ⓐ Ⓑ Ⓒ Ⓓ

57. Ⓐ Ⓑ Ⓒ Ⓓ
58. Ⓐ Ⓑ Ⓒ Ⓓ
59. Ⓐ Ⓑ Ⓒ Ⓓ
60. Ⓐ Ⓑ Ⓒ Ⓓ
61. Ⓐ Ⓑ Ⓒ Ⓓ
62. Ⓐ Ⓑ Ⓒ Ⓓ
63. Ⓐ Ⓑ Ⓒ Ⓓ
64. Ⓐ Ⓑ Ⓒ Ⓓ
65. Ⓐ Ⓑ Ⓒ Ⓓ
66. Ⓐ Ⓑ Ⓒ Ⓓ
67. Ⓐ Ⓑ Ⓒ Ⓓ
68. Ⓐ Ⓑ Ⓒ Ⓓ
69. Ⓐ Ⓑ Ⓒ Ⓓ
70. Ⓐ Ⓑ Ⓒ Ⓓ

TURN YOUR COLLEGE DREAMS INTO REALITY!

From acing tests to picking the perfect school,
The Princeton Review has proven resources to help students
like you navigate the college admissions process.

Visit PrincetonReviewBooks.com to browse all of our products!

1634b

The Princeton Review is not affiliated with Princeton University. Test names are the registered trademarks of their respective owners, who are not affiliated with The Princeton Review.